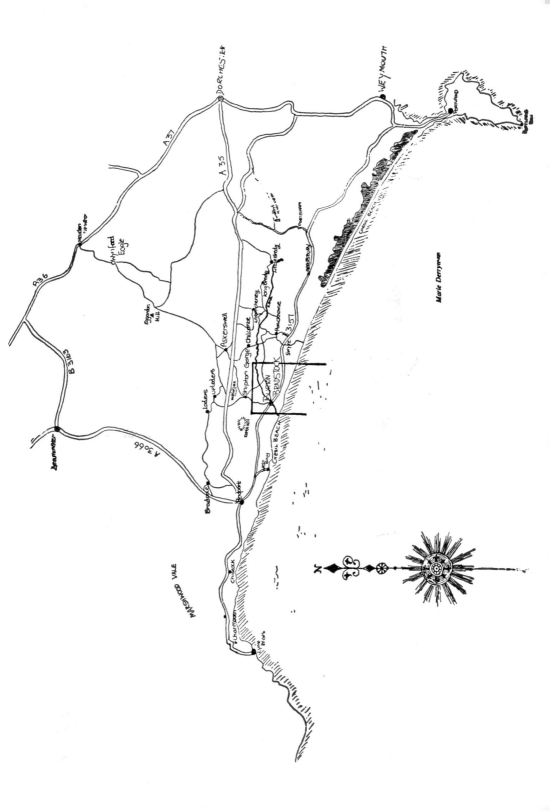

THE VILLAGE OF BURTON BRADSTOCK

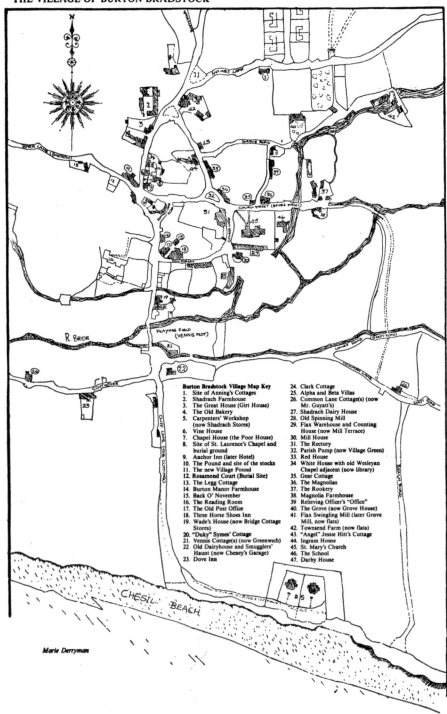

Burton Bradstock Village Map Key

1. Site of Anning's Cottages
2. Shadrach Farmhouse
3. The Great House (Girt House)
4. The Old Bakery
5. Carpenters' Workshop (now Shadrach Stores)
6. Vine House
7. Chapel House (the Poor House)
8. Site of St. Laurence's Chapel and burial ground
9. Anchor Inn (later Hotel)
10. The Pound and site of the stocks
11. The new Village Pound
12. Rosamond Court (Burial Site)
13. The Legg Cottage
14. Burton Manor Farmhouse
15. Back O' November
16. The Reading Room
17. The Old Post Office
18. Three Horse Shoes Inn
19. Wade's House (now Bridge Cottage Stores)
20. "Duky" Symes' Cottage
21. Vennis Cottage(s) (now Greenwich)
22. Old Dairyhouse and Smugglers' Haunt (now Cheney's Garage)
23. Dove Inn
24. Clark Cottage
25. Alpha and Beta Villas
26. Common Lane Cottage(s) (now Mr. Guyatt's)
27. Shadrach Dairy House
28. Old Spinning Mill
29. Flax Warehouse and Counting House (now Mill Terrace)
30. Mill House
31. The Rectory
32. Parish Pump (now Village Green)
33. Red House
34. White House with old Wesleyan Chapel adjacent (now library)
35. Gear Cottage
36. The Magnolias
37. The Rookery
38. Magnolia Farmhouse
39. Relieving Officer's "Office"
40. The Grove (now Grove House)
41. Flax Swingling Mill (later Grove Mill, now flats)
42. Townsend Farm (now flats)
43. "Angel" Jessie Hitt's Cottage
44. Ingram House
45. St. Mary's Church
46. The School
47. Darby House

Marie Derryman

Farmers, Fishermen
and Flax Spinners

The Story of the People of Burton Bradstock

By Elizabeth Buckler Gale

Bride river winds in the midst, and her bright waters throw a loop round the eastern frontier of the hamlet, pass under the highway, bring life to the cottage gardens and turn more wheels than one. Blooth of apple and pear are mirrored on her face and fruit falls into her lap at autumn time. Then westward she flows through the water meadows, and so slips uneventfully away to sea, where the cliffs break and there stretches a little strand. To the last she is crowned with flowers, and the meadowsweets and violets that decked her cradle give place to sea poppies, sea hollies, and stones encrusted with lichens of red gold, where Bride flows to one great pool, sinks into the sand and glides unseen to her lover.
"The Spinners", by Eden Phillpotts.

1st Edition   1983
2nd Edition   1984 — Revised

© 1984   Elizabeth Buckler Gale

ISBN 0 9508717 0 2

Published by
Elizabeth Gale, Higher Kingsland Farm, Salway Ash, Bridport, Dorset.
Typeset in the Marshwood Vale by Kathy Creed and printed by Thomas Farnham
for C. J. Creed, Printer, Broadoak, Bridport, Dorset.

TO MY PARENTS

REGINALD MILMAN BUCKLER
from whom I inherited a pride in the people
and the place

and

GLADYS BUCKLER
who taught me the joy of reading and writing

She had taken up
The employment common through these wilds and gained
By spinning hemp, a pittance for herself.
And for this end had hired a neighbour's boy
To give her needful help.

There, to and fro, she paced through many a day
Of the warm summer, from a belt of hemp
That girt her waist, spinning the long drawn thread
With backward steps ......
The little child who sate to turn the wheel ......

from "The Ruined Cottage"
by William Wordsworth, 1770-1850

Another poet of this period, William Cowper, 1731-1800, was said to have visited North Hill, Burton and spent some time musing in the stone cider house off Shipton Lane. Cowper is known to have wandered for many years and is recorded to have visited Southampton and Weston Super Mare, so his travels could have brought him in this direction.

An alternative explanation is that Farmer Brown, who owned the land, was interested in Cowper's poetry and had a line from a poem carved on a stone tablet. This tablet was last known to have been in the garden of the present North Hill House. Cowper's Lodge, long ago disused as a cider making house, now lies in ruins.

CONTENTS

The photographs for this book appear by courtesy of:-

Front Cover, 1, 16, 29, 34, 40, 41, 45 — The Curator, Bridport Museum (from the Ouseley Collection).

6, 7, 8, 9, 12, 14, 15, 22 — The Curator, Bridport Museum.

2, 25 — Mrs Dorothy Mansfield

3, 33, 35 — Mr. A. Rodway

4, 32, 46 — Mr. and Mrs. W. Cammell

11 — Mr. P. L. Hutchings

13, 23, 37 — Mr. A. J. Aylott

18, 19, 20 — Mrs. Doris Klopper

21 — The Commanding Officer, H.M.S. Victory, Portsmouth.

24 — The Rev. Toby Salisbury, B.A.

27, 39 — Mrs. Daphne Bartlett.

28 — G. A. L-F. Pitt-Rivers, Esq.

30 — Mrs. Greta Heal

36 — Mr. A. E. Williams

42 — Mrs. Freda Moore

43 — Vera MacLean (Mrs. Saunders)

47 — Mr. E. F. Norris

All other photographs from the writer's collection.

Photographs 11, 18, 19 and 20 were taken by Paul Stevens.

Peter and Mary Payne reproduced photographs from original prints.

Mrs. Blanche Everett, née White, born and brought up in Burton Bradstock, now in her 88th year, and Mr. & Mrs. R. W. Guyatt provided additional information for some photographs.

The maps were drawn by Marie Derryman and the sketch of "Chapple House" by Juliet Bugler.

Thanks must be extended to Mrs. Winifred Mitchell who assisted with proof reading.

FRONT COVER: SHADRACH "CARNER", BURTON BRADSTOCK.

ACKNOWLEDGEMENTS

I am indebted to Mr. John Sales, Curator of the Bridport Museum, for sparing time to read the original draft and for his encouragement and valuable advice.

Great help has been afforded to me by Miss Margaret Holmes, M.A., County Archivist, Miss Jennifer Hofmann, B.A., and the Staff of the County Record Office, Dorchester.

The Editor of the Bridport News, Mr. David Cozens, allowed me the free run of the Bridport News Archives which was a rewarding and fascinating exercise. My thanks must also be recorded to the Staff of the Bridport News for their kind help.

I received much co-operation from the Reference Adviser, Mr. N. G. Lawrence, A.L.A., and the Staff of the Dorset County Reference Library, Dorchester and Mr. H. E. Radford, F.L.A., County Librarian. The Staff of the County Library at Bridport must receive my thanks for much help and advice given.

The Curator of the County Museum, Dorchester, Mr. R. N. R. Peers, M.A., F.S.A., F.M.A., and Mr. R. M. Alcock, the Conservator, provided me with much useful information on Burton Bradstock.

Miss M. Allen, B.A., D.A.A., of the Wiltshire Record Office, Trowbridge, The Director of the Royal Navy Museum, Portsmouth, the Business Manager of H.M.S. Victory, Portsmouth, Mr. Jonathan Horwich of Christies, South Kensington and Miss M. P. Boddy, Assistant Reference Librarian, Weymouth, have all contributed to my research.

G. A. L-F. Pitt-Rivers, Esq., has so readily allowed me to quote from his family papers, deposited at the County Record Office. I count this as a great privilege for the research involved has provided me with many happy hours, without which a great deal of this book would not have been possible.

The notes on Burton Bradstock, by the late Maurice Ouseley, M.A., were presented to the Dorset County Record Office, by his widow, Mrs. M. Ouseley and my gratitude goes to her for permission to quote from them.

Heinemann, Publishers, readily gave their permission for inclusion in this book of passages from "The Spinners", by Eden Phillpotts and I am grateful to Mrs. Polly White of Hughes Massie, Ltd., Copyright Agents, who gave valuable advice and put me in touch with Eden Phillpotts' daughter, Mrs. Adelaide Ross.

John Murray, Publishers, Ltd., sanctioned the letters to Roberts after Trafalgar (from the book Nelson's Hardy, by Broadley and Bartelot) to be printed in full.

The Trustees of Dove Cottage, Grasmere, Cumbria have allowed "To A Sexton" and lines from "The Ruined Cottage", by William Wordsworth to be used.

Mrs. Dorothy Mansfield, née Gear, has so kindly put her manuscript of her father's memoirs at my disposal and the descendants of the Chilcott, Clark, Gale, Hutchings and Symes families have contributed considerably by allowing me sight of their family trees. Mr. L. O. Bealing has provided details of the Loveless family and Mr. M. A. Hansford has given permission for publication of some of his findings concerning Lt. William Hansford, R.N.

Mr. Louis Brown, the late Mr. Frank Wrixton, Mr. and Mrs. Arthur Bartlett, Mrs. Doris Klopper, Mrs. Freda Moore and Vera MacLean have given much of their time to recall events with me and provided and identified photographs.

I wish to thank them and the many other people whose willingness to pass on their local knowledge and memories has enabled me to record much that would have been lost for ever: Mr. & Mrs. A. J. Aylott, Mr. C. J. Bailey, Mr. R. Bailey, Mr. R. F. Bailey, Mr. M. Barry, B.A., Mr. & Mrs. A. Bartlett, Mrs. V. Batten, Mrs. M. Beavis, M.A., Mr. A. Broughton, Mr. & Mrs. L. Brown, Mrs. G. L. M. Buckler, Colonel and Mrs. P. G. Bushell, Mrs. S. Bugler, Mrs. V. Bull, Mr. & Mrs. W. Cammell, Mrs. J. Chick, Mr. F. S. M. Clarke, Mr. J. R. Collins, Mr. A. Gale, Mr. V. Gale, Mrs. M. Gillham, Mrs. J. Guppy, Miss R. Hansford, Mr. D. J. Hawkins, Mr. L. Hawkins, Mrs. G. Heal, the late Mr. E. Hitt, Mr. & Mrs. L. C. Hope, Mr. & Mrs. P. L. Hutchings, Mr. & Mrs. W. S. Jarman, Mrs. D. M. R. Klopper, Mr. A. Legg, Miss A. J. Legge, Mr. J. M. Lenthall, Mrs. R. Loving, Mr. D. G. W. Lyall, Mr. J. S. Mallinson, The Rev. Peter May, B.A., LL.B., Vera MacLean, Mrs. F. Moore, Mr. S. Northover, Miss M. Rendall, The Rev. Cyril Buller Ridlar, M.B.E., M.A., B.D., Mr. A. Rodway, Mr. G. Rosamond, Mr. P. Saunders, The Rev. E. Basil Short, B.Sc., The Rev. Norman Skinner, B.A., B.D., Mr. & Mrs. L. Starkey, Mr. P. Stevens, Mr. A. E. Williams, Miss E. Williams, and the late Mr. F. Wrixton.

The completion of this book would have been impossible without the support and interest of my husband, Guy Gale, and daughter, Amy, whose lives have revolved around its writing for some time, and my typist, Ita Larcombe, who has deciphered reams of illegible handwriting and tolerated continual alterations and additions to her careful work.

7

THE REASON FOR THIS BOOK

How fortunate I was to have been born in Burton Bradstock at a time when seine net fishing from the Chesil Beach was still a full time occupation and when the whir of the belts at the spinning mill had only just stopped.

I can easily remember hay being cut and worked by men in collarless shirts, breeches and leggings and thick "whiskits" and hauled home in horse drawn waggons. Women in pretty cotton bonnets stood braiding in their doorways as we walked to and from school where we still observed Empire Day. On Ascension Day we climbed the winding steps of the church tower and sang hymns from on high. I wondered, from that lofty position, at the tale I knew, of Steve Northover who, in his youth, had run around the periphery of that parapet for a dare, and how he would slip over the top of the cliff, to the ledge below, to collect sea-gulls' eggs.

As children we learnt history unconsciously. We knew about the coming of the Danes, the Spanish Armada, the Battle of Trafalgar and the local connections with those events. We had been told about famine, fire and flooding in the village. The stories passed down from generation to generation.

My Grandmother, who was born in 1861, told me much. I listened repeatedly to her telling how she walked to Bridport over the frozen snow drifts, which covered the hedges, after the Great Blizzard.

At home and school we were made aware of our heritage and history. For me, I think, it all began when I was just six years old and attending Burton Bradstock School. Andrew Collins and I had been moved up from the security of the Infants' Class to the Juniors. We sat together facing the south wall of the main classroom. Through the glass partition we could see the imposing figure of the Head Master, at his desk, perched on its dais, peering over his half-rimmed glasses; the Master of all he surveyed.

Directly in front of my desk, high as it seemed then, on the wall, was a memorial tablet to all the boys of the School who had fallen in the Great War of 1914-1918. One of the surnames on that memorial board was the same as mine and I realised that my family unit must have been bigger than I imagined. It did not take long to find out that the Robert Buckler commemorated there was also named on the headstone under the yew tree in the churchyard. Daily, as I passed by, I observed that even older headstones dotted the grass and bore my surname, marking the graves of others from my paternal family.

The war we were in then swamped our thoughts and efforts and the quest to discover more about these other members of my family had to lay dormant, although throughout my growing years I began to piece their relationship together. My father had vivid memories of his grandparents but the story went back much further than that.

In my teens I tried to obtain access to the Parish Registers but met with little response from the Rector. Perhaps he thought my pocket money would not run to the amount required to resurrect my many ancestors in Burton!

So it was some thirty years later before time became available to delve into the history of my family and to experience the joy of discovering that we

8

had been in Burton Bradstock for a very, very long time. Not content with names and dates, I longed to equate their lifetime with local and historical events and to build up a picture of the social and economic life of the generations of people of Burton Bradstock.

The researching has been unbelievably rewarding and interesting and it is my wish now to share my findings with those, who like me, are well rooted in Burton Bradstock, or who have ties or interests there.

Every care has been taken to present the true facts. Some inaccuracies and omissions may come to light. I make no apology for listing many names; for history concerns people and for me and Burton Bradstock these people are as important as those whose names are boldly written in our National History.

This can never be the complete story of Burton Bradstock. Much has had to be purposely omitted. Some subjects require research, others are still being investigated but it is my greatest hope that those who read this book will develop an understanding and high respect for the men and women of Burton Bradstock who built, and laboured to fashion a place that attracts so many to visit or settle there, or keeps yet another generation in the village of their forebears.

ELIZABETH BUCKLER GALE
1982

I

IN THE BEGINNING

Burton Bradstock, called Brideton in Domesday Book, meaning the farm (tũn) on the river Bride, (pronounced Briddy), lies some three miles east of Bridport and about half a mile from the mouth of the River Bride. This river starts its meandering journey as a spring from the chalk hills above Bridehead, Little Bredy, and falls out into the sea, south of Burton Bradstock, at Burton Freshwater.

The village is set in a "rift valley" bounded on three sides by the rolling West Dorset hills and on the fourth by the English Channel, caught up at this point into a bay known as Lyme Bay or in bygone years, by some, as Deadman's Bay.

The village meets the sea with imposing yellow cliffs of inferior oolite rock, standing some 60-80 feet high. Further east these give way to low blue cliffs of clay towards Cogden.

The soil, locally, is heavy, slow draining clay in the valley and of stonebrash, in places, on higher ground. This stony topsoil is shallow, difficult to work and grows poor crops. Before modern cultivation this land sported acres of furze bushes and brambles.

The Lyme Bay is flanked by the famous Chesil Beach (chesil means pebble). One of the largest bays in the kingdom, of remarkable formation, it exceeds any other in Europe. This bank of pebbles gets deeper from West to East as it stretches from Bridport Harbour (West Bay) to Portland. The pebbles increase in size in this direction too, being pea-size at Burton Bradstock and as big as saucers near Portland. These pebbles are like those found in the westerly valleys of Chideock, Charmouth, Lyme and Sidmouth and they travel along the Chesil coast against the prevailing wind.

The Chesil Bank checks the waves as they crash or glide in. After a heavy storm a "ground sea" is often experienced. The blue clay underneath the pebbles is exposed and the pebbles recoil with a grinding action and produce a loud, rumbling sound which can be heard well inland. At other times when the sea is calm only a peaceful ripple is heard.

This bank forms a natural barrier and has protected the land from encroachment from the ever hungry sea and the people from many invaders who have attempted to land on this dangerous coast. Because of this Burton Bradstock has managed to retain a mark of individuality. For its farmers, fishermen and flax spinners the sound of the sea, in all its moods, was never far away. For the many mariners it spawned it was their total livelihood.

West Dorset has always been isolated and remained so until the arrival of the branch rail line in 1857 from Maiden Newton to Bridport and later on to Bridport Harbour — renamed West Bay at that particular time.

Fortunate to have had natural defences it was fairly safe from early invaders. The Chesil Bank and the cliffs to the east, backed by dense forests protected the area. Only a small section of Powerstock Forest remains which once stretched from the base of Eggardon Hill to the sea.

The open Weymouth Bay was the most vulnerable site and whilst providing a shelter from the storms that beset this coast it gave easy access to those who sought to conquer.

Poole Harbour provided a way for small rowing craft but was probably a swamp and made any real navigation very difficult in the early days of the first invaders to our shores. Likewise the River Bride, at Burton Bradstock, winding its way out to sea, at Burton Freshwater, would have been choked and swampy.

Having remained in such isolation the customs and characteristic ways of speech were well preserved.

II
OUR EARLIEST ANCESTORS

Our earliest forebears would have been stone age men, similar in appearance to the Basques of the Pyrenees, long headed, dark skinned and haired and of shortish stature. These people buried their dead in the long barrows which can be found in certain areas of Dorset. One being near Winterbourne on the Bridport/Dorchester Road and another near Portesham. They used stone axes ground to a sharp edge. The chalk-lands provided considerable flint ideal for shaping into tools and implements, and these people inhabited this land when the Thames was a tributary of the Rhine and the Straits of Dover did not exist.

These savages were dependent on their skill as hunters and fishermen and would migrate to the coast following the river beds at certain times of the year, supplementing their diet with roots and berries. They collected pebbles for various uses and these have been found far distant from the shores from whence they came. Pebbles from the Chesil Beach were found in thousands at Maiden Castle, some used in slings to fire at attackers.

In due course the country became an island when the glaciers retreated and the sea level rose, and invaders arrived. These people were round-headed, fair, blue eyed and taller. They buried their dead, often after cremation, in round barrows, found in great numbers in Dorset. They were of the Celtic race and were at a more advanced stage of civilisation. They had better weapons and tools and over-ran the savages and were known as the DUROTRIGES by the Romans or to many school children as Ancient Britons.

Restricted by the natural defences of the area and the forests and swamps, they lived on the slopes and obtained water from the valleys. Rainfall was much heavier than today and the rivers ran slowly through the dense undergrowth.

They fortified the crests of the hills on which they lived. Eggardon, Pilsdon, Maiden Castle and nearer home our own North Hill, Bind Barrow Hill, Hamilton Hill, Shipton Hill and Chilcombe come easily to mind as we consider the possible habitations of our ancestors. This system of settled agriculture was to be found in Southern England around 2000 BC. Their daily economy was based on stock-rearing and the finding of numerous bones of cattle, sheep, goats and pigs is proof of this. Excavations of caves at Portland have yielded a mass of these bones.

The skins were used for clothing and ropes. No proof of spinning or weaving flax has been found for this period and although evidence of flax growing is numerous, it seems that flax was grown for its oily and nutritious seeds rather than fibres.

The Barrows of Burton Bradstock are to be found (1) to the east of Burton on the hill overlooking the beach and (2) N.W. of the church on North Hill. The latter has been disturbed over the years but large, slab stones appear to have been used to build it. In these mounds were buried the Chieftains or more important members of the tribe[1]. The people set up farms and the square Celtic type fields were laid out.

1. ½ ml. E.N.E. of **Bind Barrow** is another mound — probably a third barrow.

At Burton Bradstock the upper stone of a quern (corn grinder) was found at Green Hill on the cliff top, also a piece of red ware marked with an illegible potter's stamp. The upper part of a human skull, of low development, was found at the same place, pointing to the fact that early man was living on the heights of Burton Bradstock. A piece of black ware from there indicates possible Celtic origin. Romano British pottery was discovered in the low cliff, by the river, near Freshwater and a leaf-shaped flint arrow-head, of the Neolithic type, was found in the vicinity of the Coastguards.

A road leads from the Barrow, on North Hill, to Burton Bradstock. Its name is a permanent reminder of the earliest Burtoner. What is now known as Barr Road, to the west of the village, was previously better known as Barr Lane and in much earlier times Barrow Lane. Records of the 18th Century refer to it as Barrow Lane.

When the Romans arrived, these people lived on with them and advanced their mode of life alongside their captors whose state of civilisation had already reached high standards. The Romans settled in certain towns and established military stations linked by their superb road system. Stoke Abbott, near Beaminster, has yielded many finds to show Roman occupation. Part of Vespasian's campaign against the Durotriges was carried out somewhere not far from Bridport and this was most likely to have been at Stoke Abbott, the site of a military camp.

* * * * * *

Vespasian was born in AD 9 in a hamlet east of the old Sabine town of Reate. His paternal ancestry was humble. After entering the Senate at the age of 34, by the influence of Narcissus, the powerful favourite of Claudius, he received a military command in Germany and in AD 43 he was sent to Britain.

* * * * * *

Roman coins were found when foundations for the villas on the cliff at Burton were being prepared. (A rare coin, struck about 94BC was excavated at Chisels, Shipton Gorge, together with several others). The coin found at Burton was a common and worn one. It was struck by P. Ælius (or Allius) Paetus about 201 BC. The reverse side showed Castor and Pollux, twins, who fought for Rome at the battle of Lake Regillus.

By 70 AD a Roman Capital was set up in Dorset where Dorchester now stands and they called it Durnovaria. This "city" prospered under the Romans and remarkable evidence of fine houses and hoards of coins indicate the wealth therein. At Maumbury Rings the Romans built an ampitheatre which could hold some 10,000 spectators.

The cliff top at Burton would have been a fine look-out for the Romans and we can picture sentinels standing guard, gazing out to sea, keeping a watch against invading forces and our early ancestors in the village of Burton Bradstock going about their daily tasks, alongside their Roman captors. Of interest to us is that the Romans probably brought the art of rope making to this country.

Other invaders to our shores were the Jutes, Angles and Saxons who came to the east, north and south-east and drove westward into the Celts. The

Saxons advanced on into Somerset and into North Dorset and from then on the Durotriges came under West Saxon rule, holding an inferior place under them.

West Saxons were living on Hardown Hill near Charmouth. The numerous place names ending in "hays" or "hayne", (Old English derivation for enclosure), in the Marshwood Vale, which lies spread out below this hill, indicate settlement. They set up numerous small farmsteads enclosed from the woods and it seems probable that much of Dorset survived as upper class Celtic longer than the extreme west of the county. Evidence found at Hardown Hill dates that settlement at the 6th century. Finds included an axe, a knife, spear heads and a bronze brooch. One of their kings was Ine who reigned from AD 688 to 728. These people called themselves Dornsaete or Dorsaete.

For a time the Danes who had stolen into the north and east of this island conquered the larger part of Wessex. This was only for a short while and the boundaries of Dorset formed in the 7th Century stayed intact.

By then Dorset had become Christian and was under the control of a West Saxon Bishop. In 705 a Bishop was appointed — St. Ealdhelm, Abbot of Malmesbury, whose seat was at Sherborne. He died in 709 but following Bishops were seated at Sherborne, many falling in battle to the Danes, until Herman, a Fleming, brought over by Eadward the Confessor transferred his see to Old Sarum in 1075.

The Danes harassed the area around Poole Harbour, and Swanage Bay saw much fighting. Religious houses were burnt in Wareham and Wimborne but King Ælfred won victories there and peace prevailed for a while.

After the murder at Corfe Castle Gate of Eadward by his step-mother, Elfrida, the Saxon King, Ethelred, struck a bargain with the Danes and many settled here in Dorset. However, he then gave orders for a massacre and on November 13th, 1002, men, women, children and the Danish King Swegan's sister met their tragic end.

This brought the Danes full fast across the North Sea and they wreaked terrible vengeance on the whole of Southern England. Towns were razed to the ground and the whole length of land was set ablaze. The town walls of Dorchester were demolished, Wareham was in ashes and the Abbey at Cerne robbed and destroyed.

The Danes are known to have attacked along the coast at Portland and further west at Charmouth. Legend has it that a party of invaders landed at Burton Freshwater but the men of the village were ready and waiting in ambush on what is now the road to Bridport, just west of Burton Lodge. A dip in the hills ran red with the blood of the Danes and has since been known as Red Bottom.

The Danish King Swegan reigned followed by his son Canute. For a time the land was at peace. Not until 1068, after the Battle of Hastings, when Harold was killed, was further battle seen when William decided to subdue the rebels in the west. He marched westward to the seat of the rebels in Exeter, through the towns of Dorset; Shaftesbury, Wareham, Dorchester and Bridport.

Throughout this long period, of some five hundred years, Burton

Bradstock was caught up in the invasions and events that followed them.

*　　*　　*　　*　　*　　*

The Viking raiders presented a formidable picture. They carried swords, axes, spears, bows and arrows and iron knives. The two edged broad sword was their principal weapon, early ones often being simple, and later, spendid in decoration, colourful and ornamented.

The Viking, standing over 6ft. tall and red headed carried a wooden shield with which to defend himself. He wore an iron coat of mail and a leather and iron helmet, a long cloak and a bracelet given by a king or earl to his retainers.

One kind of Viking Warrior was a violent fighter who went "berserk" when worked up to a battle fever pitch. The word "berserk" means "bare sark" (shirtless) or without armour. These warriors were recruited for their great strength and ferocity.

As skilled craftsmen the Vikings rated the blacksmith as the most important of them. They were also glass and silver manufacturers. Their women were spinners, weavers and needlewomen and they used iron kitchen utensils and wooden bowls, and wore a great deal of silver jewellery.

The Viking ships reflected the very high technical skill of the builders. One ship recovered from clay in Scandinavia in 1867, of the 9th Century, was 65ft. long, 14ft. in the beam and 4½ft. deep from its gunwale to underside of the keel. Made of oak, its rudder was of pine.

Another such vessel was found to be 76ft. long, 17½ft. wide and 6½ft. deep. Sixteen pairs of oars propelled the ship, 32 shields covered the oar holes. The rudder entirely of oak proved the formula for safe sailing in all weathers. The mast was 40ft. high, made of pine, as were the oars — some 17ft. long, others 19¼ft. The gangplank of spruce was 24ft. long and planks, whose ends were of fiercesome carved animals, were used to frighten off intruders when the ship was moored. These ships got larger and larger and the vessels of Canute the Great may have been twice the size of these listed.

*　　*　　*　　*　　*　　*

Of interest to Burton Bradstock folk is the voyage of one Erik the Red, a Norwegian, who in 982 found Greenland and settled there for a while, naming a fjord after himself, following banishment for committing a murder in his own country. This famous voyager's name was to be linked with the village of Burton Bradstock nearly a thousand years later.

III
THE MANOR OF BRIDETON

Then the Conqueror sent his men all over England into the Shires to record how many hundreds of "hides" of land there were. They had to enquire how much land and livestock was owned by the King himself and what annual dues he was able to collect. The land owned by the Archbishops, Abbots and Earls was also noted and all the land and livestock owned by every other landowner in the county and what was its total value.

The Domesday Survey, ordered by William, records that half of the houses in the towns of Dorset had been destroyed between 1068 and 1086.

The Survey of Brideton (Burton Bradstock) states that in the demesne were 8 ploughs. Forty one Villeins, 7 Colberts, 20 Serfs, 30 Borders and 74 Cottars had between them 27 ploughs. It would appear that Burton was surveyed with several other Royal Manors and therefore these numbers probably denote persons engaged at some five other manors. Eight mills paid 4 pounds and 35 pence. There were 111 acres of meadow and 800 sheep on the Western slopes of the downs.

A wake was held in Mill Street and on the land in the front of Burton Farm (now Manor Farm). This gradually died out, although well into the present century a Burton Feast (Veäst) was held, commencing on the last Sunday in August.

The Manor of Brideton, Dorset, was given by King Henry I to the Abbey of St. Stephen of Caen to redeem regalia which his father, on his death bed, had given to the Abbey. It later belonged to the priory of Bradenstoke, (or Bradstock), in Wiltshire, hence the second part of the name of the village. In due course, when foreign monasteries were suppressed, it was given to the Dean of Canons of the collegiate church of St. Stephen at Westminster, founded by Edward III, in the twenty second year of his reign. The priory of Frampton was a cell of the abbey and college and so it was included in the liberty of Frampton. Frampton then a busy market town, near Dorchester, which later fell into decline.

It is recorded that, prior to the Norman Conquest, Brideton was held by King Edward the Confessor and therefore he was the most ancient landlord of the village that we know by name.

The arrival of Christianity had necessitated a house for worship and meeting, and churches were built; their shape based on that of the pre-Christian shrines and temples. Much is already written of the history and architecture of St. Mary's Church, Burton Bradstock so that here it is sufficient to give only the relevant basic facts. The late Mr. Maurice Ouseley, M.A., in his notes on Burton Bradstock, mentioned the possibility that there are some corner stones of the Saxon period used in the building of the later church.

At Burton Bradstock the church suggests Norman origin and its plan resembles that at Bridport and Symondsbury. The round shaft and square base of the font are late 12th Century, and the oldest known features of the Church. Two 14th Century windows in the north wall of the church are of St. Mary the Virgin. The central tower, transepts and porch are believed to be 15th Century.

To the N.W. of the church there is a cottage, opposite the side entrance of the Anchor Hotel, which is on the site of St. Laurence's Chapel, later converted to a Poor House from the remains of the Chapel. Somehow, down the ages, it was told that a stone cross lay buried beneath the Chapel House, Hutchins states that it stood in the gardens. Was it here that the first symbol of Christianity was positioned? It would seem very probable that this mound in Burton was the ideal site for the village cross and later for a place of worship. A burial ground was found beside it and many human bones were dug up there.

In 1736 a skeleton 7ft. in length was discovered. In all probability a path ran from there to the church. Across the road, on the site of the present Rosamond Court, further skeletons were uncovered in 1962/3. Unfortunately, no burial furniture was retrieved and dating the remains was therefore impossible. More original Burtoners must still rest in that part of the village. It is to be hoped that they remain undisturbed for ever more.

There was also a chapel to St. Catherine on the outskirts of the village where the village boundary hedge runs from Bennetts Hill Farm, along Rudge (Ridge Lane) to St. Catherine's House. The Chapel was situated at St. Catherine's Cross (Roads). Or was there a cross there, too? Here the coffins from Shipton Gorge were rested on their last journey, for burial at Burton.

Another Chapel to St. Luke was situated to the south west of Lower Sturthill Farm. The inhabitants of the ancient manor of Lower (Nether) Sturthill were usually buried at Burton for which 6s 8d a year was paid to the Rector of the parish of Burton Bradstock.

After the dissolution of the monasteries the Burton Manor belonged to the Crown until 1570. There has always been much speculation, locally, that the house, now known as The Rookery, had monastic connections. An underground passage reputedly runs from The Rookery to the church but no real evidence has been forthcoming.

In 1452 the Dean and Canons of St. Stephen's sold the tenancy of this Manor for three lives. Shortly after 1590 the tenancy was granted to John Taylor who was a merchant and Alderman in London. His daughter and heir, Elizabeth, married Sir Thomas Freke, of Iwerne Courtney, Baron of the Exchequer and M.P. for Dorset.

Together with the Burton Bradstock Manor went the hamlet of Graston. Graston had been a holding since Saxon times and its name is derived from Old English and Saxon GRAESTON meaning a grassy farmstead[1]. Shipton Gorge was surveyed with Brideton in Domesday Book together with the chapel dedicated to St. Martin. Other hamlets included with Burton Bradstock were Sturthill, Broad Sturthill, Innsacre and Upper and Lower Sturthill where there were two more farms, Middle Sturthill and Rose's Sturthill. It can be supposed that each of these farming hamlets employed a dozen men and were completely self-contained but now all reduced to farm houses. The Manor of Bridy, now Bredy, was within the parish, with mention of a Chapel of Ease to Burton in 1320.

Throughout the middle ages the working people could be found ploughing, sowing, reaping, threshing, grinding, rearing animals, salting

1. Hutchins. Fägersten suggests 'Grey Stone'.

meat, brewing ale and in this area making cider. Battling against wind and rain, sunshine and drought they fished from these shores in storm and calm, already the makers of nets, ropes and lines.

The servants or slaves at these manors would live in with their lords, dining in the hall and sleeping in outhouses or later over the hall, when plank floors were inserted.

For some 400 years the peasant of Burton Bradstock, as elsewhere, lived under the Feudal System which meant that in return for protection from the Lord (of the Manor) he would be obliged to work to produce food. The slaves who lived in at the Manor were not free men and all their energies went to serve their Lord and his needs. Men called Villeins held a fair number of acres of land and in return for this they gave 3 days' work a week to the Lord. The Cottars, Colberts and Bordars held much less land and they provided work for the Lord one day each week.

By the 12th Century we can visualise our lovely village of Brideton, an ampitheatre, snuggled 'midst the surrounding hills, the River Bride curling its way from Little Bredy through Litton Cheney to Berwick, Bredy and onwards to the sea.

Much of the land along this valley would be heavily wooded and trackways would be the only communicating system between farms, villages and the unknown, the river banks covered with thick growth and bordered with the trees that grow well in this area. The oak grew in abundance and the ash and elm were found in forests and hedges. Much wild life inhabited the woods and banks and wild animals such as the fox, badger, otter, stoat and weasel, deer, polecat and even the wolf would find good cover all around.

Documents for Burton Bradstock of the 12th and 13th Centuries are preserved in France, one being a charter of Henry II which states, 'Those who assail this charter are denounced and those who uphold it blessed'. The original rests in the Archives of Seine Inférieure and it concerns land of Brideton in 1156/57.

In 1275 the Abbot of St. Wandrille was summoned to answer Master John de Bridport in a plea that he permit him to present a suitable person to the church of Brideton which was vacant in his gift. However, it seems that the place was already filled by Master William de la Wyle.

Thomas de Lodres, chaplain, and others, took growing corn from the Prior of Bridenton, valued at 100 shillings in 1287 and there is record that in 1302, Master Robert de la Wyle, parson and prior of Bradenstoke was tenant of one messuage and 67 acres of land, 7 acres meadow, one pasture for 10 oxen, one horse and one cow in Brydeton

The Feudal System was used in England from Norman times until the 15th Century. The Lords and higher members of the Society provided military service, when required, and they in turn provided land for the non-free peasants who tilled their own strips of land besides alloting a certain proportion of their energies to working the land and caring for the stock of the Lord of the Manor.

The land most likely to have been cultivated and grazed in Burton Bradstock during the Manorial System days would have been the land under North Hill Barrow, behind Barr Lane houses and the meadows along Bredy Lane. Land below Bind Barrow may have been worked too, the higher land being well out of the range of the frequent floods.

On the 1840 tithe map narrow strips of fields can be seen along Bredy Lane. An ancient roadway ran past the church over Timber Bridge and probably led to some of the first "farm land" of Burton Bradstock.

A castle is reputed to have been sited 2 miles east of Bridport Harbour and more investigation is required to trace the validity of this statement. Should there be truth in this, then, the castle lay between Burton and Cogden.

The soil of West Dorset was well suited to the growth of hemp and flax, and the villagers would spin and weave and men and women alike twisted ropes from the hemp and braided nets.

IV
THE BLACK DEATH

King John in 1213 commanded that 'at Bridport ropes for ships, both large and small and as many cables as you can and twisted yarns for cordage should be made night and day'. Our village would have been involved in the wars through the demand of tackle for the ships.

The wicked King John, who hunted in Powerstock Forest, quarrelled with the church and caused much pain to free men and the Feudal System in general. During his absence, fighting in France, a protest was raised because of his appalling mode of governing which resulted in the signing of the Magna Carta in 1215, affecting the village by a clause it contained, that no free man was to be punished, except according to the laws of the land. The Medieval Society distinguished between servile and free men.

In due course Edward I set up a Model Parliament in 1295 summoning representatives from the nobility, clergy, knights and burgesses and Parliament became an established way of running public business. Records state that corn was gathered in Brideton (Burton) in 1297 to aid Edward in his wars.

*   *   *   *   *   *

During this time Bridport was not the only place to which the people of Burton would travel to buy and sell goods and for means of amusement or learning.

Abbotsbury, only six miles distant, in an easterly direction, from Burton Bradstock was a thriving town in the Middle Ages. A swannery, for which it is now famous, was in existence then.

Particularly well settled in Neolithic and Iron Age times and later having a substantial castle and occupied by Romans, where its high vantage points made it a perfect signal post, it was later ravaged and plundered by invading Danes and Saxons.

By 650 AD the Saxons had taken occupation of Abbotsbury and it became a retiring place for the West Saxon kings. Orc, who was Danish, restored the decayed church of St. Peter and established a monastery there. The date of this founding by Orc and his wife, Thora, was 1026. (Others put the date at 1044) and with this the village of Abbotsbury grew and prospered. A Guild was formed and a Guildhall built, a market being held there every Friday. With a thriving monastery, whose lands and wealth grew under the protection and benefaction of kings, the nobility and the gentry, the town became a centre of learning, scripture and commerce. On the surrounding hills and pasture-land sheep were reared, as wool was an important commodity in the district.

The flat road, one cart width wide, from Burton to Abbotsbury, avoiding the very steep hill, stretched along behind the Chesil Beach and provided very easy connection between the two villages. This track still remains, in places, and was in use and accessible until the Second World War when all fishing trade was suspended along this coast, defences of iron and concrete erected and the sea and shingle encroached over it.

The Black Death swept through Abbotsbury in December 1349, on its perilous journey throughout the land, from Weymouth, where it was brought in by a seaman. Abbotsbury fell victim to poverty and again the ravages of sea rovers and was eaten out of house and home by the forces sent there to defend the coast.

By 1400 the desolate town had begun to pick up, due to activity at the monastery again and new building took place. For some hundred years Abbotsbury thrived and for certain its prosperity was reflected in the adjacent villages.

The dissolution of the monasteries finally set the seal on Abbotsbury, a busy little town. The buildings and lands of the monastery were leased to Sir Giles Strangways on condition that 'all edifices be thrown down' and this was a job done well. Sir Giles used part of the monastic buildings to build a family mansion, half of the magnificent barn was destroyed and medieval masonry was used in the building of cottages which may still be seen today.

In 1774 a fair was still held at Abbotsbury on St. Peter's Day and fishing for mackerel was a full-time occupation for many. Over the years a great affinity grew up between the men of Burton, Swyre and Abbotsbury. They knew full well the difficulties and dangers of the Chesil Coast and yet continued, until the present day, to put to sea to glean harvests from its deep and shelving waters.

*   *   *   *   *   *

In 1323 six ropers (ropemakers) were sent to Newcastle-upon-Tyne from West Dorset, to teach the trade to others, Bridport already working at full strength could not cope with the navy's demand for tackle.

With the Hundred Years' War, from 1337-1453, the people of Burton would have been conscious of the conflict between England and France. Men from Dorset were on board ships provided by Dorset ports, including Lyme. The Dorset coast was often raided and the villages of West Dorset did not escape, Bexington especially.

When the Black Death struck, half the population of the villages was wiped out. Those along the coast from Weymouth were the first to succumb to this plague. A rapid increase in wages and prices followed the Black Death and there was a peasants' revolt in the country led by Wat Tyler. The villager would have learned too late of this uprising and although perhaps sympathising could have done little to support the cause. The Black Death completely disrupted the Feudal System. There were not enough workers to work the land and by 1500 most peasants became free and paid rent to the Lord for their land.

The fall in the size of the population, as a result of this plague, led to farms and villages falling into decline and eventual ruin. Much of the land which had been in cultivation since very early times was left untilled, with less people to work it, reverting to rough, overgrown marginal land, much of it lying on upland slopes and hillsides.

Two deserted villages can be traced in the vicinity of Burton Bradstock. At Lower Sturthill a medieval village stood close to the chapel of St. Luke. Footpaths and bridleways abound in this particular area leading to and from the site of this village. Now nothing remains of this former community.

Only a mile distant from Sturthill lies Modbury Farm on the Burton Bradstock/Litton Cheney road in the Bride Valley. 12th Century pottery was uncovered during pipe laying operations there and yet another deserted village site came to light. These two villages are connected by an ancient trackway. Besides pestilence, the expansion of sheep farming, often led to villages becoming void when land was taken for pasture by the landlords.

V

BURTON AND BRIDPORT HARBOUR

The Wars of the Roses, Henry V's renewed wars with France, Richard III's murder of the two Princes and his subsequent death in battle in 1485 and the arrival of Henry VII to the throne of England uniting the Lancaster and York Houses by his marriage to Elizabeth of York could only have affected the days and years of Burton's men, women and children in a snail-like fashion. The land would still have been ploughed with oxen, seeds sown, plants gathered in due season. Cattle and sheep were reared to produce milk, butter and cheese and eventually slaughtered as meat for the long winter months. Pigs would have grubbed under the oak and beech trees and more sheep wandered over the uplands. The blue flower of the flax would have wavered in the spring and the hard, narrow stalks harvested in the summer and prepared.

The ascent of Henry VIII to the throne did have more influence on the district for Henry continued to create an effective navy which his father had begun. A dockyard was made at Portsmouth and by the time of his death Henry had added some 80 ships to the naval strength making our navy a challenge to the maritime supremacy of Spain.

Bridport had always made all the great cables, ropes, hawsers and other tackling for the Royal Navy and most other ships in the land, but in the countryside around Bridport men had taken farms and moved out of the town to buy hemp and make inferior goods. Henry VIII decreed that hemp grown within 5 miles of the town was to be sold there on forfeiture of the hemp, (if sold elsewhere) and that only the inhabitants shall make cables etc.

A market was held in Bridport and annual fairs too. The people from Burton Bradstock trudged to the town to make purchases or sell any wares they had made during the year. There they relaxed and enjoyed some form of entertainment.

These labouring people owned a few stock and grazed them on the common land. A huddled and muddled existence of people and animals prevailed. Time and tide pulsed on as it had done since time immemorial and the river often silted up and flooded as it does today. The sea, when rough and angry lashed up over the shore, sweeping inland across the meadows.

*　　*　　*　　*　　*　　*

Flooding in Burton Bradstock was, and still is, often the result of an accumulation of heavy rain and a rough sea. When this occurs Freshwater "bays up". This is the term given by the local people when the shingle bar, at Freshwater, builds up and blocks the mouth of the river. Before the days of mechanical diggers the men of the village would battle their way to Freshwater, usually in driving rain and high winds, to shovel out hundreds of tons of shingle in order to try to free the river and allow the large volume of water to escape. Within hours of the work being done, to open the river mouth, the shingle would be piled up again by the pounding and churning sea.

*　　*　　*　　*　　*　　*

News of the brief reign of Lady Jane Grey, of 9 days, hardly reached the village before Mary seized the throne of England and tried to enforce the Catholic religion on her people.

Queen Elizabeth I ascended the throne in 1558 when England was in a sad state and the kitty was empty. Our people of Burton Bradstock welcomed her strong influence and were a loyal and royal community. Voyages of discovery, expansion of trade, a strong navy and more settled religious activities were topics for conversation, certainly amongst the learned lords, knights and yeomen. Tales of worlds away from Burton Bradstock, the arrival of potatoes and the tobacco weed, would have touched our locals.

The Bridport rope industry thrived and ship building and trading was carried on from Bridport Harbour (West Bay). This haven had yielded tolls to the crown from the time of Edward I. There are no early maritime records for this port and there is no mention that men or ships were sent to assist Edward III at the Siege of Calais in 1347 but there are continual records that the port was in need of repair. It was indeed a haven for ships, merchants and mariners seeking shelter from our treacherous sea.

Subscriptions were collected from neighbouring villages to facilitate repairs but it seemed that no amount of 'art or industry' from the inhabitants could prevent the barring up of the harbour with sand. For many years the battle against Nature continued. Public subscription, even on a National scale, was poor and the elements gradually won the battle.

The fortunes of Bridport and its harbour have for a long time been strongly linked with those of Burton Bradstock and its inhabitants, the eastern side of the marshland there being within the Manor of Burton. The rights to extract gravel already established.

Burton Manor had passed back to the crown in 1469 and by 1578 was in the hands of John Taylor the merchant and Alderman of London. By 1692 it came to Thomas Freke, a gentleman, from whence it passed eventually to the Pitt/Pitt-Rivers family who held the Manor and a greater part of the village, including land and property at Bridport Harbour, until 1958.

By the 16th Century many men had established themselves as tenants of the Lord of the Manor, building houses and setting up farms of their own. Nova Scotia and Newfoundland had been discovered!

The spinning of flax and hemp for linens, thread and ropes was well established in Burton Bradstock, as a cottage industry and it is known that a rope walks (a length of land which was long enough to draw the ropes) is to be found between the Mill Terrace cottages and the back of the present school. As well, the gardens backing on to Mill Street were long and thin and ideal for ropemaking.

Men were certainly collected together in gangs as fishing crews and would put to sea to catch mackerel, sprats, herring, whiting and other local fish in their season. One can imagine the menfolk leaving off tilling the land when the call of "vish strayen" echoed across the valley.

VI

SPANIARDS ALONG THE CHESIL

John Russell of Berwick, in the parish of Swyre, was descended from the noble de la Tour (or Turri) family whose seat it was, and who, by marriage, to the Russells of Kingston Russell, Long Bredy, increased their fortunes.

John Russell was living at Berwick in 1506 and had previously spent some time in Spain and knew the language, when a ship bound for Spain from Flanders carrying Philip, Archduke of Austria, only son of the Emperor and Joan, daughter of the King Ferdinand and Queen Isabella of Spain, whom he had married, was driven ashore at Weymouth in a storm.

Sir Thomas Trenchard of Wolfeton, near Dorchester, took these royal personages into custody and sent for Russell to act as interpreter. Henry VIII was most impressed with this man and in due course created him Lord Russell and bestowed on him the monastery of Woburn in Bedfordshire making his heirs the future Dukes of Bedford. The manor and lands at Berwick have, until quite recent times, belonged to the Bedford Estate.

The Manor at Berwick seems to have been a well fortified house and a sanctuary for its owners during the Wars of the Roses or against French invasion, but the French pirates who frequented our coast did not let it escape and it seems to have 'been forsaken by its noble owners for safer houses inland'.

Many tales still exist of sightings of Spanish Galleons off our shores, or doubloons being washed up and that the wooden reredos in Chilcombe Church is reputed to have been made from wreck from a Spanish ship of the Armada.

Stories passed down through the centuries tell of shipwrecks off the Chesil Bank and Spanish sailors coming ashore at Swyre and settling there. Curious too that the christian name, Alphonso crops up from time to time in the local registers. The last known being Alphonso Bartlett, born in Burton Bradstock in 1902, who was a superb footballer in West Dorset, a fine singer in church, village entertainment, or the bar of the local inn. He became a village baker at Puncknowle, baking and delivering bread throughout the Bride Valley, in all weathers, until his death.

*   *   *   *   *   *

Queen Elizabeth ordered regular musters when the Spanish invasion threatened. In July of 1560 over 9,000 men were mustered in Dorset, of which some 3,000 were described as 'able bodied' and they were encouraged to practise with bows and arrows on Sundays. Ten years later lists were drawn up of all the mariners from every village and preparations for war became even more serious. By the mid 1580s practice, after church on Sunday, was compulsory and the preparation and maintenance of the beacons enforced.

In 1588 Drake commanded the English Fleet against the invasion of the Spanish Armada. A sea battle was fought off Portland on the 2nd August (Old Calendar date) when the Spanish Fleet became becalmed just offshore. On such a peaceful summer's day the noise of guns off Portland would have been heard easily at Burton, gun smoke clearly visible and no doubt many villagers rushed to the cliff top at Burton and unwittingly became participants in the fight against the so called 'Invincible' Spaniard. Another naval engagement was fought in sight of Lyme, visible from Bridport Harbour, in 1672 between the English and Dutch Fleets.

VII

SHEEP FARMING IN WEST DORSET

In 1554 Queen Elizabeth I granted the right to hold a market in Bridport on Saturdays, for the sale of cattle, from the Friday before Palm Sunday to Midsummer Day and the right to hold three fairs each year. The April and October Fair Days at Bridport were to be a memorable occasion for everyone in West Dorset for nearly 400 years.

How enthusiastic the adults and children of Burton must have been to walk to the town and partake of the excitement to be found there on Fair Day. The jugglers and strolling players, card tricksters (for playing cards were a new invention), performing animals and colourful, well laden stalls (or "stannins") all along the streets. This would also be a time for trading and business transactions and a time for employing men and changing masters.

A weekly cattle market opened up the way for the buying and selling of animals — sheep, pigs and horses, as well as cattle, would change hands. The animals were led or driven to market by drovers. Drovers' ways, or tracks, are still to be found all over the country.

We can be certain that sheep farming was well established in the whole of West Dorset and in Burton Bradstock in the 16th Century. These sheep not only provided meat and milk but wool for spinning and weaving into cloth, skins for clothing and bedding.

The hills and downlands surrounding the villages of the River Bride were ideal grazing ground for the forerunners of the pure Dorset Flocks we see in evidence today. On Portland a breed of sheep existed, a lean, hardy type, used to the rigours of the weather and sparse grazing to be found on the island, similar to Mediterranean breeds.

In 1598 Nicholas Darbye farmed at Sturthill — to the north east of Burton Bradstock and at the Manor of Burton, Robert Mason and Richard Arnold were 'seised of the site and demesnes of the Manor and had possessed 600 sheep for the past two years.'

On the night of the 21st September, John Greene of Dorchester, an ironmonger, Thomas Moundyn of Burton, husbandman or smallholder, and Henry Allen of Charminster entered the village to convey away the sheep in secret by night. They had assembled between ten and twelve at night and armed and arranged themselves with long staves, picks, swords, daggers and other weapons and munition. They entered the sheep fold and drove away the 600 sheep.

The sheep were driven a long way before daybreak, towards the sea coast and into a secret ground of Nicholas Darbye. The field was in an obscure corner of the county near the sea, surrounded by hills; perhaps a 'coombe' between Sturthill and Swyre.

The Under Sheriff was alerted, (when we are not told) and with his men went to seize back the sheep. Darbye, with fifteen people, rescued the sheep from the Sheriff and assaulted him. Darbye had clapped his hands and set dogs on the sheep to run them from the Sheriff!

Subsequently, a case was brought to the Court of Star Chamber where Darbye stated that he bought 100 sheep from Moundyn who came with the

27

Sheriff, and drove them away with 200 of his own sheep. He denied being guilty of any riot and said he was worth £20,000 and prayed to be discharged from the Court.

A charity was set up in 1655, to benefit the people of Burton Bradstock, by a Matthew Derby, who was probably connected with the Darbyes of Sturthill. A William Darby was Rector of the parish in 1564.

VIII

EARLY RECORDS

For Burton Bradstock very early taxation records survive, preserved in the Public Record Office. In the reign of Henry III taxes were levied on goods of all classes to cover the expenses of the Crown in governing the country but from 1334 onwards the taxes no longer bore any relationship to the wealth of the individual or a community as they had before.

The Lay Subsidy Rolls of 1332 were the last of that kind to be prepared. The earliest Roll for Dorset of 1327, although damaged, is an important and unique document. We have the Burton Bradstock list of those taxed and to what amount as follows:-

Brideton

Nicholao in the Port XIId	Edwardo Roger IIs
Willelmo Nieuman IIs	Johanne Ostelir IIs
Richardo le Schynnere XIId	Johanne Roger IIs
Hugone Wybardi XIId	Johanne Chauntour VId
Johanne Scruwel VId	Richardo le Ver VId
Willelmo Stille VId	Roberto Rikafes XIId
Roberto Storm XIId	Roberto le Hert IIs
Thoma Wybardi XIId	Johanne de Bradenham IIs
Thoma Pynel XIId	Stephano Crul XIId
Thoma Clench XIId	Johanne Tonkere VId
Willelmo Chyuerston IIIs	Amicia Touere IIs
Johanne Kic XIId	Johanne Gys (Jnr) IIs
Johanne Cayser IIs	Johanne Denys XIId
Johanne Iwan XIId	Johanne de ... (probably Wottone) VIs
Thoma Co.. (probably Coky) XIId	Willelmo Hynebest IXd
Johnne Cobbe XIId	Willelmo le Yonge XVIIId
Hugone Frogemor VId	Willelmo Cryne XIId
Ricardo Penson VId	Richardo Touere VId
Johanne Ramesy VId	Roberto Vpsturtel VId
Johanne Daunz XXd	Johanne Gys XVIIId

Goods taxed in rural areas were horses, sheep, pigs, grain, hay, honey, and other agricultural produce. Poorer people were protected by a taxable minimum. Subsidies on land and goods were levied periodically from 1524-1642 and this was followed by a tax on hearths. Various other commodities were taxed in later years.

Henry VIII ordered Muster Rolls to be drawn up in 1539/1542, listing all men over sixteen years, their equipment and certificates of their names, to be returned by the Parish Constables and from this we see the surnames having become more the familiar type of surname we have today. The threat of invasion usually prompted a muster. Listed, too, we find the men who owned harnesses, (armour) and/or bows and arrows, pikes or billhooks and whether they were able (skilled) archers or able billmen or just archers or billmen. Some hundred men are given for Burton Bradstock. For instance John Walter was a billman and possessed a bill, a bow and 6 arrows. William Crome had a whole harness, a bow and a sheaf of arrows whilst William Boyes possessed only a bill. John Peche was an archer with a bow and 6 arrows. William Partryge had a bow and 2 arrows and Nicholas Denys, Edmund Palmer and some 44 others made up an alternative list — possibly the "second battalion".

In 1625 Thomas Gerard of Trent travelled through the county of Dorset recording the people and places that he visited. Journeying from Eggardon Hill to Little Bridy and on to 'Kingston Ruffel, Swier and on to Brideton corruptlie called Burton', he unfortunately left no reference to anything he had seen in Burton itself but he observed that Berwick House had 'fallen victim to French Pyrates'. The manuscript was one hundred years old when it was published by the Reverend John Coker in 1732. This was the first book of Dorset. A second edition was published in 1980.

Burton Bradstock's earliest surviving Parish Register dates from 1614. On crisp, faded parchment the first entries are written in Old English hand, difficult to decipher. There, too, we can see some names of the ancestors of people still living locally.

The first decipherable entry, in the earliest register, is the burial of Agnes Fry in 1614. Other surnames that are legible are Croome, England, Darby, Summers, Dennys, Polden, Beere, Batten, Miller, Hart, Hallet, Ridgway, Porter, Hooper, and Bonner.

For a period from 1667 it is recorded in the registers that the body was 'buried in woollen'. This Act, first passed in Charles II's reign was brought about to promote the use of woollen cloth; its production once a staple industry, particularly in the West of England. A fine of £5, for the use of the poor, was imposed when a body was not interred as directed.

For 1662-1664 there is another recorded source of information for the village and its inhabitants. This is a tax which was imposed on householders according to the number of hearths in their house or cottage. This 17th Century tax was imposed on fire-hearth and stove, usually a baker's oven, but certain households were exempt on grounds of poverty.

In Burton Bradstock Nicholas Ridgway possessed 10 hearths, Ann Pawing, a widow — 2, Christian Batten, another widow — 1, Dorothy Bowring — 4, William Beere had 5, of which 2 were stopped up — even then one took measures to avoid taxation. In all, the total hearths recorded were 64.

From the beginning of the 17th Century we are fortunate to have many registers and records to consult for information. These are safely deposited at the Dorset County Record Office, Dorchester.

The first register has been badly damaged by damp and two leaves are missing. A large portion of the entries of the christenings, marriages and burials of the people of Burton Bradstock and those who chose to marry, by licence, are recorded. To see and handle these ancient documents closes the gap in time and gives a great sense of pride and affection for one's native parish.

Another register is for the period 1658-1740. The entries are confused and some entries are missing. The 1754-1812 register contains an entry concerning the Act of 1753 for better prevention of clandestine marriages.

As this register contains the entries of marriage banns a fascinating entry is found telling of a Jane Buckler, who in 1809 on July 9th stood up to challenge the banns of Stephen Symes and Elizabeth Haycroft, at their second "calling home". Jane Buckler stated to the stunned congregation that Symes had promised to marry her and after the service she brought forward a witness who 'confirmed her assertion'.

The Rector later reported the facts to the Bishop on September 6th and he 'desired' the banns to be published for the third time and that the parties were to be married, if required. Any redress was to be got by a civil action. The banns were duly called for the last time on the 10th September 1809, and as they were uninterrupted the couple wasted no time and were married the following day.

It is interesting to find that Stephen Symes was almost fifty when his forthcoming marriage to Elizabeth Haycroft was held up by Jane Buckler. Elizabeth was thirty one years old and Jane thirty eight. One can imagine a prolonged romance, or friendship, between Stephen and Jane only to be wrecked by a fresh affair when the younger woman swept Stephen off his feet. Who knows?

Jane Buckler died suddenly in 1814, to quote from a marginal remark in the parish register, 'died by the visitation of God'. Stephen and Elizabeth's union would appear to have been meant to be for it was a fruitful one and some of their descendants, six generations later, are now living in Basingstoke, Hampshire, other Symes of this line probably in West and South Dorset. Four of the Symes children were born in Burton, possibly somewhere in Shadrach when it is recorded that Stephen was a butcher, the other two children were born there as well but the father's occupation is given then as labourer.

*   *   *   *   *   *

In addition to these Church Registers are the Churchwardens' and Overseers' of the Poor Accounts dating from 1699.

The Burton Bradstock Manorial Court Rolls recorded purchases and surrender of copyhold. A man could buy a tenancy, keeping a copy of the agreement, from the Lord for 3 lives and on his death it would pass to the second named — usually a relative and on that death to the third life. Copyhold had to be surrendered on the re-marriage of a widow, who was a holder, or for mis-use of land or property, or for perfectly ordinary reasons such as moving away from the village. Other manors may have had different rules. A fine was paid when the Lord or tenant died or surrendered his tenancy.

The Rolls also recorded the misdemeanours of Copyholders concerning land or property and the culprit would be brought before the Steward and Jury appointed to the Court. The Jury consisted of tenants of the Manor. In Burton Bradstock the Court could impose fines on those committing a nuisance or breaking the laid down rules of the Manor.

IX

THE CIVIL WAR

The Civil War, which came to a head in 1642, brought fighting very close at Lyme Regis and Abbotsbury. In 1644 the Royalists, under Prince Arthur, were billeted on Beaminster. A week after, Palm Sunday, a musket was discharged into a thatched roof in North Street with the intention of burning out the army. This certainly succeeded as a high wind took the fire through the whole town destroying it in two hours.

For the army throughout the land, who were engaged in the war, the new disease, called "influenza", raged, causing loss of strength to its victims and was classed as a 'venemous disease'.

In October 1644 the Strangways' house at Abbotsbury was stormed by the Parliamentarians and there was terrific fighting, resulting in the family mansion being burnt to the ground, by the use of furze faggots to fire it and an enormous explosion when the gunpowder, stored nearby, blew up, blowing some 80 people into the courtyard. All the Strangways' soldiers were taken prisoners. In the fire which followed the monastic records were destroyed. Later Strangways was imprisoned in the Tower of London. Fighting had also taken place in the church and the scars of bullets can be seen there to this day.

The war was a struggle for supremacy between the King and Parliament, between the High Church and the Puritans and was waged for four bitter years. The middle classes and the tradesmen were Parliamentarians and generally the nobility and their peasant workers supported the King. Charles I lost the day, in the end and was beheaded.

The effects of the Civil War came right home to Burton Bradstock when Nicholas Ridgway was ousted as Rector in 1649. Ridgway was a Royalist and was replaced by a Mr. Henry Lamb, as Rector, by Parliament.

Lamb, being a Parliamentarian refused to give one fifth of his tithes to support the Ridgway children. Most of the Burton working folk were royalists and had little time for the new Rector. There was great local sympathy for Ridgway and in Shipton Gorge the inhabitants did not allow Mr. Lamb to officiate, but the Ridgway children had as their Grandfather one Simon Bowring who owned Down Farm, in Shipton Gorge. The matter of money was resolved by Bowring paying his £20 tithe direct to the Ridgway children.

Soldiers galloped through Burton when another note of discord was being sounded at Bredy Farm owned by Alice Paulett, a Royalist, when she refused to pay £40 that was ordered by Parliament. The tenant was a Mrs. Chilcott and the farm was seized and sold under an Act of Parliament, later coming into the ownership of the Ironside family. A Chilcott descendant is still living in the village at the present time.

During renovations, at The White House and a cottage at the bottom of Donkey Lane, weapons were discovered buried in the cavities. It is possible that these were hidden there during the time of the Civil War.

Prior to this period we find that 144 Burton men signed a protestation against the Popish Church and vowed allegiance to the King's Majesty in 1641. The list of those signing this Protestation is given in full, for it is, in fact, a roll of the men of Burton. Those tracing family histories or with a particular interest in the people of Burton Bradstock will find it a valuable and fascinating record.

Protestation Returns for Dorset February 1641.

"I .... doe, in the presence of Almightie God, promise, vow, and protest to maintaine and defend, so farre as lawfullie I may, with all my life, power, and estate, the true Reformed Protestant Religion ...."

Mr. Wm. Chilcott	James Cox	Tho. Farwell (Jn)
Thos. Dunford	John Stevens	Rob. Charles
Tho. Croome	George Bonner	Wm. Lawrence
Rob. Bonner	Wm. Foster (Jn)	John Wood (Jn)
Wm. Thurman	John Vennice	John Batten
Ed. Jay	John Bonner (med)	Henry Beere
Chris Darby	Trustram Foster	Nicholas Batten
Wm. Foster (Sen)	Philip Davy	Wm. Darby
Rob. Stevens	Tho. Thurman	Steven Ennett
John Rowland	Richard Davy	John Perratt
John Ennett	Giles Bonner	Peter Raynolds
Tho. Farwell (Sen)	Tho. Pater	Tho. Batten (Sen)
Rog. Clarke	Edward Foster	Hy Russell
Rob. Miller	John Miller	John Foster
Victorius Stiby	George England	John Curtice
Wm. England	John Orchard	Henry Fry
John Rowland (Jn)	Rich. Rendell	John Craford
John Hendy	John Batten	Rich Michaell
Ellis Fry	George Hart	Tho. Batten (Jn)
Morgan Daw	John Hallett	Wm. Birchell
Osmand Ridgway	Rob. Moody	John Birchell
Tho. Miller	Steven Way	Trustham Porter
Nicholas Thurman	John More	Jesper Medway
John Beere	Rob. Rolls	George Croome
Silvester Vennice	Rob. Hounsell	Rob Bonner
Wm. Tissar	Tho. Sanford	Henry Greeninge
Nich. Pitcher	John Metyard	Mathew Martin
John Lea	Hy. Stevens	Tho. Dyar
Wm. Roman	Stev. Fry	John Hart
Wm. Cake	Tho. Jeffant	John Warren
Tho. Hart	Wm. Hockett	Rich. Beagan
Barnard Porter	John Vennice	Rich Payne
John Haggard	John Trivett	James Hendy
Wm. Rowland	Joseph Ridgway	Tho. Cake
Sam Paul	Tho. Jerviso	Goer. Ridgway
Steven Ennett (Sen)	George Beere	Roger Winsor
Daniel Polden	Ralph Hurden	Tho. England
Rob. Moody (Sen)	Rich. Bonner (Sen)	Joseph Byshop
John Rummon	Rob. Paine	Peter Rumman
John Foster	Roger Porter	Walter Knight

Rich. Bonner (Jn)	Rob. Pilton	Henry Basing
John Wood (Sen)	George Basing	John Prince
John Bonner	Ed. Paine	Rob Crabbe
Alex. Creedy	Tho. Basing	Wm. Porter
John Rendell	John Bonner (Jn)	Wm. Bas
Edw. Beere	Mathew Waad	John Strowbridg
Nicholas Ridgway (Rector)		
Symon Bowringe		
Tho. Barrett	Churchwardens	
Abraham Bryant		
John Croome	Overseers	
Thom England —	Constable	

* * * * * *

Excitement must have mounted in tranquil Burton when it was learned that King Charles II had passed through Bridport and thence to Broadwindsor on his escape from the Battle of Worcester in 1651. The town, at the time, full of soldiers mustering to advance on the Channel Islands.

* * * * * *

Some 40 years after the Civil War, West Dorset took a central position in the Duke of Monmouth's Rebellion in 1685. On June 11th Lord Grey, in charge of 400 of Monmouth's men, marched overnight from Lyme to Bridport with a party of 40 horsemen and surprised the 1,200 foot soldiers and 100 horse stationed in Bridport. Under the cover of mist they arrived at Allington Bridge early on a Sunday morning. Fierce fighting followed. Many of the King's soldiers lay out of the town in a meadow so that the town was not well defended.

Amongst those killed was Edward Coker and Wadham Strangways, gentlemen officers of the King. Cross fire ensued at the Bull Inn and one of Monmouth's officers, Colonel Venner, was severely wounded. Advancing further towards East Bridge they were met by the militia, camped in the meadows and were repelled, retreating rapidly but in good order, back to Lyme with 23 prisoners.

By July 6th Monmouth was fighting a fierce battle on Sedgemoor, in Somerset. Bedraggled and starving, he was captured in a field near Horton and eventually met his ghastly end on Tower Hill, London.

The Bloody Assize followed, over which the harsh Judge Jeffreys presided. Some 2,611 people were brought before him at Exeter, Taunton and Dorchester. Out of 300 tried at Dorchester only about 50 escaped punishment for their alleged part in the rebellion. One man who met his death was a Mr. Lancaster of Bridport. He was hung at Melcombe Regis in 1685. There, at Greenhill, Weymouth, the gallows were erected and the rebels executed, no doubt, by the "Bridport Dagger", as the hangman's noose became known. Their heads were then severed from their bodies and these, together with their quarters, were distributed to various villages in the area, where these gruesome exhibits were put on display.

From Burton people walked to see a dozen others hung. Some 25 men from the Bridport district were Royalist soldiers involved in the battle and were eventually rewarded for services rendered to the King. Barbaric execution, transportation and whippings were the penalties for the rebels and terrifying reports of this were brought back to Burton Bradstock.

*   *   *   *   *   *

It seems local disagreements, as well as National ones, were not uncommon for we read that around 1635 a petition was filed by one Robert Ryves, who was an officer in the Royal Army, to the King. Ryves set out the details of his side of the story concerning a quarrel and struggle he had with the Rector of Burton Bradstock, **Mr. William Hastings (1623-1635). As** Steward to Mr. Freke, the Lord of the Manor, Ryves had been sent to Burton to divide the tithe lambs between Mr. Freke and the parson on St. Mark's Day.

Shortly after the incident Mr. Hastings had quit the Living and village and journeyed some 300 miles, stopping at sheep shearings along the way. Riding about the country, Mr. Hastings was taken ill and told his physicians that he had been swimming late in the evening in the sea, which had 'brought him to shaking' and later this had developed into a fever. Eleven weeks after being taken ill he died.

The Rector's son had accused Ryves of causing hurt to his father which Ryves in his petition to the King firmly denied. The prosecution of Ryves had been engineered by Mr. Tregonwell who had married a Lady Ryves, widow of Sir John Ryves of Damory Court, Sheriff of Dorset. This marriage took place at Burton and is recorded in the Parish Register of 1625.

The Reverend Hastings was the grandson of George, Earl of Huntingdon and the Lady Ryves was his sister. Her second marriage was to the son of John Tregonwell of Milton Abbas. This John and his sons gave several decayed tenements at Milton Abbas to erect a school house. The elder son, John marrying Jane Freke, a daughter of Sir Thomas Freke of Shroton, sometime Lord of the Manor of Burton Bradstock, and his sister Alicia married George Hastings a brother of the Rector of Burton.

X

THE BURTON BRADSTOCK HOMESTEADS

During the 17th Century violence and theft were common. Murders were committed but suicide was rare. By various means many escaped any punishment and even hanging was not much of a deterrent. The consumption of alcohol was heavy and drunkenness rife. Women, too, were heavy drinkers of alcohol. Illegitimate children were not always baptised and this complicates tracing family lines. Fevers were the most serious diseases, smallpox, in particular. The elderly were very dependent on their children for support in their old age or infirmity. The wealthy could afford doctors and apothecaries but the poor went to amateurs for their medicine. Bankruptcy, often as a result of heavy drinking, was common, causing a chain reaction in business. Such happenings would have occurred in Burton Bradstock, too, to a greater or lesser degree.

*   *   *   *   *   *

In the county of Dorset in 1629 the total of seamen was 900 of which over 50 came from Burton. With so many of the population engaged in this occupation one is given an idea of the type of life many Burton families would be living. Men away for long periods sailing from Bridport Harbour, Lyme, Weymouth or Poole leading a hard, rough life, ill paid and dangerous; but Burton youth and men are well known for their durability and spirit of adventure and many a tale and trinket would have been brought back to the rustic home from over the seas.

Other rough, one storeyed cottages, would have housed the families of farm labourers or those enjoying a degree of self-sufficiency by renting a few acres, garden or orchard, (apple orchards were by now being planted), keeping a few cows, pigs or sheep. Oxen and a plough were needed and these were shared, in return for help with labour on the farms.

The home manufacture of ropes and linen sheeting brought in a little extra money. Flax and hemp were grown, not only by the Lord of the Manor, merchants and independent farmers, but in the smaller acreages and gardens of the labouring folk and the goods produced sold locally.

In addition to the local hemp and flax trade there was a small woollen industry at Beaminster and gloving also, as a cottage industry, was carried out in Bridport and other adjacent towns, supplying a larger set-up in Yeovil.

It is known that sheep were still plentiful and formed an important part of the economy. Grazing on the slopes by day, folded near the farmstead at night, they produced useful mutton and fine wool, their manure acting as valuable fertiliser, their skins (wool fells) also in much demand. Annually taken miles to a Sheep Fair for sale, shepherds and their boys from Burton trudged along the tracks of the Bride Valley and over the Longbredy Downs to Martinstown or Dorchester, taking several days each way.

*   *   *   *   *   *

At the farms on the outskirts of the village in 1620 the Pauletts of Melplash were at Bredy Manor, paying Church and Poor Rates to Shipton, Burton and St. Luke's. Graston paid tithes to St. Luke's Chapel, Sturthill, dedicated in 1502. At some time it belonged to the Abbot of Abbotsbury. In the time of Henry VIII it was owned by Thomas Clark whose heirs held it until it eventually came to the Strodes of Parnham, near Beaminster.

The Earl of Ilchester owned the Manor at Shipton Gorge after 1645 and it later came to the Maureward family. It takes its name from the Gorges family who subsequently owned it.

Hutchins gives plenty of information, if somewhat confusing, with regard to the Manor of Sturthill which lies nearer to Shipton Gorge than Burton. The Hides of Walditch and Loders and their family owned Upper Sturthill for many generations and also Lower Sturthill which came to them through the Mores and Cheveral families eventually selling the latter to John Every of Wootton Abbas.

In 1618 the Pauletts of Melplash and Bredy sold Broad Sturthill to Giles Stoodley of Broadwindsor in whose family it remained until 1721, coming then, by a sale, to the Mills family of Beaminster. Lower Sturthill came to the Henleys through an heiress and was purchased by William Bull. His son William Bull, M.D., had no male heir and it passed to his daughter who was the wife of Andrew Buckler. Rose's Sturthill obtained its name from its owner, a Mr Rose of Lyme Regis and would seem to be presently known as St. Luke's Farm.

Taking its name from the river on which it stands, Hutchins states that Bredy originally belonged to the Bonvils. It was in the hands of the Chilcotts, at the time of the Civil War, possibly leased from the Pauletts, but was seized and later sold to Major John Ironside, son of Bishop Ironside. By 1753 it had come to John Tucker of Weymouth.

Berwick, in the parish of Swyre was once a manor. It originally was held by King William as given in Domesday Book. Eventually, as previously stated, the seat of the de la Tours, it came to the Russells, the last being John Russell who became the first Earl of Bedford.

From 1600 Berwick was let; at one time to the Squibb family when in 1687, by a Squibb heiress, it came to be leased to George Gollop of Strode which subsequently connected it further with the Hansfords and history of Burton Bradstock.

*   *   *   *   *   *

A time of wealth or increase in population brings forth a period of building and restoration and it has been found that a fair number of houses and cottages were built in Burton Bradstock during the 17th Century.

The houses and cottages in Burton Bradstock, seen today, have, on the whole, been restored and repaired tastefully. Most properties are a mixture of periods which date from the 17th-20th Centuries.

The cottage home of our villager was single storeyed until the 16th Century. Fashions in building prevailed then, as they do today, and a design fashionable in London might take several years to filter through to the West Country and be used locally.

The original cottage consisted of a hall which was the total "house" and used as a living-room, bedroom and kitchen. There was a hole in the roof to serve as a chimney and later a chimney stack was built on the end wall.

Wealthier people added rooms either side of the hall for storage of food and ale. Later a bedroom (chamber) was built above the hall or one of the extensions. The kitchen was often completely detached. Further sleeping accommodation was found in the side room (parlour) and it was not until the 18th Century that this room became the sitting-room and the buttery (or ale house) was turned into a kitchen.

The design of this type of cottage often resulted in a long, narrow building. Originally windows would have been shuttered openings and thatch would hang low and thick. A door would open straight into the living room and often a back door was opposite it.

The size of the cottage was measured by the wealth of its owner, and so for the 16th and 17th Centuries the majority of the cottages of Burton Bradstock were extremely humble. They were built by the village people on the Lord's land and remained his property. The farmhouses reflected the wealthier position of their particular owner occupiers.

A treasure of a document rests in the Pitt-Rivers' Archives! It is the inventory of the goods and chattels of widow Mary Miller of Burton Bradstock taken in 1718. From it can not only be assessed the furniture and utensils found in her simple farmhouse, but as the rooms are listed, probably in order, a plan can be drawn of the building.

A true and perfect inventory of all and singulor the goods and chattles of Mary Miller widow lately deceased of Burton Bradstock in the County of Dorsett taken and apraised by Daniel Polden and Simon Ridgway the 14th day of October 1718.

	£ – s – d
her wearing aparell	3 – 00 – 00

IN THE CHAMBER WITHIN THE HALL

one feather bead - one feather bolster and one beadstead - one feather peelo - one rugg	*1 - 05 - 00*
one truggle beadstead - a bad feather bolster - a dust bolster - a chest - a box and two old coffers.	*0 - 12 - 00*
four course sheets - pelebed - one diaper napkin - one woulen napkin - a small bourd and cloath and 2 cheeseclouth - one hard baskett.	*1 - 00 - 00*

IN THE HALL

One table board frame and furmer - 2 settles 2 chayres	*0 - 05 - 00*
one iron frying pan - 2 hooks - one friepan - one pair of tongs - one tosting iron - 2 shelves - a spit and fire pike -	*0 - 10 - 00*
2 small brass pots - one iron pott -	*0 - 10 - 00*
2 kettles - one skillett -	*0 - 13 - 00*
one warming pan - 13 puter dishes - 6 puter plates - and puter candle stiks -	*1 - 14 - 06*
10 earthen platters - a copper cup - 2 stone jugs - 2 earthen jugs - a chamber pott - 3 cups - one earthen dish.	*0 - 05 - 00*

IN THE BUTTERY
five barrels 3 of them quarter barrels and 2 of them
half quarters.   0 - 08 - 00
2 churnes - 2 bad tubs - 4 small chees vats -
a breake - a renge - 2 earthen pans -
2 pailes with other lumber.   0 - 12 - 00

IN THE MILKIN HOUSE
One old cubbord - a lantern - a pair of butter weights -
2 dozen of trenchers - one coole dish - a trencher case
and 2 skimming dishes - a brass ladle - six spoons - 4
earthen dishes - a latten pudding pan.   0 - 06 - 06

IN THE CHAMBER IN THE WEST SIDE OF THE ENTRY
One chest - one quoffer - a beadstead and chair an
old tubb - one old small silver spoon.   0 - 13 - 06

IN THE CHAMBER OVER THE HALL
.... and 2 peels one sheet and half one coverled
and blanket - one beadsheet -   2 - 00 - 00
2 dust beds - one beadstead - one rugg - one blankett -
one sheett and half one dust bolster - one dust pillow -   0 - 12 - 00
One trunke - one chest - one quoffor - one cup - 6
milk pans - 2 small feather pillows - a pillow and
coveren.   0 - 11 - 00

IN THE BREWHOUSE
One furnese - a table board - 2 frames - a silting
tray - a covell - a cheese stand - a washtub with
other lumber.   1 - 08 - 00

                                                                     £16 - 05 - 06

*   *   *   *   *   *

The main section of the Rookery can be dated as 17th Century. It has interesting doors and side posts. Also, a plaster ceiling and the drawing room fireplace are important features. An ice house, built at a later date, exists towards the Back River but has been covered over.

Several other properties were built in Burton at this time, too. The Three Horse Shoes and The Dove Inn have revealed interesting period features during renovation. Shadrach Dairy Farm, in Mill Street, Shadrach Farm, at the bottom of Shipton Lane and the Manor Farm Houses have held farming folk for several hundred years. Ingram House was probably a farmhouse, too and was built in the 1600s but later greatly altered around the end of the 18th Century. The Rookery Cottage has all the signs of being an early farmhouse, as well.[1]

The Mill House falls into the same era as these other properties leading one to think that its position near the mill, points to the mill having had much importance then.

The White House, beside the Village Green, and adjacent to the old Wesleyan Chapel, now the library, was built around the year 1635. The south west wall holds a gable stone marked "S.B. 1635". Showing some original stone mullioned windows and containing some original fireplaces, it forms a fine visual aspect, in the centre of the village. The story of its building can be pieced together from information found in the late Maurice Ouseley's notes and other records.

Nicholas Ridgway was the Rector of Burton Bradstock and, as revealed in a previous chapter, he was a Royalist and by command of parliament was ordered to be relieved of this post.

The Ridgways were farmers and clergymen and Jane Ridgway owned a mansion house called Graston and lands in 1639. She married Simon Bowring, who owned Down Farm, which included St. Catherine's Chapel, in Shipton Gorge. The family was further linked when a second Nicholas Ridgway married a first cousin, Edith Bowring, daughter of Simon, in 1636. This wealthy family was in a good position to build such a fine property as the White House and it is certainly not speculation to attribute this to Simon Bowring, possibly Steward to Sir Thomas Freke. If its name is original it may have been a farmhouse (white house or milking house).

Graston House is dated 17th Century but has been greatly altered and is now much smaller. Manor Farm Cottage, at the top of Donkey Lane is of the same period, Bridge Cottage Stores and other cottages were also built during the 17th Century and a variety of local materials go to make up their structure. In the deeds, the former, is referred to as "Wad's". A Matthew Waad signed the Protestation Returns in 1641.

It would appear that the present Rectory has been used as the Rector's home since Elizabethan times. A smaller property than it is today, it was flanked by a courtyard, on the south side, where there was a well. The adjoining cottage used as a carriage house.

In these houses and cottages oak was used for the main timbers, the oak tree growing well in West Dorset. Sometimes ash poles were used for roof timbers, under thatch, which would have come from Cogden were the tough water reed (called "speer")[2] grows. Elm, which grew locally in abundance, was used for floor boards. Oak, and later pine, were the materials for partitions.

Many walls were made of cob, a mixture of clay, horse hair, chaff, broken twigs and pebbles. The mixture was made to a soft consistency and placed between wooden shutters and trodden until it hardened, like concrete. Split hazel was used as the woven base for wattle and daub inside walls and partitions. "Wattle and daub" is the term used for the method of making partitions, usually in the roof space, or as interior walls. It was used for exterior walls in some parts of the country but in West Dorset cottages it is more often found inside. Upright hazel sticks are positioned and then woven with horizontal split hazels. This "hurdle" was then daubed with a mixture similar to that used for cob walls and completely covered. When hardened this produced an excellent wall.

Other wood was obtained from wreckage found on the beach and a fine example of this is to be found in Donkey Cottage, facing Manor Farm Cottage, at the top of Donkey Lane. Ship's timbers having been used in one of the walls. Wreck ("rack") was also a good source of fuel, spitting and glowing green as it crackled in the fire.

The stone for building was drawn from the quarries handy to the village. The nearest one being just beyond Mr Guyatt's Cottage on the coast road to Abbotsbury. The top stone is called rubble and is inferior to the better stone found lower down. Rubble was used for the main stone work in most of the local houses and cottages. Through the Bothenhampton area runs a strata of Forest Marble, layers of lime-stone divided by thin seams of clay and calcerous bands which contain tiny shells used as stones for flooring, roofing and fencing, and called "flag" stones (large flat stones 2-3 feet in length and breadth). All old cottage floors, particularly kitchens, were made of these flagstones.

The larger houses in the village are built of similar materials throughout but the better quality woods and stones were selected and more carefully cut. In the late 18th and during the 19th Centuries some additions and alterations were made to the larger village houses and cottages. At Grove House Richard Roberts purchased Purbeck and Ham Stone and much valuable timber. Lesser quality wood was used by him in the cottages.

1. Three 17th Century cottages, adjacent to the present Post Office, indicate that they were once a single property of cruck truss construction. An open chimney being put in later.
2. As written in the records, probably from spear-grass.

XI

THE BROADMAYNE CHARITY

The 1600s were also the years when local benefactors chose to set up charities and in Burton Bradstock The Broadmayne Charity was established by the will of Matthew Derby of Bockhampton, near Dorchester, in 1655.

The Derby family had long been associated with Burton Bradstock and it is to be supposed, until further research into the Derby (Darbye, Derbie) family is carried out, that Matthew was a member of the local branch.

Matthew Derby, by his will of 1655, gave to the poor of Bockhampton, where he was born, 20s yearly for ever. Also to the poor of the parish of Burton, near Bridport, 20s yearly for ever.

He also gave £3 yearly towards placing poor children apprentices to handicrafts — men out of the several parishes before named the first £3 and yearly payment to be made to Bockhampton, the second to Main Martin and the third to Burton.

20s yearly to prisoners in County of Dorset in the prison to be bestowed in bread, at or near the usual feasts in the year.

20s annually to the free school Dorchester master and his successors.

20s per annum to the overseer of Broadmayne for distribution in bread or clothes.

£3 to be given every third year allowed to accumulate to £10 for Binding an apprentice.

In the Burton Bradstock accounts we find continual reference to apprentices being bound to an employer to learn his trade, the fees being met from the money of the Broadmayne Charity.

Richard Bryant, gentleman, of Litton endowed a charity in 1638 as did Robert Crabb, a baker, of Burton Bradstock in 1653, but these have long since been discontinued.

*   *   *   *   *   *

In November of 1688 William of Orange who had married Mary, the daughter of James II, landed at Brixham, Devon, to head a strong army. Being mainly a maritime village, and still smarting from the memories of the Monmouth Rebellion, the male population of Burton Bradstock, like others in the West Country would have been slow to join William's army. However, the army gathered strength as it headed towards London and James fled leaving a vacant throne. William and Mary were crowned in 1689 and between them led the country through a difficult period into the next century.

News of Mary's death, from the all too common smallpox, reached Burton Bradstock in 1694 and of William's death, in a hunting accident, at the opening of the 18th Century.

The Coronation Day of the new Queen, Anne, in 1703 called for the payment, by the Churchwardens, for 'five dozen of beer for the ringers'. Further afield, in the Capital, St. Paul's Cathedral was being built of Portland stone. It was indeed a period of consolidation and the uniting of England and Scotland, to form Great Britain, was an Act of Union for which Queen Anne's reign will be remembered.

XII

THE MANORIAL ROLLS AND "CHAPPLE HOUSE"

After waiting on Queen Anne's death, Sophia, of Hanover, who was the nearest Protestant relation to the Stuarts, herself died a few months before Anne in 1714 and her son George became George I of England.

Notable during his reign was the Jacobite uprising in 1715. Their intention was to supplant the King with James Edward Stuart, son of James II, but they were unsuccessful. In 1745 they tried again to restore the Stuarts to the throne and in 1746, with George II on the throne, we read that the Burton ringers rang out the church bells, which echoed through the village and valley. The Churchwardens provided drink for the ringers 'for the good sucksos in Scotland over the robles'. There were known to be four church bells, from a record of 1552, and a lych (gate) bell at Burton Church. (Further details about the bells can be found in the church)

*   *   *   *   *   *

For the 18th Century far more light is thrown upon life in the coastal village of Burton Bradstock. A vast amount of recorded, written, information is available.

The Steward continued to oversee the Manor and its inhabitants and with a non-residential Lord of the Manor the homestead and lands were all tenanted, under the Copyhold system. The farms at Bredy, Graston and the Sturthills continuing as separate farming units but paying tithes to Burton Church and poor rates.

Some other small acreages were privately owned and occupied by their owners or sub-let. The tenants of the cottages on the Lord's land all had at least a garden, some an orchard, as well, and many had pockets of land varying from 3 to 30 acres spread all over the parish.

The Manorial Rent record for Burton Bradstock for the period 1744-1752 has survived. Miss Ridgway rented a large acreage of land and was the highest contributor to the Manorial coffers. Fields she tenanted had names like Southmead, Oxhaze, Corner Close, Mouth Ground and Porters. John Angel gave one shilling annually for half a barn, as did Hester Mudford for a house and garden. Henry Symes and the Widow Fisher each paid 4d for a small cottage. William Hallett's 'small house adjacent to the pound' cost 6d annually. Two acres and 27 perches of land were let to John Lawrence for the sum of 4/5d. Abraham Lawrence had the 'fishing rites' at 2/8d. These were rights to fish from the sea and he most likely charged a fee to other fishermen. A shop was let to Benjamin Barber at 4d per year and one is left to speculate as to what property John Arcerman had for which he paid only 1d annually!

Daniel Polden rented Corncroft and Larkfield (names still in use today of fields beside the river), costing him 6d. Abraham Lawrence had a mill at 15/2d and Miss Ridgway was charged 6/- per annum for the South Mills. Most of the cottages and land went under the name of previous occupiers such as *Bowrings, Nappers, Lawrences, Longs, Wades, Barretts, Farwells, Frys, Bonners, Basings and Porters.*

Many of the tenants were employed in agriculture or allied trades. Others were glaziers, stonemasons and carpenters. Their small wage was supplemented by being self-sufficient from their garden or land. Like a century before they kept a cow or two, pigs, sheep, geese, ducks and bees. Some had a horse which was very useful for pulling a plough or cart. The animals were also grazed on the Common, which in Burton stretches from the Beach Road to Burton Mere at Cogden, or roadside verges and any wasteland in and around the village; this being the right of tenants of the Manor.

The Manorial Court was held regularly in the village and conducted on the Lord's behalf by his Steward. A Hayward was appointed by the court to see that things were carried out according to the laws of the court. His duties were to take care of the boundary fences, keep lanes clear and impound stray animals — usually an annual office. Early records have not survived for the Court in Burton, the first information available is for 1752.

A jury was summoned to consider the matters which came before the court. The main business before them was the transferring and surrendering of copyhold, keeping the rivers clean and the highways and hedges, bridges and village stocks in good repair. They were also concerned with the safety from fire and the general state of repair of the cottages, together with keeping the peace amongst the inhabitants.

'Burton Bradstock Manorial Court Leet and Court Baron — for and in the name of George Pitt, Esq., Lord of the said Manor — held on the eighth day of November 1752.'

This is the first Manorial record of Burton Bradstock that has survived. William Jeanes, Gentleman, was the Steward and the Jurymen were:- *Ralph Maynard, John Lawrence, William Hyne, Joseph Swaffield, George Miller, Matthew Camell, Benjamin Barber, Joseph Greenham, John Symes, Henry Symes, John Gover and John Long.*

*   *   *   *   *   *

The care of the poor of the village had been the responsibility of the Overseers of the Poor since the end of the 16th Century. The poor were those who because of age or infirmity could not support themselves. The responsibility was that of the parish and the Overseers were elected each year to carry out the duty of supporting them.

The Overseers' accounts for Burton Bradstock are available from 1699, as are the Churchwardens' accounts. Originally, money was used for the poor from the church funds but later the Overseers had the use of a poor rate which was levied on all land and property owners of sufficient means to qualify as ratepayers.

The 1758 list of Estates in Burton Bradstock eligible for rating for the Poor Funds were *Sumner's, Soper's, Tucker's, Polden's, Lawrence's, Hind's, Barber's, Steven's, Mynton's (later Best's), Waldron's, Willshire and Lawrence's, Nic. Darby's, R. Maynard's, Stone's (later Mr Hansford's), J. Symes', Woody's, Greening's of London, Jo Miller's, Barrett's and Pitfield's and the Widow Northover's.*

The Tithes, too, at that time are most interesting. Mr. Greening was to pay £3-2-6d per annum and an 'hogshead of cyder' every other year. At Bredy one fleece in 30 and one lamb in 30 were part of that tithe. Burton Farm paid

Fig. 1

THE RIVER BRIDE AT BURTON BRADSTOCK

Fig. 2

"THE PARISH PUMP" (L). FOREGROUND (R) WESLEYAN CHAPEL NOW A LIBRARY, ADJOINING THE WHITE HOUSE BUILT IN 1635

Fig. 3

THE ROOKERY LIES TO THE N.E. OF THE CHURCH, IN THE OLDER PART OF THE VILLAGE. DOCUMENTS, WHICH MAY HAVE REVEALED MORE OF ITS HISTORY, WERE DESTROYED IN THE BLITZ ON EXETER IN THE SECOND WORLD WAR.

Fig. 4

VENNIS' (NOW GREENWICH) COTTAGE BUILT IN THE 1600S PICTURED HERE BEFORE THE DRAMATIC RESCUE IN THE GREAT FLOOD OF 1886 WHEN THE BRIDGE AND WALL IN THE MAIN STREET WERE WASHED AWAY. THE CENTRE BLOCK OF BUILDINGS IS ALSO 17th CENTURY. THE AUTOCRATIC MR "DUKY" SYMES LIVED IN ONE OF THE COTTAGES.

Fig. 5

"CHAPPLE HOUSE", REPUTED TO BE ON THE SITE OF ST. LAURENCE'S CHAPEL, USED AS THE VILLAGE POOR HOUSE.

Fig. 6

A FLAX RETTING POND

Fig. 7

A FLAX HECKLER (OR HACKLER) AT WORK

Fig. 8

DR. GILES LAWRENCE ROBERTS, 1766-1834, METHODIST PREACHER AND
DISPENSER OF MEDICINES TO THE POOR

Fig. 9

SHADRACH FARM (L). TOWNSEND FARM (R). THE ROAD LEADS ON NORTH TO
SHIPTON. GAGES LANE BRANCHES OFF (L) AT THE COTTAGE, TO PARSON'S HILL.

Fig. 10

A FISHERMAN MAKING HIS NETS.

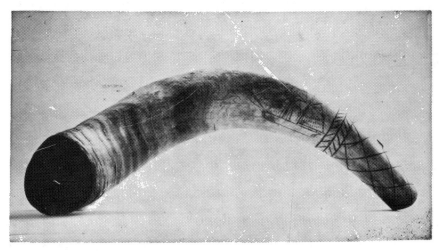

Fig. 11

IN THE MACKEREL SEASON A HORN WAS USED TO SUMMON HELPERS AND BUYERS TO THE BEACH. NOW SAFELY IN THE HANDS OF A DESCENDANT THIS ONE IS INSCRIBED. "THOMAS HUTCHINGS" (BORN BURTON BRADSTOCK 1828)

Fig. 12

BURTON BEACH WHEN FISHING WAS STILL A FULL-TIME OCCUPATION. BEHIND THE ROUTE DOWN TO THE BEACH STAND ALPHA AND BETA VILLAS, IN FRONT THE CLIFF PROMONTORY KNOWN AS "LOOK OUT"

Fig. 13

SOUTHOVER — THE STREET OF MARINERS. THE SIX COTTAGES (L) BURNT DOWN IN THE LATE EVENING OF THE 13th SEPTEMBER, 1898.

Fig. 14

SHIPWRECK ON THE BURTON SIDE OF BRIDPORT HARBOUR.

Fig. 15

EARLY CAMPERS AT FRESHWATER, WHERE THE RIVER BRIDE PERCOLATES THROUGH THE SHINGLE. THE LYNCHETS, (OR IN DORSET: LANCHETS), CUT IN THE HILLSIDE, WERE CULTIVATED IN THE MIDDLE AGES. LATER FLAX WAS SPREAD THERE TO BLEACH.

4/- yearly to the Rector, in lieu of tithe milk and a calf and 8 cows depastured on a piece of ground, called Pain's Ground, otherwise known as Burt's Ground.

Parson's Hill, amounting to 23 acres, 3 rods, 39 perches was Glebe land. The furze there reserved for the Rector. At Graston the Rector was entitled to cut an acre of hay. Mr. Tucker, the owner, could cut two swaths first, the full length of the acre.

At the time, Burton Farm was let to Mr. Best at £70 per annum, Bredy Farm in 1764 to Francis Roberts at £12 per annum, for 3 years, increasing to £14 per annum in 1766.

The Churchwardens' accounts for 1701 were signed by William Maynard and Henry Pittfield. In 1713 we find William Toogood, Simon Ridgway, Abraham Lawrence and Ralph Maynard, in 1721 Silvester Vennis, and the name of John Northover appears in 1729. Mid-way through the century the accounts are signed by Morgan Chilcott.

Beggars were a common sight scrounging their sad way through the villages and countryside. The Churchwardens found it less expensive on the parish if a sum of money was given to them to send them on their way and out of the area.

'1744 gave a poor woman 6d to rid her out of the parrifh' (parish).

In 1754 we find that a man named Spurdle was paid for digging and walling a well and paving it round. It seems that some sort of local collection was made towards this because it was a communal well and 22 subscriptions were collected. The amount we are not told. Still in connection with the well, Ralph Maynard was paid for fetching the pump from Bridport and removing the robell (rubble) in the rode (road).

£6 was voted in 1755 to erect a handsome pump on Doll's Napp. The village green, which lies between the W.I. Hall and the present library, is known as "Parish Pump" and it can be presumed that here was where the villagers of 1755 and thereafter came to draw water, until piped water flowed through much, much later. The larger houses had their own wells.

About this time it was 'unanimously agreed to prosecute and punish as far as in us lie any person or persons who shall be found breaking of hedges or carrying off gates, stiles or committing any felonious act whatsoever'.

(Old Mrs. Gear remembered children from Swyre being sent to prison for taking sticks from hedges outside their parish in the 1800s).

Women laboured in the fields for long hours or worked at home spinning and weaving or braiding nets. Children ran at their heels or weighed heavily on their backs or in their bellies. These women bore the continued life of the village, suffering the agony of the births, the rearing and often the loss of many infants. Some were fortunate enough to have hard working, healthy husbands, others were the victims of drunkenness and abuse or were widowed early due to disease or accidents.

During the 18th and 19th centuries caring for the poor presented an immense problem. With the folding up of the old Feudal System and enclosure of land, by the end of the 18th Century there had been a great growth in the number of people unable to support themselves. Old people worked as labourers as long as possible but many eventually found themselves ending their days in the Poor House.

The parish had a Poor House — the Burton Bradstock one, known as "Chapple" House, still stands at the Pound. Built from the remains of the Chapel of St. Laurence, it retains an original window. The front door, now filled-in, had a doorstep which was well worn consistent with continual use. Numerous old clay pipes were found in the garden, no doubt dropped by its many inmates. The Village Stocks stood at the Pound too. From the 14th Century every parish was commanded to erect and maintain village stocks. Although their use has fallen off the law has never been amended.

On entering the Poor House, as an inmate, the person surrendered his or her meagre possessions to the Overseers. The money raised from the sale of these few goods and chattels went towards the upkeep of the place. At this time a bed was the owner's most valuable possession.

For the benefit of this history extracts from the Overseers' Accounts have been selected to best illustrate the necessities and conditions of the people. They are collectively termed "poor" but were in fact the working people of a parish, who, because of old age, illness or accident could no longer perform their work. Orphans and base born children also received parish aid.

In the Burton Bradstock accounts of 1755 the first month's entry lists six people obtaining parish aid each receiving between 2/- and 8/- each per month. In January 1760 the month's accounts state that the following payments were made: *Henry S 6/-, John L 4/-, John B 4/-, Sarah B 4/-, Agnes M 4/-, Mary S 4/-, Mary C's child 3/-, Elizabeth N 3/-, Katherine F 2/-, Thomas D's wife 8/-*. Mr. Maynard, an Overseer, received 4/6d 'for journey to bimester for Waywardin's Warent,' and Thomas D's wife received an extra 2/- payment. There was also Richard Spurl's bill for repairing the highways amounting to 19/5d. The accounts were approved by Richard Roberts, John Boys (or Boss) and Francis Roberts.

By 1763 the list of those in need had become longer and it was stated, by way of a note, in the account book that Old G shall have a shirt and Robin S a warm coat. In April of that year Widow M and Edith B were docked 6d a week from their allowance and Rebeccah D received 1/- a week. Was this robbing Peter to pay Paul?

In August of 1764 Judith D had reached the point of going into the Poor House and an inventory of her possessions survives:

Woon long bord	*1 fether bed*
Four chears	*1 dust bed*
3 larg puter dishes	*1 bolster*
4 puter plates	*2 pellors*
2 bras sclets	*2 blankets*
2 bras pots	*2 cheats*
2 tubs	*2 bedsteds*
3 barels	*1 chest*
1 fourm	*1 box trunk*
1 cemer	*1 cobered*
6 trembras	*1 chest*

A list of the goods of Sarah C has also survived from the year 1779

1 large squear tabel
3 large puter platers
3 puter plates

1 corner cobeard
1 bead and beadstead
1 rog and 1 blanket
2 sheats   1 bolster
2 chears   1 settel
and 1 squear tabel
1 lettel brafs boyler
1 blackean rek
1 dreasear of shelves

Had they lived today these old women would be called Senior Citizens and qualify for a State Pension, their goods valuable antiques.

There were 'rayles upon cleff' which needed repairing in 1765 and that cost the Overseers 12/8d. By December it was agreed to allow John T 1/- per week and to put Roger W into the 'Chapple' (Poor House). Schooling fees were met and the children dependent on the parish cost 9/- for their education.

5/8d was paid for 'two pairs of shuess for Mary S and her dafter'. When Martha A's goods were listed, she possessed 'a pail frock, candlesticks, sasers and two looking glasses together with a glass tea canster and pothoks'. Besides these "luxury" assets she had simple furniture as did Judith D. John T had amongst his goods 'billows' and tongs and a Bible.

*   *   *   *   *   *

A rate was collected in 1765 to repair the road to the Harbour, now West Bay. It is interesting to learn that the main road from the Harbour to Bridport ran via Marsh Barn. There were trackways from Bridport and Bothenhampton over North Hill (over the Quarries as locals would say) to St. Catherine's Cross. Branching off at Bennetts Hill Farm a packhorse way led off south across Parson's Hill and thence to Gage's Lane. Mrs. Henrietta Williams, née Hitchcock, told of the packhorses and travellers' loaded donkeys coming to the village by this route.

At St. Catherine's Cross the trackway went north to Shipton Gorge and **South to Burton Bradstock and on eastwards to Bredy meeting Annning's Lane which ran from the east end of the village, also to Bredy. This track route over North Hill, via St. Catherine's Cross, towards Burton, was a common highway, or ridgeway, known as Ridge or Rudge Lane. Certainly a drier route** than the other possible ways would have been in olden times. The present Shipton Lane being only a farm track, intersected by gates from Burton to Shipton, usually impassable in the winter.

*   *   *   *   *   *

Death was a common intruder into the homes and lives of all in Burton Bradstock in the 17th and 18th Centuries. The Overseers of the Poor provided the money to buy many coffins for children and paid out 30/- for a funeral black cloth for the use of the poor.

In 1772 a list of expenses for John T's funeral (probably the John T whose inventory was listed in 1766) reads as follows: *Coffin, bell and grave 9/6d. After Dave (affidavit) 6d. Shroud etc. 2/6d. Beer, bread and chees (for the bearers) 2/10d. Laying out 2/-.*

29 people paid a rate in 1770 amounting to £2-18-11d per collection. 11½d of this came from John Tucker for mills. The year's rates in 1773 amounted to £78-10-8d from 16 collections. The Overseers' costs totalled £71-13-0d paid to the poor and with other small expenses came to £76-9-3d.

In 1750 the Lord's Steward and jury of 12 village elders were informed that the Poor House, called the "Chapple", was in decay and likewise the Bakehouse. The Lord of the Manor would repair the latter as this would have been a communal bakehouse for the village. The Back River was to be raised and repaired by the Way Wardens, who were responsible for keeping the ways free.

Joan Collins did not carry away the rubbish which lay near Joseph Stone's and she was ordered to remove it within 10 days on pain of a fine of 6/8d. Elizabeth Acreman was having a squabble with Mr. John Lawrence. It was reported that 'she had thrown dung rubbish and other offensive stuff to his annoyance before his door'.

To the inconvenience of many parishioners, Mr. Soper had been placing turnstiles at Church Path and Market Road, now High Street, and he was brought to the Court and ordered to remove them.

Thomas Allon had altered the water course and was ordered to return it (put the water on course). Several bridges were out of repair in 1757 and they had to be put right within 6 months and the stocks were broken. Pigs were not allowed to run about the streets without being first yoked! In 1759 all highways in Burton Bradstock were out of repair and Larkfield and Bank Hedges wanted plashing (remaking). Edward Chapple had also been obstructing footpaths to the backsides of cottages.

The river from the Bakehouse down to the Beach wanted scouring. It was therefore ordered to be done well and 'sufficiently' by the respective persons who had lands adjacent.

Bathsheba Thurman's house had fallen down and had to be rebuilt by Lady Day next, and Jane Northover, now widowed, surrendered her tenancy with the Lord of the Manor, of the Blacksmith's shop and stable with the appartments. This was then taken over by David Knight.

Yearly the ringers rang out the bells from the church to remind the parishioners of the success over the rebels on November 5th.

The Manorial Court Rolls of the 1760s still show that the river was a constant problem — the Back River between the lands of the Widow Polden and John Lawrence 'wants cleansing'. Besides this the Back River was to be made wider. The road to Timber Bridges and Back River was out of repair and in 1763 three bridges in the parish needed mending.

The Steward and Jury at the Court heard that Sarah Vennis, a widow, had remarried. By the rules of the Manorial Court she was enforced to forfeit her widow's estate which she was holding for her widowhood. A year later Richard Akerman, a carpenter, about 36 years old, had taken over Vennis' Plot and other premises. Vennis' Plot is now the village Playing Fields.

In the same year, 1764, Elizabeth Lawrence's chimney was very bad and dangerous to her neighbours. Another copyholder, Elizabeth Fryer, had gone the whole hog and pulled down her cottage house!

Repeatedly we read the order that 'no naked light or flame is to be carried in the street on pain of fine.' The hotchpotch thatching, and timbers overhanging the eaves, would soon burst into flames and fire would spread rapidly. John Diamond's dwelling house had fallen down in 1768. As he had done nothing to rebuild it, by the following year, he was ordered to forfeit it to the Lord of the Manor.

The Court of 1770, when George III had been King for 10 years, named David Knight as Bailiff, of Burton Manor. The Bailiff's, or reeve's, duties were not so important as the Steward's. He could perhaps be best called a deputy.

The Pound was an important feature. It obtained its name from its purpose which was a place where stray animals were impounded. Burton's first pound was in the vicinity of the present Anchor Hotel and that area there is always known as "The Pound". Later it was moved to the bottom of Shipton Lane, as shown on a map of 1840. In 1771 the Hayward, Valentine Gardinor, 'should receive sixpence for every pig that shall be found in the Highways of the said Manor for Impounding'.

There was a certain amount of trouble caused by wandering animals or those untethered. In 1772 it was recorded in the Manorial Court Rolls that 'no person (except the Lord's Tenant or occupier of lands) shall feed any horse on the Highways on pain of a fine of 10/-.'

When the Manorial Court was held in 1796 the jury of local men consisted of *Samuel Gale, John Bishop, Thomas Hutchings, William Bishop, Henry Buckler, John Spurdle, Richard Bowles, Thomas Moggaridge, Richard Bustle, George Chilcot, William Buckler, Edward Coombs, John Knight and Nicholas Bagg,* and yet again there was trouble with the Back River.

Nathaniel Morrish had made a dunghill against the wall of his dwelling house and had been given a short period of time in which to remove same on pain of a fine. A considerable number of chimneys were out of repair in 1799. Those belonging to Robert Woodcock and Mary Sponsford were only one foot from the thatch; a definite fire hazard.

Bushes in Vennis' Plot, occupied by Mr. R. Roberts, were obstructing the river and so were some bushes in Soper's Orchard, which lay behind the cottages adjoining the present Bridge Cottage Stores.

The water course from Barrow Lane, now Barr Road, to the New Inn (Anchor Hotel site?) was totally stopped. Thomas Hutchings, Benjamin Williams and John Williams were ordered to cleanse same, opposite their respective houses, within one month or be fined 30 shillings.

There had been flooding within that year, as Kittle Bridge, across the river beyond Southover, had been swept away and would have to be replaced. Again and again the 'clift' rails needed repairing.

It can be seen that the rules of the Manor Court kept the village and villagers under control and ensured a safe and peaceful way of life, as far as possible. The Overseers provided sustenance for those unable to fend for themselves and provided an existence of sorts for the old, infirm and sick, as well as the many orphans who found themselves without parents and home and dependent on the parish.

*   *   *   *   *   *

XIII

THREE THOUSAND SKULLS

The 18th Century parish registers tell us much about the population of Burton Bradstock and it can be estimated that there were some 500 inhabitants in the parish. The Bridport Harbour area was known as Burton Marsh and little habitation was there apart from a few cottages and Marsh Barn, although it was a busy harbour when the waterway was not silted up. There were some 100-130 able bodied men working from Burton Bradstock either in agriculture or as tradesmen and labourers and a large proportion as mariners.

Several mariners' wills have survived, in which they bequeathed their goods to their wives. For Burton Bradstock the will of Andrew Topp, 1725, Joseph Maniard, 1742 and Thomas Willshire of 1746, all described as mariners, remind us that 'Burton's sons were always brave'.

Families were limited in size by the high mortality of infants and from other wills available it appears that two or three children made up most family units. Couples married in their mid to late twenties, governed by the completion of apprenticeships, often 7 years, in trades such as painters, glaziers, masons, shoemakers and so on and they were solely dependent on a cottage becoming vacant, or building one of their own, together with the need to have saved £20-£30 to set up home and "farm". Those not bound by apprenticeships relied on irregular work on farms and a very small wage from which to make savings. Young people did not have the financial "where-withal" to enter into early marriage.

The women were restricted, to a certain extent, from bearing too many children by marrying later. They regularly became pregnant and the live children they bore and the number reared, to the age of five, was small. It is reckoned that about two thirds of all children born to the labouring people died before reaching the age of five years and even the families of the gentry were not exempt from this. (A memorial tablet to five year old John Best can be found in Burton Church.)

The parish register for 1740 lists 7 baptisms, 5 burials and 3 marriages. The surnames of those baptised were *Hayward, Barber, Northover, Waldren, Anning, Bowles* and *Williams.* Of the burials three were of the same surname and probably of the same family, dying from some disease.
Burials 1740:
September 12 Margaret Barber
November 5 Henry Barber, who was baptised the previous July.
November 11 Frances Barber
The following year the pattern is similar with 6 baptisms, 7 burials and 2 marriages.
Marriages 1741:
Samuel Symes to Elizabeth Polden 17th February
Robert Tucker to Mary Lawrence 28th September
For 1745 other surnames appear in the register of Baptisms:
Robert son of Thomas and Elizabeth Akerman
Richard son of Joseph and Xten Greening
Hester daughter of John and Barbara Hooper

Sarah daughter of John and Hannah Gale
Joseph son of Matthew and Elizabeth Hind
Jenny daughter of Edward and Thamzin Bagwel

No deaths were recorded that year except that of The Reverend Mr. Williams, the Rector.

An interesting entry by the Rector for 1746 records the Baptism of 'Martha daughter of John and Martha Nicholls of Bridport born in the fields near Burton and privately Baptised in my house'.

In 1747 the burials leapt to fifteen in number and included Mrs. Best.

Drownings at sea, due to shipwreck, along the Chesil Coast were frequent and in 1753 'was buried Peter Strhom, Master of a Hambourg Vefsel'. In 1763 the body of a lad about 4-5 years old was washed up at Burton and from his clothing it was presumed he was the son of a lady washed ashore, near Abbotsbury, several days earlier and a Frenchman, name unknown, was buried at Burton in 1768. From time to time the burial of mariners, drowned at sea, some unidentified, is recorded in the Parish Registers. (In 1837 and 1838 footnotes in the registers refer to the incidents that led to the deaths.)

The marriages for 1755 have been cut out of the register and one can only speculate as to the reason for the removal of these entries and by whom.

The baptisms for the years 1760, 1770 and 1780 are 15, 17 and 11 in number and reveal the following surnames listed in the order in which they first occur: *White, Maby, Angel, Lovelace, Hawkins, Hind, Thurman, Hooper, Crabb, Swaffield, Payne, Anning, Richards, Moores, Warren, Hallett, Miller, Pitcher, Chappel, Horseford, Crew, Whittle, Trevice, Knight, Akerman, Nicholas, Cammel, Hansford, Gale, Perrot, Summers, Fudge, Burch, Woodcock, Syms, Swaine and Spurdle.*

Burials in years taken at random were 17 in 1756, 12 in 1762 and 13 in 1773. Other surnames that occur here are *Hardy, Chilcott, Bowles, Bishop, Best, Tibbs, Richards, Samways, Burchell, Polden, Farr, Gardiner, Russel and Nurse.*

There were 2 or 3 marriages each year. On the whole, both parties being from Burton Bradstock and from this paricular register we find a fairly regular pattern throughout pointing to an increase in population in the latter half of the century and that no particular heavy outbreak of disease struck in the village during the century, except 1747, when there may have been an epidemic or hard winter. That smallpox, tuberculosis and cholera and the like were always present, wiping out families or the weak who had no immunity to these killing diseases, is a known fact.

The last entries in that register are for 1782 and record the burials of Maria Chick, Elizabeth Fudge, Thomas Symes and William Lacy.

*   *   *   *   *   *

The families living in Burton Bradstock in the 18th Century were able to supplement their wages not only from their smallholdings and plots of land or the common for grazing but by growing flax and hemp and spinning and weaving in their homes. To this could be added the benefit of fishing from the sea.

By the mid-century, wages for men were from 10d to 1/3d per day, more for the very long hours in summer. It must be remembered that for most men the work was not regular. They were hired for a specific job and the winter months could prove a very slack and lean time. This then would be the time when the spinners and weavers would get busy, the products being sold to local merchants.

Younger men did work annually as farm labourers. Living in, part of their payment was included as board and lodging, as, in fact, it still can be today. This also applied to the young women who were farm servants but there were also seasonal jobs for women, as we learn in Thomas Hardy's novel "Tess of the d'Urbervilles". Tess was a dairymaid employed for the spring and summer months, when the milk yield was at its height, in the Blackmore Vale.

Women and children would help in the fields during the busy periods with sowing, haymaking, harvesting, hoeing and scaring birds. The latter was also a job for small boys. Another Hardy novel, "Jude the Obscure", describes a lad in the fields scaring the birds. Although receiving only half the wage of men for their work, the women and children provided additional income essential to the economy of the home.

After harvest women and children would glean from the corn fields. The grain they collected provided a welcome addition to their larders. This was usually a "perk" and done in their own time but for them it was an essential item in their food store.

Reference is found to the growing of potatoes. At the turn of the century George Forsey's will refers to a small plot of potatoes in a field called Barrow and Richard Roberts, the mill owner, speaks of the labourers harvesting their potatoes. "Tiddy" or "spud" growing has been a part of rural economy for many generations and a great pride was taken in being the first villager to dig potatoes and the one to produce the best crop. Good Friday, being a holiday, was the usual day when the seed potatoes were planted. Anyone who had not planted the seed by that day was considered very lazy.

*   *   *   *   *   *

Throughout the second half of the 18th Century the Overseers of the poor continued to administer their aid and the Manor Court met to transfer copyhold tenancies and supervise the well being of the property and persons in the control of the Lord of the Manor.

The Overseers obviously encouraged helping oneself for they paid in 1773 'for a spining whele for Hannah Wheadon 2/8d'.

Sweeping the chimneys of the poor cost 1/- on one occasion and '116 sheves (of) reed for Mors house' cost 11/4d in 1780 with labour and spars 8/1½d when the roof was thatched.

In 1770 12 people received from 2/- to 10/- per month and John Woodman who was caring for James C's children received 9 weeks pay and shifts were bought for the children costing 5/4d. Mending their shoes set the Poor Rate back a further 1/2d. Later the children received 2 pairs of 'stokens'. Mary S did not go without stays, a pair was provided for her costing 5/-.

Payment was made to women who sat with the chronically sick and dying and for laying out the dead. A common form of treatment, for many ailments, was bleeding and we read of David Knight, a blacksmith, who was paid 1/6d for bleeding James Anning's wife 3 times.

In 1770 the wall from Green Cliff to the Common had to be brought back into its former place. Timber Bridge, beyond what is now The Rookery, was not fit for passing and was to be repaired without delay. Mary Symes had not kept her chimney in repair, as ordered by the Manor Court and 'the river from Burton to Burton's Mouth was out of repair and for want of being cleansed many houses are overflowed'. One month was set for its cleaning. It was ordered that 'no person shall make a dunghill in the streets' and no grain was to be 'whinnowed' in the road.

At this Court of 1770 David Knight was the Bailiff and the Jury was made up of:- *Ralph Maynard, Thomas and Richard Akerman, Thomas, Henry and John Symes, Thomas Bartlett, John Lawrence, John Anning, Joseph Waldron, Edward Williams and Thomas Russell.*

In the Churchwardens' Accounts of 1791 it was agreed at the Easter Vestry Meeting, to pay by Church Rate, prosecution for 'murders, burglarys, felonys and thefts which may be committed within the said parish'. We read that the Churchwardens, when away from home, on parish business, for one day or any part of a day, shall be allowed three pence per mile and a crown a day, when away from home, for more than one day.

It was agreed 'to sign no certificate for licensing any additional public houses and if any strolling players or people exhibiting shows and slights of hand tricks shall reside longer than one week in the parish then the Churchwardens shall put a law in force'.

A decision was made to give George Gale 15/- per annum for the use of a house to keep fuel, to be sold out, once a week, to the labouring poor, at 'prime cash by them'. This fuel was provided to prevent the hedges and fields from being ruined. Seven guineas was the sum agreed to be laid out for the store of wood, furze and coals which were to be purchased.

These accounts were signed by Robert Hunter, the Rector, and Thomas Marsh, Jacob Brown, Daniel Stone and Samuel Best, the Churchwardens and Overseers of the Poor.

*　　*　　*　　*　　*　　*

The labourers of the 18th Century were constantly changing masters and as the century wore on and many lost their independence when their land was incorporated into larger farming units they were forced to become more dependent on being hired on a more permanent basis. As the industrial scene became more organised and centralised some workers found employment at the factories and moved on less frequently. With the setting up of the flax and hemp spinning mill in Burton Bradstock around 1790 the village escaped from losing too many of its original families.

The increase in population put a heavier burden on the Overseers of the Poor and poverty increased or declined as and when the harvests were good or bad and the fixed price of bread rose or fell.

Those who became dependent on the parish qualified for relief by way of birth, marriage or employment for over one year. Apprentices could become qualifiers and later we shall read of the mill owner, Roberts', concern not to burden the parish with poor people after completing their apprenticeships. Anyone who did not qualify for relief could be removed back to their legal place of last settlement, escorted by the Parish Constable.

Later settlement orders have survived. One concerning Charles Smith and Amelia, his wife and 3 children. Smith was born in Burton Bradstock and was stated to be 37 years old in 1854. His father, Henry Smith had been bound apprentice at 14 to Richard Roberts and had left Burton for Darley Dale in Derbyshire but had been removed back to Burton in 1824 and this order had never been appealed against, making Burton Bradstock the parish responsible for the Charles Smith in question who was, at the time of the removal order, sick and permanently disabled.

In 1858 three children were being supported by the Overseers of the Poor in Burton. After investigation it was found that their father had been born in a cottage at Shepherd's Cross, Ilton, Somerset and they were going to be removed back to that parish. These three children Fanny, Leah and William, had been brought to Bridport Harbour, Burton Bradstock and landed on the quay by a trading vessel from Guernsey where they had been abandoned by their parents.

*   *   *   *   *   *

The end of the 18th Century in Burton Bradstock, when George III had been on the throne for 40 years, was a time of reorganisation. For several generations its working people had been as independent as their land and Lord would allow. They had planted and made hedges, built houses and vast lengths of walls, tilled gardens and fields, planted orchards, plundered wrecks and smuggled in contraband goods and fished in all seasons and weathers from the steep shores. They had married, generally, from within the other village families and buried their dead in the churchyard. Generations of their ancestors had been buried repeatedly on top of each other, at least 4ft deep for an adult and 3ft for a child and after a 14 year lapse, in the same grave.

They had rung out the bells for all occasions; the threat of invasion, coronations, victories and in mourning, tolling the bell 9 times on the death of a man, 4 for a woman and 3 for a child and then as many times as a person was old, between 8 a.m. and 8 p.m.

They had rested on the Sabbath from fishing, 'if any person belonging to this place or residing in it shall shoot a sean (seine net) on a Sunday or a fish anyhow in doing so for the purpose of catching fish or who shall put a boat to sea for any unlawfull purpose whatever shall be prosecuted by the Churchwardens', and they attended the church in such force that it eventually had to be enlarged and further gallery seats provided.

Here was a people about to imprint an unique history on the village. The craft they had plied for hundreds of years was to be centralised in a mill and many of the clay fields of the Bride Valley would wave sky blue with acres of flax. Richard Roberts was living in Burton Bradstock and there he saw the potential in its people and products to establish a business.

The flax mills of Burton Bradstock were to tide the people over the hard years of the early 19th Century and this would go down in local history as one of the few villages in West Dorset to have its own flax spinning and weaving factory.

*   *   *   *   *   *

In the late 18th Century William Wordsworth, the Lakeland poet, and his sister, Dorothy, lived at Racedown on the outskirts of the Marshwood Vale, some four miles from Broadwindsor. They rented this fine house from John Frederick Pinney in 1795 for 2 years. This member of the well known local family was the Grandson of Azariah Pinney who was sent to the West Indies for his participation in the Monmouth Rebellion. However, Azariah made a large fortune in the Indies and it was his Grandson who built Racedown.

Wordsworth noted how the country people were wretchedly poor and captured the sights, scenes and atmosphere of West Dorset in some of his poetry. In his poem "To a Sexton" he brings out the feelings of a sorrowing widower. Apart from the tragic aspect of the poem, he brings to his readers' notice the village churchyard scene and the repeated use of the ground, perhaps **not** known to everyone. This poem was written in 1799.

To a Sexton

Let thy wheel-barrow alone
Wherefore, Sexton, piling still
In thy bone-house bone on bone?
'Tis already like a hill
In a field of battle made,
Where three thousand skulls are laid;
These died in peace each with the other, —
Father, sister, friend and brother.

Mark the spot to which I point!
From this platform, eight feet square,
Take not even a finger joint:
Andrew's whole fire-side is there.
Here, alone, before thine eyes,
Simon's sickly daughter lies,
From weakness now, and pain defended,
Whom he twenty winters tended.

Look but at the gardener's pride —
How he glories, when he sees
Roses, lilies, side by side,
Violets in families!
By the heart of man, his tears,
By his hopes and by his fears,
Thou, too heedless, art the Warden
Of a far superior garden.

Thus then, each to other dear,
Let them all in quiet lie,
Andrew there and Susan here,
Neighbours in mortality.
And, should I live through sun and rain
Seven widowed years without my Jane,
O Sexton, do not then remove her,
Let one grave hold the loved and lover!

XIV

BURTON BRADSTOCK IN THE 18th CENTURY

Whilst the Lord of the Manor and his Court, the Churchwardens and the Overseers of the Poor saw to the rights and welfare of the parishioners of Burton Bradstock and in return the villagers worked to support themselves for as long as they were able, the old system was beginning to fade out and a set-up remembered by our fathers and grandfathers, as the village of Burton Bradstock, was taking shape and was to remain so for some 200 years until 1958 when the village estate was split up and sold to private individuals who put their personal stamp on the cottages, streets and other old buildings and who filled the fields on the perimeter of the village with luxury properties. The people who came to settle in the village in the second half of the 20th Century had come to enjoy the rural atmosphere created by the men and women of Burton Bradstock in the 18th and early 19th Centuries but their arrival also coincided with the affluence of that particular time and to a great extent the true ruralness disappeared, most of the small industries, that support a village community, were not required and faded out, farms were sold, split up and often put to other uses.

*   *   *   *   *   *

The 18th Century saw the reign of the three Georges. The first King George was summoned, against his will from Hanover. He retained many of his Hanovarian customs and spoke little English. Having banished his wife for her adultery, whilst committing it frequently himself, he arrived in England with two, far from attractive, mistresses. Much of his reign was occupied warding off various wars and maintaining trade routes but for the working men of Burton Bradstock, their concern, their weekly wage, amounted to a mere 6 shillings.

George I's son, George II, reigned from 1727 for 33 years. The troubles with the Jacobites continued and war was declared on Spain in 1739. A series of wars was to last right through to 1815 and mid-century saw the Anglo/French war in North America with the storming of the heights of Quebec and seizing of Montreal. The North American Colonies were later lost and independence was established on July 4th 1776.

George II's son, Frederick, had met an untimely death in 1751 and the succession came to his 22 year old grandson, another George, who became George III. His long reign from 1760 took him into the 1800s. His devotion to his wife and fifteen children, family life in general and love of furniture, music, gardening and farming and his patronship of the arts endeared him to his people and brought to this country a period of progress and creativity leaving us a legacy of fine buildings, paintings, music and literature.

The King and his family, mainly the elder children, frequently visited Weymouth and gave fame and fortune to the town, making it a favourite spa and establishing it as a centre for holidays.

*   *   *   *   *   *

Back in Burton Bradstock the reigns of these three kings and their involvement with wars and foreign trade provided a living for those who were mariners, sailing the seas of the world, much of which was comparatively new, and those engaged in making ropes and other ships' tackle, including sailcloth and hammocks and those making nets for the fishing trade in the New World, mainly Newfoundland.

During the reigns of the Georges, landed gentry enjoyed much prosperity and held positions of importance as members of Parliament or Justices of the Peace. Many were wealthy merchants accumulating vast fortunes both here and abroad and with this money they built fine houses some of which can be seen today throughout the country, still intact as they were then, others vastly altered, destroyed or greatly reduced because of their size, which in later years became a liability to their owners.

*   *   *   *   *   *

During the Georgian period agriculture and methods of farming progressed. George III enjoyed playing at being a farmer and by then a rotation system was established which resulted in better crops being grown. This method had been introduced by Viscount Townshend who was nicknamed "Turnip Townshend" — turnips being one of the crops used in the four year rotation.

The popularity of mutton continued to keep up the numbers of sheep and from an observation of livestock by George Culley, a Northumberland farmer, in 1794, we get a fine picture of the Dorset breed of sheep. The extract was taken from Mr. J. M. (Bunny) Lenthall's book of the Bradstock Dorset Horn Flock that he had kept at Burton Bradstock until his emigration to Australia in 1967.

'In 1794 the Dorsetshire breed were mostly horned, white faced and stood on high, small, white legs with long, thin carcasses. Many had no wool on their bellies. The mutton obtained from them was fine grained and well flavoured and they lambed twice a year.'

George Culley went on to say that fat lamb could be obtained at any season and was found early in the year at the tables of the nobility and gentry, and even amongst tradesmen 'in these luxurious times'. Lamb was sold in the London markets, even before Christmas, and was, from then on, in constant and regular supply. Ranging in price from 15/- to ½ guinea a quarter hundredweight these lambs were imprisoned in little dark cabins, never seeing the light of day. They were brought out to be suckled by the ewes which were oil cake fed, supplemented with corn, cabbages and turnips and other available green food. The lambs were kept in very clean conditions in deep, fresh straw which contributed a lot to the high success of rearing fine lambs. Culley also remarked on the good Dorset pastureland.

*   *   *   *   *   *

A change in the calendar took place in 1752 when the year began on January 1st. In the days of the Saxons and Normans December 25th had been the New Year and around 1190 to 1751 the 25th March, Lady Day, saw the start of the year. Until 1752 the Parish Registers clearly show the use of the Old System.

*   *   *   *   *   *

XV

SOME BUILDERS

A further time of prosperity and increased population produced buildings of all types and not least in Burton Bradstock a considerable number of cottages and houses were built and others altered or repaired around this period. The most important of these was the building of the Great House, near Shadrach, in Burton. Queen Anne in style, this fine house still stands elegant and imposing at the end of the village. At one time it stood adjacent to a row of cottages which burnt down in 1926 and were replaced by two modern houses set further back from the road. The name of the Great House became corrupted into the local dialect and is now known as "Girt House". It may have been built by a Captain Ingram and was certainly inhabited by him at some time.

During the 18th Century it is documented that the men of Burton were building and rebuilding their cottages, some at their own expense. These cottages remained the property of the Lord of the Manor being built on his land and mostly from materials taken from the Manor lands. A small rent was payable to the Lord for the property and legal documents were drawn up and exchanged.

Silvester Vennis, born in 1688, held the deeds of two cottages one of which had been erected by Thomas Vennis. There was a Thomas Vennis born in 1690 and these two were brothers. Very likely the cottages were where one nows stands on the corner, in Vennis' Plot, or the Playing Fields, opposite Cheney's Garage, at the beginning of the Lower Road. The cottages are now one and known as Greenwich Cottage. Could this be a corruption of Vennis' Cottage?

Magnolia House (later called Farmhouse), below the school, was built in 1765 possibly on the site of an earlier building and much altered and improved in the 19th Century. It is said that these alterations were carried out by an old sea Captain, a bachelor, who lived there alone except for his manservant. The carved lid of the Captain's sea chest was put to good use as the door of the front staircase. Recent renovations there have revealed the original doors and windows, now blocked, a fine cut stone floor in the main room and the exciting find of a George III coin, dated 1765, embedded under the hearth stone of the original fireplace. It is well known that the builders placed a penny in the hearth when building a house and other finds relating to witchcraft and superstition have, from time to time, been found behind hearths or lodged on a stone in a chimney or in the roof space of cottages.

Only a few yards above Magnolia House, opposite the Church, is "The Magnolias", both properties sport Magnolia Floribundas, planted in the early days of these houses. "The Magnolias" would possibly have been a cottage altered to a large house around 1795. From the outside it can be seen that the height of the building was raised and a fine portico and date stone marked "AH 1795" are to be found on the north side of the house.

The initials AH can possibly be attributed to Ann Hansford, daughter of Lieutenant William Hansford of the Royal Navy. An alternative explanation would be that the A stands for Adney and the H for Hansford. William

Hansford having married Mary Adney, a widow, at Burton Bradstock in 1762. Her maiden name was also Hansford and she is stated to have been of Swyre, her family living at Berwick at one time.

There were certainly others with an H as an initial in Burton about that time who could have built "The Magnolias". In the 18th Century, we find Hunter (another daughter of Lt. Hansford, Charlotte, married Robert Hunter the Rector of Burton), Hounsell, Hyde, Hallett, Hine, and Hazard were all tenants of the Burton Manor — several of them paying large rents for their land and property; but the Hansford connection is by far the most likely.

The Grove may have been renovated for the marriage, in 1777, of Samuel Best, son of Mr Best the tenant of Burton Farm. Some of the land that went with the tenancy lay in that part of the village.

Darby House, nearby, is Georgian in style and may have been built by the Darby (Derby, Derbie) family who were long associated with Burton Bradstock or on land owned by them, or William Derby, the Rector of 1564/67.

* * * * * *

Ingram House was either two cottages or a farmhouse with cottage when Captain Ingram carried out alterations there at the end of the 1700s. It would be expected that this was for his retirement.

Like all good sailors he wanted everything "ship-shape" and the mud in the street outside his door was not to his liking. He decided to pave the whole length of the front of the house, keeping the frontage and doorway clean. It also provided a "quarter deck" for the old man — a Rear Admiral by the time of his retirement. Ingram would pace up and down the stone pavement to take his daily promenade.

His walkway later proved an annoyance for the children of naval Captain Collins who lived there some hundred or so years later. Like Rear Admiral Ingram, Captain Collins ran his home as a ship and his children were required from time to time to weed the "quarter deck".

Holding a Master Mariner's Certificate both for sail and steam ships, seeing service all around the world and having been blown up, losing his ship, 54 men and his leg when only in his thirties during the First World War, it had come as a bitter disappointment to Captain Collins to be forced to retire from what promised to be a brilliant career; at least in Burton he was able to follow in the wake of an Admiral.

* * * * * *

Many deeds, lodged in the Pitt-Rivers' Family Archives at the County Record Office, relate to properties and land rented from Burton Manor in the 18th Century. Wade's House on the bridge, with buildings and parcels of land, was tenanted in 1759 by one Samuel Soper of Burton Bradstock. The deeds refer to a dwelling house, tenement barn, stables, garden and orchard and large acreage of land at Cogden and the common, some 80 acres, and adjoining South Mills. This must be the property known as Bridge Cottage Stores, a village shop in the S.W. end of the village and built by a member of the Wade family in the late 1600s/early 1700s.

During the years 1759-1784 John Anning, a carpenter, was in possession of a cottage with garden and orchard, 'lately rented by John Northover', and then his widow, the rent being payable on the Feast of the Blessed Virgin Mary and the Archangel Michael. By 1784 his son John Anning, a 35 year old mariner, held the property, having survived his brother William on whose life it was held.

Richard Roberts the flax and hemp spinning merchant, of whom more will be written in a later chapter, was beginning to stake his claim in the parish by the end of the century. At his own expense he built a warehouse at Bridport Harbour and had erected a mill in 1778 for the spinning of wool on the ground of Mill Plot, Burton, now Cheney's Store, which had been surrendered by John Lawrence in 1794, paying a yearly rent of 8d. There was a mill there long before and Roberts either rebuilt or enlarged it and the Lawrences and the Roberts were probably connected by marriage. There is a clause in the deed giving Lord Rivers the right to pen back the water, to flood the meadows, to produce early grass. The Roberts' Family was also renting a considerable acreage of land in Burton Bradstock.

John Waldron, a merchant from Poole, held land on the lives of Mary Waldron, aged 19, and Fanny Thurman, aged 7, at an annual rent of 11/2d and one pound heriot. A heriot was a payment, or rent, paid in kind, usually the best beast. Parcels of land and a dwelling house were rented to "Mrs" Mary Miller, a spinster, at 5/2d per annum. "Mrs" was a title afforded to a spinster of some standing.

By 1800 practically the whole of Burton Bradstock, that we know today, as the real old village, had been built. A great change in the mode of life of many villagers was about to take place. Whilst many would still hold cottage and garden tenancy for the rest of their lives and that their descendants would follow the same pattern, some had lost their land to larger farming concerns. Another Master was to take charge in the village — a local industrial revolution was taking place.

*   *   *   *   *   *

XVI
MAKING THEIR MARK

The wealthy squires of the country fed themselves on salt beef, cold mutton with cabbage and carrots and pudding to follow. They drank Portugese wines and the strongest brandy, indulged in stag hunting and later fox hunting which was a new invention in the early 18th century. They enjoyed cock fighting and horse racing and although we have no record of a squire in Burton Bradstock we can be certain that the Roberts, Hansfords, Lawrences and Captain Ingram and other wealthier men of Burton fell into this category to some extent. These squires and merchants were now established and their sons and grandsons, barring ill fortune, were to inherit property and wealth on an unprecedented scale.

*　　*　　*　　*　　*　　*

Some humbler sons inherited simpler fortunes. We are able to ascertain this from wills that are available, made by the men and women of the village, whose possessions totalled £5 or more and were signed by them in the presence of two witnesses. The Peculiar Court of the Lord of the Manor could prove a will and others would be presented at the appropriate Ecclesiastical Court.

Joseph Croome signed his will in 1745. He was a miller and had two sons William and John and a daughter, Louis Brown, to whom he left the proverbial shilling. Mary, another daughter, inherited land 'situate at Litton Chayney'. William owed his father fourscore pounds (£80) and when that debt was repaid John and Mary were to receive £30 each.

John Anning bequeathed to his son, William, all his working tools (previously we had read that John Anning was a carpenter) and his best 'sute of clous' also his 'bead that I lie in'. His other son was probably a mariner and was to receive his watch and 'two tabels bordes' if 'my son John do come home safe from the Enges'. His wife 'Elisbth' was to live on in the dwelling house and messuage and on her death his daughters, Ann Cleap and Sarah Anning, would inherit it. Ann was to have 'the east end of the house that Sim Saint live inn'. This large and only house, at the time, in Anning's Lane, stood until very recently, on the south side of the lane.

George Miller, a cordwainer, bequeathed his feather bed to his grand-daughter, Mary Crabb, in 1772.

A boldly signed and sealed will of the 12th March 1771, made by Henry Symes, gave 1/- to Mary Bowles, his sister, a widow, and 1/- to his brother John. To Jane, his beloved wife, 'all my stock, household goods, furniture, all my leasehold and copyhold messuages tenaments. But in case my said wife shall marry after my decease and not continue my widow then and in such case she my said wife shall not have or be intitled unto what I have hereby said except such goods as intitled on my marriage with her. Also £100 secured unto her by a certain marriage bond entered into by me'. If she remarried everything was to go to John Lawrence, son of John Lawrence, gentleman. The first mentioned being the brother-in-law of Henry Symes.

The will of Mary Bradford of Burton Bradstock, dated 10th August 1780, gave 'to Mary Burt my green silk gown and to Jane Best my white gown and

Mrs Drapers yellow silk gown and a lace cap and to Betty Nossiter my flowered silk gown and to Mary Cooper my dark linen gown and my black coat and stays'. Edward Stevens was to be her executor.

Joseph Swaffield, blacksmith, bequeathed 'all lands and tenaments, goods, chattles, moneys and securities (except my dwelling house and household goods which I have lately disposed of by deed) to my good friends Mr. Thos. Marsh of Bothenhampton, yeoman, and Eliz. Marsh of Wyche, Bothenhampton, widow'. dated the eleventh February, 1761.

Elizabeth Akerman could only make her mark on her will of 1753 in which she left 1/- to her son, Thomas. Her largest clock to her grandson, Robert Akerman, 'when he attain one and twenty years of age'. Martha Windsor, her daughter, inherited her tenement and all the rest and residue of her goods and wearing apparel, personal estate and effects.

William Darby left his 'large brass kittle' for the general use of all the family and not to be sold for the use of any one in particular. All his wearing apparel both linen and woollen, with the exception of three of his best shirts, went to his son Samuel Darby. The three best shirts passed on to his wife.

George Forsey's son, Thomas, received one corner cupboard, all the bed things, plates and a 'tea kittle' and silver watch on the death of his father. The other son, Richard, became the owner of his father's leather boots. Forsey's sons and daughters all received 10/- yearly at Christmas.

David Knight, a farrier, stated that the expenses of his funeral were not to exceed £6 and all his lawful debts were to be paid within 3 months. His writing desk was to pass to his son and £5 to Elizabeth Cammel, or her daughter, for looking after him when ill and unable to do anything for himself.

John Gale, Yeoman of Loders, with Burton Bradstock connections and buried there, mentions one acre and quarter of flax in West-town, Shipton Gorge, in his will of 1798.

Finally, at the end of the century, Elizabeth Bartlett made her will on the 24th November 1798. Her house and garden tenancy she left to Mary Bagg, her daughter. Elizabeth Spurdle, her grand-daughter had the right to claim and possess it after her death. Mary Bagg was also to receive 'my best yellow curtains and bedstead, best tea chest, round mahogany table, best table cloth, three silver tea spoons marked MB also 10 gns owing to me by her husband.'

Four other initialled silver spoons were bequeathed to her grandchildren, as was a silver cream cup marked F.E.B. and a second unmarked silver cream cup. 'All rest money and goods to my daughter Catherine Spurdle. I do also desire and direct that my said daughter Catherine Spurdle for the loving kindness and attention she has always shown to me may have the sole management of my funeral and internment'. She made her mark which was witnessed by Richard Roberts and John Dorcen.

The wealthy Poole merchant, who had moved to Burton to live, and no doubt trade, left to John Waldron (otherwise Penny) son of Mary, the daughter of John and Eleanor Penny, of Newfoundland, £100 sterling and all clothes and wearing apparel. Various nephews and great nephews and their daughters were to receive sums of money of £10 and £20. £100 was on trust for Mary Richards and £25 each for Elizabeth and Fanny Richards. The Burton Bradstock, Poole and Newfoundland connection conjures up an intriguing story.

* * * * * *

Here by 1800 was a picture of our people of Burton Bradstock, Richard Roberts the mill and warehouse owner, John Waldron the wealthy merchant, Naval Officer Ingram at Girt House and the Hansfords at the church end of the village. Yeoman farmers in residence at Burton, and Shadrach Farms, a nucleus of better off tenants of the Lord of the Manor, the working people whose possessions did not amount to £5 and the very poor, old or unfortunates whose roof was the "Chapple House" and here in the Burton Bradstock of 1800 was a close knit community with the labouring folk contributing their hard work and skills for their own survival and because of the very low rewards they received unwittingly contributing to make their masters rich men.

XVII

ROBERTS AND THE FLAX MILLS

Domestic industries developed in Medieval times were being financed and organised by enterprising men in the 18th and early 19th Centuries. Richard Roberts, with a strong West Dorset farming background, was one of these men. He had the foresight to utilise the abundant water power of the River Bride and the suitable clay soils of West Dorset for processing and growing flax and some hemp.

Reference in the latter part of the 18th Century to South Mill, Burton Bradstock leads one to wonder if a north mill already existed. The Mill, called Lawrences, stood on the southern side of the village, below the church. It has already been noted that Roberts erected a mill on the Mill Plot in 1778, stated in the deeds to be a mill for processing wool. Was that its previous use, Roberts' original intention or an error? The woollen industry of the West Country had suffered a decline by that time. This building was possibly an addition to the existing mill or renovation.

The flax was spread to bleach and dry on the slopes at Freshwater and in earlier times the river there could easily have been dammed to use as a soaking, or retting, pond. In living memory acres of flax were grown in the fields near Freshwater. Nearby was a shed where flax was combed.

Records mention a pond at the Mill and in Roberts' time the flax would have been soaked there, with so much water available it would be probable that a pond was made for that purpose. The factories were referred to as "mills" because they needed a water-mill to power them. The method of preparing flax for spinning was to pull the ripened and by then dirty grey plant, by hand. Next it was bundled and dried and stamped with a wooden biddle (flat board with a sloping handle) to remove the seed balls. It was then retted, either by being soaked in a pond, or dew retted, which was a natural process formed when the stalks were allowed to weather in the dew and sun, as at Burton Bradstock, when the flax was spread at Port, near Freshwater. When retting was complete the substances binding the fibres were decomposed.

The material was further dried by setting light to the outside skin, called skimps, which had fallen away, under wooden frames where the retted flax was spread. After this second drying the flax was "swingled" or "scutched". The flax was laid across lengths of wood placed on the frames and beaten with a wooden tool called a swingler or scutcher.

The next part of the preparation was to dress the flax. This further separated the fibres and arranged them in parallel formation. The fibres were drawn through a series of combs and the short ends removed. The short pieces were known as tow and used for inferior work. This process was repeated so that the shorter fibres were removed until the longest and best fibres came out of the final combing. Originally this part of the process was done by hand and the craftsman was known as a flax dresser. When hackling machines came into use then the operator became known as a hackler or sometimes heckler. At Roberts' mill it would seem that the hand and machine dressing of the flax was carried on simultaneously. The lines of fibre called "stricks" were those arranged on the distaff ready for spinning. A similar process was employed for processing hemp used in rope and twine manufacture.

As trade prospered Roberts saw the need for a mill to be used solely for swingling flax and in the early 1800s he built, or possibly rebuilt, the second mill in Grove Road. In his business letters of 1807-1815 he mentions three mills but as to where the third one was situated and whether in Burton is unknown. Reference is made to a mill at Radipole in several letters. About the same time he built what is now called "Mill Terrace", directly below the church. This was initially a warehouse with a flax shop or "dressing" shop and "counting house", the equivalent to an office.

The raw material went from the Grove Road Mill to Lawrence's Mill and warehouse where it was carded and dressed and coiled ready for spinning, on the premises, or returned to the other manufacturers. Roberts processed many tons of flax for other merchants and his business accounts refer often to preparing flax.

A canal was dug from the Grove Mill to Lawrence's Mill (it runs past the school today) and the water was then harnessed, as required, to drive the wheel at the spinning mill. As a row of cottages ran from the church down over towards Timber Bridge, Roberts very likely demolished one of them to make way for the canal.

From Litton Cheney to Burton Freshwater the River Bride was intersected with hatches used to control the flow of water to the mills and also to allow the meadows to be flooded for early grass production. A man was employed to work the hatches and this necessitated walking the whole length of the river. He had to have a good knowledge of the water supply and local conditions, for on him depended the volume of water available to the mills and the safety from flooding, in the village, during adverse weather. The last man in Burton Bradstock who was well qualified to do this being Steve Northover, who was employed for many years at the Grove Mill, when it was a corn grinding mill.

Today the mills stand as edifices of the times we live in. The Grove Mill converted to flats, the Spinning Mill now a store. Devoid inside of all evidence of their former use they hold only the ghosts of weary, often hungry workers — their tasks were arduous and the hours long, pay and conditions poor. To work meant to survive and Roberts exploited his workers for his own benefit, as did other employers of the time. We read of him buying food for the poor possibly this was payment in kind for some of their work or, if not, he was feeding them to stay fit for work, or buying on behalf of the Overseers.

*   *   *   *   *   *

The mill owner's grandparents, Francis and Mary Roberts moved to Chilcombe, a hamlet above the Bride Valley, in the second decade of the 18th. Century. They are supposed to have come from Wales and it would be interesting to know what brought them there.

At that time Chilcombe held a much bigger community than it does today; but its quaint church still stands in the farmyard. The name, Chilcombe, may be derived from the Saxon words meaning "cold" or "chalk" and either of these would have reflected the Roberts' Welsh homelands, for its setting high above the valley and its suitability as sheep pasture, reminded them of the hills and valleys of Wales. The Manor of Chilcombe was held by the Bishop family and there may have been a family or friendly tie between them and the Roberts.

The Askerswell registers show that a Roberts' daughter, Elizabeth, was christened in 1717 and another girl, Damaris, followed in 1718, when she died within the year. Francis, who was later to be connected with Burton Bradstock, Henry and Richard were christened in 1719, 1721 and 1722 respectively.

Francis Roberts was lured by the rolling West Dorset countryside to take up farming and he is reputed to have first lived and farmed at Hembury, Askerswell. This afforded him the chance to cement his acquaintance with Grace Travers whom he married at Burton Bradstock, by licence, in 1748, by which time he was living at Bredy.

His Bride's family was well established in Uploders and Askerswell. Her brother, Major Richard Travers, inherited a considerable estate in Uploders and West Dorset. He was in charge of the local yeomanry, a force established in towns and villages, working alongside the Sea Fencibles, to protect the coast against the French.

Their sons Francis, 1748-1794, Richard, 1752-1820, William, 1757-1811, Robert, 1758-1827, and a daughter, Mary, were their legitimate children. A Thomas Roberts later claimed to be a brother of Richard, the mill owner; but more of that in due course.

Francis, the eldest son, had a long and exciting career in the Navy. He saw several battles at sea, was one of the few survivors of one campaign, was captured by the enemy and later escaped from prison. He saw service with the famous, which included Captain Thomas Hardy and the Great Nelson himself. This Francis Roberts' career was finally ended when he died of yellow fever, in the West Indies, on board his ship, "Success". His illegitimate son, a rover, found life in the South Sea Islands to his liking and he married a dusky princess there.

The second son of Francis and Grace Roberts made his mark on West Dorset when in 1786, at the age of 34 he was married at Burton Bradstock Church, by licence, to Mrs. Martha Best, a 31 year old widow, née Hoskins, of Symondsbury, where her family would appear to have been well settled on that side of Bridport.

Mrs. Best had been widowed for just over two years. Her first husband being Samuel Best, whose family tenanted Burton Farm (now Manor Farm) from the Lord of the Manor. They had married at Symondsbury in 1777 when Martha was just 22. Martha brought with her to Burton the promise of a handsome dowry, for her family, the Hoskins, were "well breeched".

In the will of her mother, also Martha, of 1778 she was named as the only beneficiary. Her brother John having survived three years and her baby sister, Betty, just one year. She inherited the interest from the sale of the tenement and lands and estates, stock, crops, goods and chattels which were held in trust. The money was to be for Martha's sole use 'free from control or intermedling of her said husband', (Samuel Best). Martha Hoskins, Senior, could not write and was therefore obliged to endorse her will with a mark.

With this and their already well established position in Burton, by her first marriage and his flax business, Martha and Richard Roberts started their life together in a very secure state. They moved into The Grove (House) where one or other of them was probably already living, more likely Martha, as some of the land in the Grove area went with the Burton Farm.

Roberts improved the house, which still stands today, an attractive, thatched stone building, set back off the lane. It must have been a busy thoroughfare when the mills were at work; the carts back and forth with the flax and hemp, the workers passing by early in the mornings and then late in the evenings. As for other houses, the nearest would have been John Anning's house, in Anning's Lane, where some of the Council properties now stand, North Hill House (now Norburton Hall), and Darby House.

The children of this union were Richard, the younger, born in 1787, who sailed with Nelson and Captain Hardy, Francis, born in 1789 who made the navy his career also. These sons were followed by Sophie 1791, a third son William Hoskins born in 1796, and Martha Maria Augusta in 1799. Richard, who later joined his father in running the mills, had at least 9 children and Francis fathered 6, all born between 1813 and 1839.

* * * * * *

Flax and hemp factories were already well established in Bridport and Richard Roberts was astute enough to realise that the flax that he, his brother and other farmers grew in West Dorset and the skill of the people of Burton Bradstock to process and spin it could be brought together for his benefit.

Flax was used in the making of sheeting and sailcloth and hemp for making twine, rope and nets. The climate of each season determined the quality of the flax and hemp and subsequently that determined the end products. Roberts also imported flax and seed from Russia. Russian flax bleached well and was better for finer cloth.

Linen table cloths and napkins, towelling, cheese cloth, 'of a good colour', mail bags and sheeting were produced in Burton Bradstock. There is reference to many yards of sheeting being supplied to the house of a Mr. S. B. Gundry. Bags for carrying bread were also made. High on the list of products was sailcloth and hammocks mostly for the use of the navy. At the height of the wars, with France, Roberts was assured of a market for these goods. Besides the cloth for the sails of the fleet, tarpaulin sheeting was also manufactured and would have been used on ships and by farmers.

Roberts hoped to be given a contract with the Navy Board for hammocks and there is a great deal of correspondence concerning this. He informed Mr. Samuel Hood, a navy inspector, that his flax and tow spinning mills were equal to any in the kingdom and that 200 looms were available to cope with the work. If he was given the contract he would get William Morton Pitt, Mr. Banks, Mr. Oglander and Lord Ilchester to speak for him. His nephew, married to a Princess from the South Seas, where some of the best imported hemp, used in making hammocks, grew, had offered to load several ships annually and the contract might be a very good thing for the Roberts family thereafter.

In 1814 there is mention of a fishing net being made 'roped fit to put the lead on ready to go into the water at 9-10 guineas'. A larger and deeper one was to cost 12-13 guineas. A considerable amount of wick for candles, lanterns and lamps came out of the Burton factory and golden and yellow shoe thread of different sizes. Thread was also used extensively in the making of harness and saddlery.

In 1807 Roberts wrote to A. Hutchins of Exeter, a linen draper, with regard to sending sheeting 40 inches wide at 11d a yard. Most of the goods manufactured in Burton were despatched by sea from Bridport Harbour and the sailing of the vessels depended on the state of the weather, as Roberts said, "If the wind stays fair".

In 1813 there was a letter to Colsons of Exeter, drapers, who bought towelling and sheeting and another in 1815 to Richard Hayward of West Chinnock for whom Roberts was heckling and spinning not less than 5 cwt of flax at one time. The mill was always busy in the early years and there was rarely less than a month's work in hand.

Some other firms that traded with the Burton mills were Jas. Kiddle of West Chinnock, L. Fowler of Stoke Abbott, George Parker also of West Chinnock, George Salisbury of Norton under Ham, Cox and Hine of Beaminster, Robert Lane (?) of Netherbury, John Richards of Chard, John Nicholls of Exeter.

Goods that were not transported by ship went by chaise mail coach from the Greyhound Hotel, in East Street, Bridport. This high class hostelry was also a terminus for travellers and a meeting place for the businessmen of Bridport and the surrounding district.

A high percentage of the employees at the mills were engaged from the village itself. Children were taken on as bobbin fillers and sweepers from the age of eight. The neighbouring villages provided more employees, and there were the orphans brought in from London and elsewhere.

The men were employed as retters, swinglers and hacklers (or hecklers) and older men as weavers. Women worked the spinning looms turning the fibre into yarn and seamed the sails and other such products. Children were given the menial and worst jobs and everyone worked at least a 12 hour day. An Act of 1802 laid down that poor law apprentices should not work more than 12 hours.

Eden Phillpotts has left a vivid description of three village girls working in the spinning room. Phillpotts, a prolific Devonshire writer, on a par with our own Thomas Hardy, stayed in Burton early in the present century and wrote one of a group of industrial novels called "The Spinners", set in Burton Bradstock and centred around the mill.[1] Although little had changed in processing in the one hundred years from Roberts' time to that of Eden Phillpotts', the conditions in the mills of the early 19th Century would have been far from good, the mill not so light and airy as Phillpotts saw it then, rebuilt after a fire in the 1870s.

In the novel, Raymond Ironsyde, the mill owner's younger son, was joining the business in the hope that he would mend his ways and settle down. He was somewhat keen to try the scheme proposed by his elder brother, mainly in order to catch glimpses of Sabina, his lady of the moment, who worked at the mill as a spinner.

The manager of the mill was showing Raymond around the work rooms. 'In the great buildings two sounds deafened an unfamiliar ear: a steady roar, deep and persistent' and over this a more penetrating din could be heard of the humming belts and running wheels. The floor was of stone and on it were dispersed the machines for carding, spreading, drawing frames, roving frames, gill spinners and spinning frames. The noise was so loud that one could not hold a conversation. Raymond observed that from nearly all the machines 'there streamed away continuous bright ribbons of hemp or flax that caught the light and shone'. This was called the "sliver" as it passed through the machines on its way to the spinners.

Eden Phillpotts went on to describe the women at work. Some forty women and girls laboured and the 'old people sat on stools by the spouting sliver and wound it away into the tall cans that received it'. Some girls performed 'a rhythmic dance' with their hands, tearing the stricks into three and laying 'the shining locks' on the spreading boards. Three of the spinners were Sabina Dinnett (the heroine of the story), Nancy Buckler and Alice Chick; they 'seemed to twinkle here, there and everywhere in a corybantic measure as they served the shouting and insatiable monsters that turned hemp and flax to yarn'.

It is very doubtful that Roberts was able to pin down his Burton Bradstock employees to regular work if the fishing season was in hand. He complained about the unreliability of his workers stating that they left off work in the mills to go fishing and were also given to drinking ale and cider. During harvest they were to be found at work in the fields. In August 1812 Roberts wrote, 'weather exceeding fine and reaping goes on briskly'.

Besides the local employees, Roberts gleaned from surrounding villages, putting paid to the cottage industry throughout the Bride Valley. He acquired labour in the form of children in parish care from Cranborne, Ottery St. Mary, Shepton Mallet and from the city of London. A letter to the parish officers of Westminster in July 1814 was in reply to an advertisement he had seen.

'Seeing an advertisement in the newspapers of a number of Boys and Girls to be bound out as apprentices I beg to ask the ages and numbers of each sex also if it would be agreeable that they should be bound to the linen trade and manufacturers in spinning and weaving till the age of 21 years old each if such would be admisible with your parish officers. I will give you respectable references to gentlemen in London who will inform you of all the necessary in such cases of myself situation and respectability of such servants in my employ which has been about 21 years standing. An early answer will oblige'.

Apprentices did not receive wages. A very small sum of money or suit of clothes was all they could expect on completing an apprenticeship.

That children were available from Ottery St. Mary in 1811 is very probable as the woollen mills had closed there. That same year he had written to the Cranborne officers with regard to girls, preferably 8-10 years, and he stated that he would soon have houses of convenience for taking a number. He told their overseers that they would be taken good care of, perhaps better than at home, both with raiment, food and morals and he added they would not have hard work and do no more than 12 hours a day!

These children were boarded out in the village and some on the farms. By not employing these youngsters after they reached 21 years he evaded having to pay higher wages and probably saved providing other accommodation, as the younger children could easily be cramped together in a room and bed. Small children were made to go in under the machines to retie broken yarn or do minor repairs, often at great risk to themselves, as the machines were rarely stopped.

In another letter he asks for children of a strong and healthy constitution. They would be taken free of expense, except for two suits of clothes they would need — one for working and one for Sundays. The children would be sent to church regularly and taught to read and say their catechism every Sunday for two hours.

Employing young women had its problems as we find many references to illegitimate children. These mothers gave their occupation as semptresses and net makers.

One of Roberts' male employees brought him troubles, for the man who bore the same surname as his master had implied to customers that he was a brother and partner in the business and had collected money under false pretences. He held the account books of the 'new weaving concern' in 1813 and Richard Roberts sent his clerk, Mr. R. Mudge, with a letter demanding the return of the account books that same day.

Mr. Jacobs of Portsmouth handled the Roberts' insurance affairs and other business matters in that part of the country. We find Richard Gale and a Mr. Swain concerned with the selling of flax seed in Southhampton and London and the boy Farrant, an apprentice at the mill who ran away, his home being near Wellington, in Somerset.

A letter to a would be apprentice clearly sets out the work and conditions at Burton. *'With me you will be able to learn many branches of the linen manufacturing more than any other person in this country can show you because mine is a general manufacturing of sail cloth, ducks, sheetings, table linen, napkins plain and figured, wrappings and packing cloths upon the newest and best principal. Also bleaching and my terms will be 100gns for your learning with the advantage of what work you may do whilst learning and with it you would learn the mode of book keeping also. You would have to live with my foreman close by the works in a neat house and small family either to board with them or by yourself.'* Roberts added that the yarns he used were spun by machinery or hand as best suited.

In acquiring this machinery in 1811 a representative was sent to Leeds, a man named Hoare, who had cost Roberts a considerable sum to bring up to the knowledge he possessed. However, it seems that machinery was finally purchased from Bristol, although Roberts showed an interest in machines in Belfast that came available. He certainly employed a man direct from Leeds for some 6-12 months to assist in the installation of the plant. Roberts intended to train a young man to look after the machinery thereafter and to be engaged in the repair of houses. A blacksmith was required, too. 'If he is clever he may learn something for himself' and he was to be paid according to his abilities.

1. When Eden Phillpotts was researching in Burton for his book the locals suspected him of being a German spy.

XVIII

THE BUSINESS MAN

Roberts did not enjoy good health during the years in which his letter books were written. Most of his business activities were governed by his condition at the time. Often he was unable to make firm appointments to visit London, Bristol or Portsmouth. He ailed of a stomach and bowel complaint in 1814 and also suffered from rheumatism.

He described, to a Mr. Cox, of Beaminster, a vapour bath he intended to install 'where his common boiler now stands by the fireplace'. Later he was able to report 'I am glad to say I am much better'. Prior to this he had travelled to Bath to take the waters there.

Much of the repair of cottages in Burton Bradstock can be attributed to Roberts' need to house his workers. He had erected the Mill in the 1780s and built the swingling mill in Grove Lane in 1803. Mill Street housed many of his workers and the foreman lived at the Mill House, near the Spinning Mill. We read of 400 feet of inch elm being ordered and there was an enquiry about the price of timber from Norway, 'deals of the best Norway, also middle sort and the inferior that would come cheap for poor cottages'. He brought Roman Cement to Burton in 1811. He required deal for the installation of the machinery in the mill and timber for sawing up for the cottagers' houses. Elm board 1 inch thick was needed for floating a water wheel which powered the mills. Mindful, as always, of the cost of items, he turned down the purchase of 'a long spar' which was too dear for a ladder. At another time he required delivery of sycamore board by 8 or 9 o'clock in the morning at the Coach and Horses Inn, Winterbourne, near Dorchester. It was to be as knot free as possible as the flax was to be spread on it. The price, 2/6d per foot, which was to include the sawing. We read of American pine timber imported to Plymouth to be used chiefly for building.

Roberts also imported timber to resell and there are several references to sales being held at Burton. On one occasion a sale had to be postponed as the mahogany could not be got home in time. It was at this time, 1812, that his mills were under alterations — the new machinery being put in. A complaint about faulty spindles followed.

Since the time of Richard Roberts' mills the knell of a factory bell was a familiar sound and summons — Roberts bought a 'factory bell — a small one with a sharp, clear tone in the tone of D'. As the village choirmaster he recognised a note that would alert the ears of his workers. He presumed the bell would cost in the region of 1½-2 guineas and he was interested as to what the weight of such a bell would be. That the bell was hung in position there is no doubt, as it was to call the people of Burton Bradstock until the factory closed in the 1930s.

The mills were always at full production and no time could be lost when new innovations were being fitted which were to be the best and of considerable magnitude. Imported flax and other goods for the mill came by sea to Bridport Harbour and some machinery was on board the "Mary Ann" captained by Captain Anning. Hemp, too, was imported via the Harbour.

Roberts would have nothing to do with chemical processing. He said that his materials were washed in a mill, boiled and laid out on the grass. The sun as a bleaching agent was all that Roberts used.

Gas lighting did appeal to him, most likely in order to prolong the working hours. In a letter with regard to this he asks, 'Do they (the gas lights) produce good light and are as safe from danger and are they cheaper in burning than oil?'.

The mill owner's life was not without its problems and we read of several disputes over non-payment for work that Roberts had done for other merchants. He appeared to be a meticulous business man and either by nature or need never overlooked monies outstanding to him.

He had the occasional brush with the tax man. In a letter to the Honourable the Commissioners of the Board of Taxes he pointed out that he was being taxed on two horses but one of them belonged to his son and was being used by him to ride when superintending the raising of flax 10-15 mile distant.

The demand of £100 did not please the mill owner and he wrote that he felt like quitting his country and becoming its enemy with the dreadful war, as well. He said he was £20,000 worse off because of the war. Here he must have been having a typical moan over tax payment because, shortly after, he is enquiring, in another vein, about having tokens made for his factory which would have been issued by him and therefore pointed to his prosperous position.

Roberts had trouble, in due course, with his man Hoare who originally a 'common carpenter' had been sent to the north of England, by Roberts, to learn the flax trade and machinery and had agreed not to set up for his own good. However, he had moved off to Castle Cary and taken with him the secrets of the Burton processes and machinery. In a letter of the 12th of June 1812 Roberts wrote to Hoare, who had been back to the village and trespassed on to the mill premises, surveying the works in the second room and not content with that had taken a tool and made an attempt to work with it. Roberts demanded a signed apology.

Faulty goods, whether for the mills, or his personal use, never escaped Roberts' notice and when ordering he always laid down the requirements in a very efficient manner. Roberts' detailed order for stationery is an example of his precise business attributes. In December of 1811 he was ordering *'½ 100 of good quills – the broad feather over the thumb, 1 quire of good blotting paper, ledger, good paper, vellum finish strong bound, brass corners ruled in red cross red, as this faint ink. 3 lines in an inch, 10" wide 14" in length, 600 pages in all:*

100 whole side
50 ½ side

repeat the same thro the book dividing the whole in three such arrangements. Alphabets at the beginnings, doubled at the edge where the letters are.'

Possibly, Roberts paid some wages in kind. There is much mention of cheap butter, bacon, pork, cheese and the cheapest white herrings to be given to poor families. In September of 1812 he writes to London 'I shall not want anymore bacon yet awhile the poor people are now eating potatoes, fish and their base corn'. Earlier he had been buying bacon at 54/- a cwt., 'which answers very well for poor and working families'. A year later he purchased five sides of bacon at 98/- per cwt. (hundredweight).

A few of the letters copied into the Letter Books refer to the purchase of good brandy and sugar for wine making. (He had heard that sugar was selling well). Importing French cattle was another of Roberts' transactions. A letter to a Mr. Bullen of Weymouth, in 1814, stated that 3 or 4 were required for himself and that he would sell the rest. He had ground available for 10 or 12 and a note had been sent to a gentleman in Cherbourg to get him a dozen good ones, 3-5 years old of the yellow and white spotted sort. Also at the same time he enquired about good salted pork or bacon and salted butter from Cherbourg to be sold in England. Pigs were also imported via Weymouth and Roberts intended to correspond with his man in Cherbourg, in French, the next time, in order to keep matters between themselves!

Roberts seems to have been involved, locally, in parish affairs and as the executor or trustee of several estates some of which gave cause for concern.

Somewhere in his lifetime he and his wife parted and set up separate homes in the village. It is fairly certain that Roberts stayed on at The Grove. A servant girl, called Charlotte, who had been with him eight years died from a violent cold and Roberts expressed his sorrow at losing her. The Grove House also suffered a fire in 1814 and there is a great deal of correspondence between Roberts and the Directors of the West of England Fire and Life Insurers.

Henry Gale, a manservant, was the last to bed at 12 o'clock after the family had been baking bread and his wife Martha Gale awoke at 4 am and gave the alarm. The family, (Roberts is presumed here), numbering five, made their escape naked from the chamber windows. A William Stanley appeared to be the hero of the occasion as he entered the front room and with a supply of water — a chain of human hands passing buckets — the fire was brought under control. Roberts was so grateful to Stanley that he suggested to the insurers that a reward of one guinea should be made to him. He also claimed from the insurance brokers the cost of beer and cheese for the helpers.

An interesting remark made in the letter points to the use of furze faggots for fuel for the oven. A wet 'fursen' faggot had been lying 3-4 yards from the oven and also a small quantity of damp scattered 'furse' was there and ignited. Roberts valued the whole property at £800 and claimed £7-9-10d for losses.

A very personal problem that beset the mill owner concerned his brother William, a draper of Bristol, married with two daughters. William Roberts had died mysteriously in Belgium and there was correspondence with the authorities in Antwerp. The brother had most likely gone to the Continent to avoid his creditors as his business was in a bad state, Belgium being a country, at the time, where an Englishman, in reduced circumstances, could live more cheaply. It seems he had taken the assumed name of Robinson and Richard Roberts was requesting a death and burial certificate and stated that his brother had about 230 French Louis d'ors in a belt around his body and in his trunk a bill on some house in Paris.

In 1811 Roberts travelled to Bristol dealing with his late brother's affairs and there was a meeting of the creditors in London and Bristol. He intended to purchase a house for the widow as he desired 'to give a **fair** opportunity to the two girls'. Mrs. William Roberts (Fanny) kept a school in a respectable part of

Bristol. Travelling from Burton Bradstock to Bristol was by chaise and on one occasion Roberts shared one with a lady and gentleman from the village, thereby halving the cost.

The influence of Lord Rivers was requested in 1815 to promote Richard Roberts' son, Francis, to Commander at the end of the war. Francis was brought up and educated for the navy under his uncle, Captain Francis Roberts, who had no legitimate son of his own. Young Francis had served 10 years in the navy, mostly under Sir Thomas Hardy, also a pupil of Francis senior. Roberts had letters from Sir Thomas Hardy on his son's abilities and service. Francis was at that time a Lieutenant on board H.M.S. Derwent, (Captain Williams) and seeing service at St. John's, Newfoundland.

No where in the letter books is there a word of Roberts' wife but she was still at The Grove in 1805. His daughter Sophia is mentioned quite often and so are details of his son, Richard, buying the mills, by instalments, over a period of years. Richard, junior, certainly undertook a great deal of the business work and travelling during the later years for which reference is available.

The impression of Richard Roberts, senior, unique village mill owner, choir master, Foreman of the Manorial Court Jury, Overseer of the Poor, and Churchwarden, merchant of seeds, cattle, dairy produce, meat, and timber, self-styled lawyer, farmer and conscientious parent comes through vividly in his letters. He was prepared to deal in any merchandise that would be profitable and was always alert and up to the minute in all his business affairs; keen too, to see his sons well set up.

He must be remembered as a preservationist of the 19th Century. Those who have "inherited" Burton Bradstock must thank him for bringing a measure of stability to the village when the times were uncertain and difficult. Although for his own ends, by providing work, village families were able to stay put in a place where many of them had been rooted since time immemorial. Others came to Burton Bradstock to work at the mills and established family lines that still exist. Together he and the men and women of Burton Bradstock, of the late 18th and early 19th Centuries, spliced brains and brawn and fashioned a fine village for the future.

XIX

SHIPS AND SEAMEN AND SOME SMUGGLING

The advance into the 19th Century is indeed a good time to assess the connections that Burton Bradstock had with the sea, up to this time, both legal and illegal.

Well into the 15th Century the Spanish and Portuguese dominated the maritime scene. They had discovered new oceans and continents and settled widely. That very early traders from the eastern world had reached the West Country is fairly certain and the stone head which caps a gate post at the Three Horse Shoes Inn, Burton Bradstock is reputed to have been brought by early venturers. We are already familiar with the invasions along the Chesil Coast of the French and Scandinavians and local contribution to the Navy in the form of ropes, nets, tackle and sailcloth had been established from the time of King John.

In the West Country, Bristol was the principal port from which ships sailed into the Atlantic and later under the command of John Cabot, discovered Newfoundland. The West Country ships were trading with North America, the Canaries, West Africa and the Caribbean from the end of the 15th Century.

* * * * * *

Earlier in the 14th Century, it is recorded that the nearest point to the East Cliff at Bridport Harbour and up to one mile inland, together with the foreshore, belonged to the Manor of Brideton (Burton Bradstock), the west side belonging to Symondsbury. At this time boats were able to navigate right up to the Borough of Brideport (Bridport).

The first mention of the port at Bridport was 1272 and the Abbot of Cernel and the Prior of Frampton were entitled to take all the wrecks on each side of the weir. The larger vessels lay in the haven nearer the sea and a penny toll could be taken by the Manor of Brideton from all vessels on the Burton side. Any portion of a wreck or vessel or its cargo, which was thrown up on the beach, could be seized provided that neither man, nor dog, nor cat had escaped alive.

Burton Bradstock was fortunate that, in those early days, the natural mouth of the river was close to the East Cliff and was not diverted until much later when ever since there appears to have been problems at Bridport Harbour. The river has silted up and the sea swept inland, finding the former river-bed, or demolished man-made barriers during the past two centuries, since he tampered with Nature.

John de Huderesfeld, possibly a Yorkshireman, began work on constructing a port in 1385 at the present West Bay. The familiar sand bar proved a problem and in 1445 collectors were appointed to raise funds for the port. Burton Bradstock contributed the sum of 5/3d. The port and Bridport went into decay in 1541 and outbreaks of the plague in 1544 and 1625 and further silting up of the harbour in 1548 and 1619 contributed to the fall of the importance of the port.

For the mariners and fishermen from Burton the state of Bridport

Harbour was a major concern. In 1740 the sum of £3500 was paid to erect two piers to turn the course of the river and make a harbour between the piers to receive vessels of 150 tons burden.

A further attempt to build a harbour and the intricacies and complications of ownerships and tenancies is well illustrated in a report of the Quarter Sessions held at Bridport in 1740. The case considered was between the Corporation of Bridport "V" the Owners and Occupiers of lands at Bridport Mouth, now called West Bay.

Eight acres, 3 roods and 13 perches of land at the mouth of the river had been 'piled out' and alloted for intended building of a harbour. An Act of Parliament in 1722 had been passed to restore and rebuild the harbour but it had not been carried out until 1740. Due notice of the proposed work had been given to the occupiers of the land but they and the owners were demanding compensation.

Six acres, 3 roods, 25 perches were in the possession of John Best, leased from George Pitt, the elder, Esq., Lord of Burton Manor for 21 years. The annual value of this land was 45 shillings per annum. Six and a half years of the lease were still left. A small hut had been built on the land rented at 27 shillings per annum.

Jurors appointed were *Walter Mullens, Robert Symes, Christopher Marsh, Richard Henville, Robert Hansford, Robert Greening, Edward Lawrence, John Beer, Samuel Hoskins, John Marsh, William Greening, and Henry Gould.*

Concerning the land and compensation, they awarded John Best £13-10 shillings. £31-10 shillings to George Pitt the elder. The hut was said to be worth £28-4 shillings and Jonathan Hayden received 40 shillings, John Best £6 and the residue went to the Lord of the Manor.

A second plot of land of 2 acres 25 perches was the inheritance of the beneficiaries of Thomas Strangwayes, Esq., deceased. There was also a hut built there and two sheds erected against it, taking up 25 perches, which was claimed by Robert Chilcott who held it on lease of lives of which two lives were still in being.

To complicate matters William Lawes was the sub-tenant of Chilcott and the sheds there were erected and owned by John Lea, John and William Bishop and John White on the east side of the river. The land was all sandy that Robert Chilcott possessed and only worth 3 shillings per annum. The main hut was possessed by William Lawes and let and worth 35 shillings per annum. The sheds were worth 12d. Suitable compensation was decided and awarded to the owners of the land, Chilcott, Lawes and those who had erected the sheds on the land.

One acre of meadow was Common Meadow but the owners Thomas Strangwayes Horner and others had the right to the AFTERshare (after cut) from the Monday after August 1st to the Monday after February 1st each year. This they let to Robert Chilcott.

One quarter of the FOREshare (first cut) of ½ acre 5 perches was the inheritance of William Waldron, Esq., and occupied by Henry Davie. The other three quarters were the inheritance of John Bragg, Esq., and Elizabeth, his daughter, wife of George Bethell, Esq., and this, too, was occupied by

Henry Davie. Twenty perches of the foreshare were the inheritance of Simon Taylor, Gent., and occupied by the same Davie. The remaining 30 perches were the inheritance of Matthew Hounsell, Gent., and occupied by Davie. The annual value of the whole was no more than 20 shillings a year.

Sums as follows were allocated:-

Value of 1 acre on Westside £20

Aftershare £7

to Robert Chilcott £3-5s

to Thomas Strangwayes and others £3-15s

for the 1 acre foreshare worth £13

to John Bragg, George Bethell and Elizabeth his wife £5-5s

to William Waldron £1-15s

to Simon Taylor £2-10s

to Stephen Hounsell £3-10s

Small pockets of land, such as these, were very common and were owned and leased and even then sub-let by numerous people. To make matters more difficult, people owned or leased several patches of land spread widely over an area. The holding of leases for three lives and ownership or leasing of cottages, huts and sheds on land owned and leased by others made for what appears to be very complicated arrangements!

The building of the Harbour went ahead and was completed in 1742. The building was under the direction of Mr. Reynolds who was paid 15 guineas for the plans. £5,000 was raised in sums of £1,000 and £500 lots donated by local benefactors.

For 1785/95 the expenditure for keeping the harbour and piers in repair averaged £229-17s-7d and the receipts £239-17s-9d. Receipts in the early 1700s only amounted to £18-1s-11d per annum.

In 1741 a letter written by John Best on behalf of Mr. Joseph Waldron to Mr. William Jones of Shroton, near Blandford, probably the Steward of the Manor, states, 'Sir the harbour do go on finalty'.

Ship building at Bridport Harbour was a local trade and waxed in importance well into the last century. The rebuilding of the East Pier amounted to £385 in 1815/16 and likewise the West Pier £350 in 1816/17. Repairs and erecting a breakwater in 1817/18 cost a total of £626. Following all this work, a road was made from Bridport Harbour to Bridport. The Harbour was to be a busy one during the whole of the 19th Century and many Burton men worked there as fishermen, ship-wrights, ropers and general labourers. Warehouses were built — one by Roberts of Burton in the late 18th Century. Many Burton mariners sailed from there, too.

*   *   *   *   *   *

The men of Burton Bradstock were as familiar with the ways and workings of the sea and the Chesil Beach as they were with the land and the flax that grew on it. The seine net method of fishing was and still is, employed to reap the vast harvests of local mackerel and sprats. This small meshed net, shaped like a long bag, with narrow ends, is thrown from a boat rowed parallel to the shore. A rope from the net is held on shore at either end and the net gradually drawn in by those anchoring its extremities. The fish become trapped in the small mesh of the bag and are dragged up onto the beach. Defoe was rowed along the coast from Abbotsbury to Burton in 1724 and he observed the use of this method of fishing and the enormous quantities of mackerel caught and sold at 1d per 100. Dozens, stones and bushels of fish have been sold from Burton Beach ever since and provided a reasonable livelihood, or supplement, for many a village family. Today mackerel are also caught by individuals from boats using a feathered line. Brightly coloured feathers are attached to the lines which are hooked. How the earlier men of Burton would have benefited from this simple invention.

In the damp and cold of November nights fishermen would go drifting for herring, keeping in touch with the shore only by the lone light of a lantern, flashed from the beach.

Other fish like whiting, skate and locally named blen and duncow and spider crabs were snared in the seine net or caught way out on "Bob Knight's Ground" where good fishing could always be assured.

* * * * * *

There are always times when the sea is too rough to put to sea and the breakers crash up over the pebbles lashing the cliffs and drag back everything movable into the cauldron of "boiling" water, sometimes throwing the flotsom back up and at others burying it for ever. Then the sea is no respecter of lumber, life or limb and many a ship and seaman has been lost along the treacherous Chesil Coast.

One such happening was the loss of "The Golden Grape", on a voyage from Cadiz to Dover, on the night of the 11th December 1641. The weather was recorded as 'fowle' and she was forced onto the shore at East Fleet. Seven men and boys drowned and the ship broke into pieces and in heavy seas, over the next four days, she was smashed completely.

She was laden with Spanish Port and Sherry and 2000 barrels of raisins, 400 jars of oil, 240 pieces of silk together with silver plate and bullion, bags of Spanish coin in gold and silver, pistols, Pieces of Eight and other goods. Her total crew numbered 20.

The terribly violent seas that raged that December did not prevent plundering. Bands of men from all the neighbouring villages descended upon the scene, some with carts, which were costly to hire and the barrels which were washing in on the beach were stoved in and the wreckers filled every available bag and pocket with raisins. They stripped off their waistcoats and used the sleeves as bags. Fighting broke out and the strongest men carried off whole barrels of oil, port, 'sherryes sackes' and raisins. The Authorities were also on the scene but were out-numbered. The servants of Sir John Strangways, of Abbotsbury, laid claim to their ancient right to take wrecks and over-ruled the authorities. The oranges, lemons, silk, gold and silver disappeared in every direction and many houses and cottages were searched in an endeavour to recover the lost cargo. At an enquiry which followed some 400 local inhabitants were brought for examination.

A barque from Lyme, laden with salt, was wrecked off Bridport in 1670 and in November of 1795, 1000 persons are supposed to have perished, from a fleet, caught in the rigours of the sea, on its way to Torbay and in March of

1815, the Alexander, bound from Bombay to London, foundered with the loss of passengers and troops. From this tragedy only 4 men and a woman were rescued. The night of the 23rd of November 1824 was one of the worst for weather ever recorded in the area. A large number of vessels were lost and the seas swept in at Portland, Fleet, Abbotsbury, Burton and Bridport Harbour. By the entrance to the Swannery, at Abbotsbury, can be seen a pole which marks the height of the sea that night. The village of Fleet was submerged and this subsequently provided the plot for the exciting novel, "Moonfleet", by John Meade Falkner. The storm was felt well inland, too, for in Dorchester the Reverend and Mrs. Richman were killed when their house collapsed. Eight vessels were lost off the Chesil in October 1839; a ninth escaped by being thrown up on the Bank.

Throughout the 18th and 19th Centuries many vessels are known to have been lost along the Chesil Coast. Aware of the number that put in at Bridport Harbour alone (1830: 528 vessels — total tonnage 42,386) it is possible to realise that the sea was a very busy highway.

Trawlers and trading vessels alike were swept on shore or caught in the mountainous seas and wrecked along this dangerous coast. Men risked their lives to save life whilst women and children stood by watching the pathetic, windblown scenes. A south westerly gale could be a harrowing experience for all concerned.

In November 1837, a Swedish brig, laden with a cargo of timber, was driven on shore at Burton, following a collision with another vessel during the night, when her bulwarks were stoved in and her masts carried away. The crew of four men attempted to swim to safety, after the vessel struck rocks and immediately began to sink.

The Steward of the brig — Oloff Bjorkholm — was drowned and duly buried in Burton Bradstock churchyard. The three others of the crew were miraculously saved 'by the exertions of the inhabitants of the parish'. The wreck drifted perfectly on to the beach and no doubt the wreckers from the village soon gathered timber for their hearths and homes regardless of the laws of salvage.

1838, again in November, during the afternoon of the twenty ninth, saw the plight of a French smack, Le Jean Bart. She was carrying a cargo of hides and was drifting helplessly from Bridport Harbour towards Burton. Signals were hoisted at the Harbour, on the beach, where the vessel could most likely run aground and be saved but she let go her anchor and immediately drifted eastwards to her fate.

Of her crew of nine, four men, including the Captain and a 13 year old Spanish boy were drowned. The bodies of two of the seamen were never recovered. Five others were saved, certainly by the skill and struggles of the local men, who hauled them from the angry Chesil waters to the top of the cliff, by means of ropes. Two of these rescued by that means, were boys also and were thought to be dead on reaching the summit of the cliff. Three local men named Symes, Hounsell and Sweeting worked on the bodies and revived them.

The Captain remained until the last, helping his men to safety at the bottom of the cliff. Finally, when so near being saved himself, his strength gave out and he was washed away. The terrified Spanish boy could not be persuaded to leave the wreck and one other man pitched to his death when the rope he was clinging to was severed by the rocks.

A subscription was opened and sufficient money raised to clothe the survivors and transport them from Weymouth back home. The note in the Parish Register, beside the burial entry for the Captain and the Spanish boy, states that the height of the cliffs was at least 215 feet. This would seem to be somewhat exaggerated. That the sea was coming right up to the cliff face was certainly fact and would indicate how rough the weather was that day.

*　　*　　*　　*　　*　　*

One further shipwreck must be mentioned. That of the schooner, "The Flirt", which went down off Burton in 1898. The drama of this event was at its height by 4 p.m. on the afternoon of November 23rd. The fishermen and villagers had watched helplessly as she struggled against the exceptionally high sea. The angry, foaming waves rolled in with tremendous power and height from way out to sea.

"The Flirt" was being battered just off the shore and four of the crew eventually jumped into the sea to the horror of those waiting on the beach and the cliff top. The vessel was heeling over and there was no alternative for the crew but to take their small chance against the angry water. The backlash and ebbing tide gave little chance of survival. One man had Luck on his side for the powerful sea and a huge wave threw him nearer the land.

Twenty nine year old James Gear was one of the fishermen watching this terrible spectacle and without thought for his own safety he 'dashed into the sea and at great risk and much difficulty succeeded in rescuing the man' — so reads the citation which he later received from the Royal Humane Society. It does not appear that Gear was tied to a rope held by the other men, as was often the means used in a rescue, and from that it is probable that those on shore gave little chance of anyone being saved from the vessel.

The rest of those who jumped overboard were lost and the late Mrs. Hetty Williams remembered, as a child, seeing the bodies laid out in the shed opposite the Dove Inn. Little Kate Gear seemed not to be taken aback when she encountered several bodies of dead mariners stretched out in the church when she went in to wind the clock one dark evening. (A newspaper report states that three other men who remained on board were saved and that the Coastguard rocket rescue apparatus was at the scene.)

The wreckage of "The Flirt" was purchased by Andrew Spiller of Bridport and a table was made from the hatch of the vessel which is now in the Dove Inn, Burton. Another reminder that Burton's sons were always brave. Perhaps the bodies were brought back to Southover on the hatch.

*　　*　　*　　*　　*　　*

Other Burton men were employed on fishing vessels which fished the coastal waters from Bridport Harbour. In 1565 there were 11 such craft employing 54 men and 6 boys in the Bridport area. The "Gabriel" of 6 tons and the "Shaphawke" were in the ownership of John Wylshere. The largest vessel was the "Great Anne", of 30 tons, with a crew of 10 mariners and 2 boys. In 1586 the "Mary of Birport" had Robert Bokler as her master and traded in peas and beans. A 10 tonner was the "George" trading in rope and hemp, as well as peas and beans. Similar Records appear through to the 1900s.

*　　*　　*　　*　　*　　*

These legal trades ran parallel with the illegal smuggling that was carried out. Customs were originally set up to collect taxes on exports dating from 1275 when a tax was levied on the export of wool. Poole was made a Port of the Staple in 1433 and hanging was the punishment for smuggling wool out of the country. Later wine and leather became liable to import duties and smuggling in these commodities became profitable. Other customs houses were set up around the country and in 1588 twenty horsemen were employed in keeping ward along the coast of Bridport. Important people had import exemptions but bribery went on everywhere so that by 1680 special craft, known as cutters, were put into service along the coast to prevent smuggling. The Collector of Customs at Weymouth wrote in 1718 that 'the smuggling traders in these parts are grown to such a head that they bidd deffiance to all Law and Government'.

A traveller to Abbotsbury in 1752 remarked that 'all the people of Abbotsbury, including the Vicar, are smugglers, theives and plunderers of wrecks'. That the men of Burton were any different would be hard to believe![1]

Smuggling was rife along the Chesil Beach and successful landings were constantly made from Bexington to Burton. Tracks led inland from Swyre, Cogden and Burton to the Spyway Inn below Eggardon Hill. A Smugglers' track runs from Berwick towards the Dorchester Road and the roof of a cottage at Berwick was reputed to be a hiding place. The smuggling in the area was highly organised. Isaac Gulliver, of smuggling "fame" throughout the south, controlled the illicit landing of contraband goods and at one time he owned Eggardon Farm, Askerswell and a cottage at Shipton Gorge situated where the Bridport Road converges with Cuckoo Lane. Now called "Gullivers" this imposing cottage has a commanding view of the sea from its upper rooms. Ideally situated as a look-out and signalling station, it was also on an easy inland route for getting the goods away or for temporary hiding.

In Swyre churchyard there is a table-top tomb which was opened and used as a store for brandy. In the 1940s the cellar at Norburton (formerly North Hill Farmhouse), Shipton Lane, still held broken bottles from the days of the Burton smugglers. The tale concerning this haunt is that three prominent men from Burton were caught and brought to justice for smuggling. One turned "King's Evidence" and sent his two fellows to their fate. He and his descendants lived on but never more prospered.

At the Manor Court at Burton in October 1777 a memo was made, on a deed, with regard to John Hooper, a notorious smuggler and son-in-law of John Hatwell. He had stated that he had paid George Miller of Burton the sum of £15 on a lease of a cottage. The Steward of the Lord of the Manor was very concerned that Hooper was seeking a property in the village. No licence was ever granted to Miller 'impowring' him to lease to Hooper and the Steward refused the granting of a licence, as Hooper was a very improper and dangerous fellow to be 'sufford' to gain any property or settle in the parish. About this time there were three John Hoopers recorded in the Burton Bradstock Parish Registers. Whether any of these was the notorious smuggler is unknown and would require further investigation.

*   *   *   *   *   *

Fishermen are known to be some of the most superstitious of folk and also tellers of tall stories. Perhaps the landing of a mermaid on the Chesil Beach in June of 1757 is a tall story. This monster, rather than mermaid, was some 13 feet long and possessed 48 large teeth in each jaw. Its upper body resembled a human and the lower part that of a fish, its head was half human, half hog and instead of fins it had hands.

Always sea-gulls received special consideration from the local fishermen for they never killed one, it is said, as every gull was the soul of a dead sailor.

Superstition certainly centred around the fishing boats. Beach holed stones which can often be found amongst the pebbles were used to ward off witches from bewitching the boats. These stones varied in size and would be found to have a hole right through them and were called Holy Stones by the fishermen. One of these stones was tied or nailed close to the bow of the fishing boat and the end of the rope to which the boat was anchored in the shingle would also be passed through one of these Holy Stones. Boats which did not net good catches were said to be "witched" and a mackerel stuck with pins would then be placed in the stern in the hope that this would annihilate the evil spirit that was bewitching the boat. The stern of the boat was partially covered-in and the dry net would be stowed there, when not in use, as this was supposed to be a protected place.

By the 1930s these beach-holed stones were considered as lucky stones.

*   *   *   *   *   *

Two lighthouses had been erected at the southern point of Portland Bill in 1716. They were coal fired and often went out or were not even lit. By the 1780s they were both converted to oil and one was rebuilt. Besides saving many vessels from wrecking, where the rocks and race of Portland meet, the lighthouse also became a landmark.

Lt. William Hansford of Burton, presumably living at The Rookery and owning cottages nearby, would have welcomed the Portland lighthouses during his naval career.

As yet, his parish of origin has not been located but his marriage probably to a cousin, brought him additional wealth and influence.

His wife, Mary Adney, was a descendant of Elizabeth, sixth child of George Gollop of Berwick who was the ninth son of Thomas Gollop of Strode, near Beaminster; the Gollops an ancient local family.

William Hansford joined his first Royal Navy ship, "Eleanor" as an Able Seaman in 1739. His naval career took him through the war of "Jenkin's Ear", later as a Quarter Master sailing in the West Indies. In 1753 he was Master's Mate on H.M.S. Berwick, somewhat appropriately and on H.M.S. Captain from 1753-1756, a ship aboard which Nelson served. From 1790-1794 he was still to be found as a Lieutenant in the lists of Flag Officers. He died in June of 1799 aged 82.

*   *   *   *   *   *

The fear of invasion by the French along the Chesil Beach was foremost in the minds of the inhabitants from the end of the 18th Century. As early as 1653 some fifty men had reported for service in the navy at Bridport besides those who were "pressed" into service, which included fishermen. Fishermen were excluded from being pressed into the navy by 1798 and they formed the "Sea Fencibles" — a defence force employed to defend the coast until 1810. A company was raised from Swyre and Burton to form one section of the chain around the Kingdom. In 1798 fifty three men served with Nicholas Ingram of Burton. They mustered once a week, armed with pikes, and received one shilling per muster. By 1799 there were 77 men in that section and this number remained constant until 1805 when its needs were much reduced.

Signal towers were situated at Puncknowle Hill and Golden Cap and a beacon was maintained on Shipton Hill. Furze faggots were used to fuel the fire and sufficient had to be provided to burn for two hours. Richard Roberts, of Burton, was responsible for paying the rent for the Shipton beacon of 7/- per annum. An alarm that the enemy was about to land in 1799 turned out to be false but the men had already rushed to man the batteries (guns).

*   *   *   *   *   *

The enemy were eventually beaten without having set foot on Dorset or English soil, yet the folk of Burton Bradstock found themselves fully involved in the defeat.

Richard Francis Roberts, son of the Burton mill owner, was in the navy and was following in the footsteps of his uncle, Captain Francis Roberts who had an honourable and distinguished career tragically dying of yellow fever on board the "Success" in the West Indies. Captain Francis Roberts had served with **Captain Thomas Hardy**[2] **of Portesham, born at Kingston Russell** House, Long Bredy, in 1769, who also had a long and very distinguished naval career, to whom a monument stands sentinel above Portesham.

From Burton, too, came Rear Admiral Ingram who lived at, and possibly built, Girt House. In 1802 Hardy wrote to Ingram from the flagship "Victory" 'I find the Burton fish, etc., has been too good. However, a touch of gout in September sometimes is a pleasant thing for the partridges'. Hardy also pointed out to a would-be naval officer all the inconveniences attending the profession and the numberless hardships. It seems that Admiral Ingram and the Captain of the Dorset Yeomanry, Richard Travers of Loders, were the leading characters in West Dorset. The Dorset Yeomanry were recruited as another defence force against a landing by Bonaparte, and the men were from the coastal villages; Weymouth to Burton and inland from Little Bredy and **Shipton Gorge. (Ingram being in command of the "Fencibles").** Travers was connected to the Roberts family by marriage. The distinguished Sir Evan Nepean, Secretary to the Admiralty, lived at Loders Court, which he had purchased in 1799. These gentlemen of Loders and Burton Bradstock seemed to enjoy good living and good wine for we read of Hardy's brother-in-law

83

being plied with wine by Travers enough to lay him up for three days!

From the Victory, laying off Antigua in June 1805, Captain Thomas Hardy wrote, 'I saw young Roberts of the Jason yesterday, he is very well but I do not think he will ever set the Thames on fire'. Roberts had certainly had a first class education possibly at Wimborne, Milton Abbas or Dorchester and he had volunteered as an A.B. on Nelson's ship, the Victory, on May 10th 1805, at the age of twenty. Hardy promoted him to midshipman two days before the Battle of Trafalgar and he was also employed as Captain's Clerk. Very fortunately, for historians, Roberts kept a personal Remark Book which at the turn of this century was in the possession of a Roberts' descendant, Miss Roberts, also living at Burton Bradstock. Miss Roberts gave permission for the Remark Book to be used by two historians Broadley and Bartelot whose book "Three Dorset Captains at Trafalgar" was published in 1906.

The people of Burton shared fully in the anxiety and triumph of the Battle of Trafalgar in October 1805. With Young Roberts on board Nelson's Flagship, they eventually received a full account of the battle. To quote letters to Roberts from his father and family is sufficient to convey the feelings of those caught up in war from the usually peaceful village.

The day after the damaged Victory tied up in Portsmouth Richard Roberts wrote as follows to his son:-

Burton. Bridport
5th Dec. 1805

My dear Richard,

I have just received the happy news of the arrival of the Victory at Portsmouth and I sincerely hope you are well. I have only a few days since received your letter written the day after the battle and also Mr. Kenway's dated the 27th Oct. from Trafalgar Bay. You cannot conceive the pleasure and happiness it gave your Mother, your brother and sisters and myself to find you had so happily escaped the fate of the 21st Oct. I will assure you that it was no common feelings that agitated the sensations of the whole family to which you may add a great many of your friends and acquaintances at Burton, Bridport and elsewhere as soon as it was known that you were safe. We had the pleasing gratification of congratulations from many friends both by person, letters and messages. This you may be assured was highly gratifying. I have news further to tell you that your mother, myself and Sophia will very soon be up to see you, Capt. Hardy, and all the brave fellows of the Victory whom I have any personal knowledge of; to all of whom I sincerely beg of you to give my most hearty and sincere congratulations for this happy escape. I am told that Capt. Hardy is soon to come home as his health is very indifferent. I hope it will not be so before we get up. I have written to Mrs. J. Jacobs to try and get me some lodgings with two beds at least and if three the better. I have also written to Capt. Rogers to ask leave for Frank to come to Portsmouth to meet us, which I hope and trust he will do. I beg you will write to me by return and say how your own health and Capt. Hardy's is, also to say what are your proceedings with the corps of Lord Nelson and where the ship is or likely to be etc. I leave the other part of the paper for you to receive the congratulations of your Mother, brother and sisters. I am with the greatest affection,

Your father, Richard Roberts

Then followed letters from the young Roberts' mother, brother and sisters.

My dear Richard,

I sincerely congratulate you on your late preservation from the perilous situation you have lately undergone. It is not in my power to describe the painful anxiety I have felt for your safety or the joy I felt on hearing you were safe and well, on the receipt of which I returned my thanks to your Almighty Preserver and hope you did not forget to do the same. Hoping to see you in a few days.

Your affectionate mother, M. Roberts.

Burton, 5th Dec. 1805

Our dear Brother,

We beg to offer you our most sincere and earnest congratulations for your late fortunate escape from the dreadful battle you have lately had, and also the lucky escape of shipwreck and hope soon to have a pleasing answer from your own hand. We are your loving and affectionate sisters and brother.

Sophia A. Roberts, W. Roberts, Ag. Roberts.

The following day young William Roberts wrote to his sailor brother relating the excitement and sadness of the occasion, together with the usual sort of domestic news a boy of any century might pen.

Burton, Dec. 6th 1805

Dear Brother,

Your kind letter of the 22nd Nov. (i.e. Oct) we were all very happy to receive, and to find you were alive and well. We gave away beer to almost every man in the parish. I was almost drunk myself. Mr. T. Fish brought the news and deprived old Jemmy of the pleasure, but we were afraid old Jemmy would not be quick enough. Augusta wishes she could write. Father has bought a little black pony and gave £9-19s-6d for it. It is not broke in yet.

We have raised at Burton and Bridport a subscription for the widows and orphans. They collected at Bridport £14 at the Church door Thanksgiving Day, but they got a great deal more than that the day before. We at Burton collected £6-8s-1d. Mr. Hunter (Rector) and father are going all round the parish to those people who were not at church. Jno. Cheney wants to see you and for that matter so do I too. You will see Father and mother and Sophy. I still remain your affectionate brother.

Wm. H. Roberts.

P.S. Please write soon and give me a good account of the battle. We had bell ringing and beer drinking the night that we received the list of the killed and wounded and likewise when we received your letter. The colours were hoisted on the tower. Mother had hard work to keep the beer barrel a running. Our family is increased very much for we have had no less than 13 puppies: Blossom 7 and Clara 6. Ralph, Gipsy and all are well and hearty. We have been talking about your taking Ralph with you but I suppose you have enough. I expect you home to Burton but none of rest don't. All the Bridport volunteers went to church on Thanksgiving Day. I do not think there is any person in your place. Father will write you soon; he received your letter on the

6th inst. This is all I have at present to say.
Addressed Mr. Richard F. Roberts, H.M. Ship Victory, Portsmouth
To the care of Mrs. J. Jacobs, Ordinance Row, Portsea.

Mr. Kenway, a family friend further expressed the feelings of people of the village.

Burton, Dec. 7th 1805

Dear Friend,

'Tis impossible for me to express the happiness that I feel in having to congratulate you on your safe arrival. The many anxious weeks that have elapsed seem for a moment forgotten. I am truly thankful to the Almighty for your preservation. What must have been your feelings in the dreadful conflict you have witnessed! It chills my blood when I think of it, and I am already to conclude I should not have been able to have endured such a terrible scene. When I consider your never having been to sea before and the short time that elapsed between your sailing and the battle, together with the distressed condition of your ship since; it seems to me sufficient to determine anyone to leave it. However, knowing your determination it probably will have the contrary effect, and be the means of your persevering in the line you are in. If so, I sincerely wish you every success and that you may become a dignified character in the British Navy. We first heard of the engagement on the morning of the 5th. Nov. The account was sent by Mr. J. Hounsell to Burton soon after Lieutenant Lapinoture passed Bridport. It informed us of the death of Lord Nelson and that 19 ships were taken and one blown up. Our feelings were extremely racked; all deploring the loss of the hero; all measurably pleased the victory was so decisively in our favour. But at the same time our minds were much distressed on your account. For my own part I never experienced such incoherent emotions in my life; one minute hoping you were safe; the next doubting it from the dreadful carnage that was inevitable in such a situation. From this dilemma nothing could relieve me but hearing immediately from you. Every post was looked for, with indescribable anxiety. Our disappointment was great in not having the particulars of your ship in the first Gazette; and the impractibility of it did not appear till other despatches arrived. During the interval (which was extremely tedious) every means was used by all your friends to obtain the earliest information. Capt. Blackwell of the Euryalus desired Mrs. Fish to present his compliments to Mr. Hardy's family and your father saying Capt. Hardy was safe and he had no doubt you were likewise. This was some consolation; but nothing equal to what we experienced when your name was not to be found amongst the list of killed and wounded. The news flew like lightning through the village. The bells rang and everybody seem actuated by one general sentiment of joy. But this however was not the positive intelligence I wanted; for afterwards a doubt crept in whether your name might not have been omitted, and this was not dispelled till the receipt of your very acceptable letter dated Oct. 22nd (to your father) which he received in Bridport and immediately sent by Mr. Fish to Burton. The bells rang again until several of the ropes broke! They were repaired next morning. Your father's colours were hoisted on the tower and continued flying several days. I was really astonished to find you were collected the day after the action as to be able to write such a letter. It gave me great pleasure and it does you infinite credit. Your favour to me of the 27th came at the same time. I should have written you sooner but did not know where to direct as we expected the Victory home some time past. I should have thought that you had been so much agitated by the transactions of the 21st that it would have been impossible to collect your ideas on paper.

It is not to be wondered at that at the time you did not know the particulars of the action. This has been pretty well supplied by the public prints, which is astonishing.

What would the English Nation have done with your gallant Commander had he survived the action and brought home all the captured ships! Not that it is wanting in bestowing every encomium on him and on all those under his command. But surely a new vocabulary must have been formed, for however verbose our language may be reckoned it would still have been wanting in epithets. Great, magnanimous, illustrious, would appear too hackneyed and common. It must have been more than Invincible Admiral of Admirals and perhaps Lord of Lords; for I think the people would have run into idolatry and absolutely worshipped him. Pray God may have taken him to Himself and given him a crown of glory.

I have no doubt that the subscriptions now making in the kingdom to help the widows, orphans and wounded will be followed up by others for a remuneration to the officers and crews of every ship in action. However I shall be most happy to hear that you come in for a share of prize money; for I am such a novice that I do not know whether clerks have any share.

Dec. 8th — I left off writing last night thinking there would have been a letter to your father informing him that you were in harbour which would have fixed the day of your mother and sisters leaving Burton but am informed that there was no letter. It therefore being uncertain when you will come into port, I thought it best to send this and write again by then. I am happy to inform you that your relations and friends in general are well. Mr. R. Roberts of Gorwell was here and told me he thought he should go up to see you, but I heard yesterday he has the gravel and is otherwise unwell. I have many times been requested by your friends and acquaintances to present their love and kind remembrances to you when I wrote, which I do unitedly with my own, and remain

Your affectionate friend, J. Kenway

Mr. R. F. Roberts, M.D.,
H.M.S. Victory
Portsmouth, or Elsewhere

Village legend has always maintained that there was a young mariner, named Hawkins, from Burton Bradstock, at the Battle of Trafalgar also. He was not serving on the Victory, according to the ship's roll but he could well have served on board one of the many other vessels engaged in the fight. This requires further research. A John Buckler from Burton is known to have been on the Victory in 1799.

No more need be said of Burton and her connection with the sea for the present. She had shared full fathom in a great adventure. The bells rang out until the ropes broke, signalling the joy that a sailor son of the village had come safe home. The people of Burton knew only too well what young Roberts and other mariners had experienced that October day.

1. Since the first edition of this book was printed Roger Guttridge has written a superb book about smuggling in Dorset. Smugglers from Burton Bradstock are listed and certain events recounted.
2. Admiral Hardy, by the time of his retirement.

Fig. 16

POST OFFICE CORNER.
ROCK HOUSE (L) WITH THE READING ROOM *ADJOINING*.
ENTRANCE TO MANOR FARM (R) WHERE A PARAFFIN *OIL STREET LAMP IS*
PROMINENT. C 1900.

Fig. 17

COTTAGES AND SHOP (L) BURNT DOWN IN 1926 WHILST A SALE OF BOATS WAS
BEING HELD ON THE BEACH. GIRT HOUSE (CENTRE). TOWNSEND FARM HOUSE (R).

Fig. 18

A SAILOR'S JUG. THIS ONE WAS PRESENTED TO CAROLINE CLARK BY HER SWEETHEART IN 1834.

Fig. 19

Fig. 20

BILL CLARK HOSKINS, MARINER, 1833-1854

H M S VICTORY H M DOCKYARD PORTSMOUTH HAMPSHIRE

Fig. 21

H.M.S. VICTORY, H.M. DOCKYARD, PORTSMOUTH, HAMPSHIRE, AS SHE IS TODAY, LAUNCHED IN 1765, AT A COST OF £57,748, ON WHICH MIDSHIPMAN ROBERTS SERVED UNDER NELSON, AT THE BATTLE OF TRAFALGAR.

Fig. 22

BURTON FISHERWOMEN

Fig. 23

GERTIE CAMMELL, NÉE SPONSFORD, BRAIDING AT HER COTTAGE DOOR IN
MILL STREET.
NELL WARD STANDING BEHIND.   C 1920

Fig. 24

ST. MARY'S CHURCH, SOMETIME PRIOR TO ALTERATIONS IN 1897, AND THE SPINNING MILL CHIMNEY, AT ITS FULL HEIGHT.

Fig. 25

THE STREET BEYOND THE CHURCH ONCE KNOWN AS BRIDGE STREET. TWO COTTAGES BELOW THE CANAL WERE BURNT DOWN IN 1902 WHEN A SPARK FROM THE FACTORY CHIMNEY IGNITED THE THATCH. THE MAGNOLIAS (L) RISES ABOVE THE OTHER DWELLINGS.

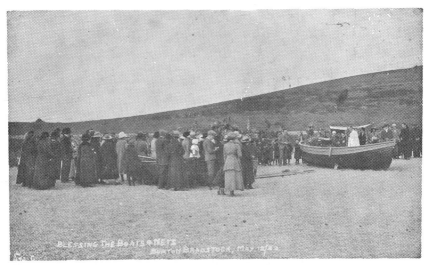

Fig. 26

1922: BLESSING THE BOATS AND NETS ON BURTON BEACH. AN AGE OLD CUSTOM
CHILDREN HOLD GARLANDS OF FLOWERS IN THE BACKGROUND.

Fig. 27

DAPHNE LEGG (NOW MRS BARTLETT)
AND OLIVE HITT (MRS AYLOTT) HOLDING THEIR GARLANDS
DAPHNE'S MOTHER LOOKS ON. C 1913.

Fig. 28

*LT. GENERAL AUGUSTUS PITT-RIVERS, F.R.S., (1827-1900)
AN ARCHAEOLOGICAL PIONEER AND LORD OF THE MANOR OF BURTON
BRADSTOCK.*

Fig. 29

THRESHING AT BURTON MANOR FARM IN VICTORIAN TIMES.

Fig. 30

THE VILLAGE FÊTE DAY 1920.
ROOKERY COTTAGE(S) (R) FOREGROUND WHERE A STONE STAIRCASE **HAS**
BEEN REVEALED, TOGETHER WITH OTHER INTERESTING FEATURES, DU**RING**
RECENT RENOVATIONS.

Fig. 31

WHITSUNTIDE FAIR ON THE EAST BEACH, BRIDPORT HARBOUR, NOW WEST
BAY, 1860.
THE SHIP BUILDING YARD CAN BE SEEN IN THE BACKGROUND.

XX
VILLAGE SCHOOLING

Like so many other aspects of their lives, the education of the children of Burton Bradstock in the late 18th and early 19th centuries depended on the benevolence of the wealthy. As early as 1786, in the returns of Parliament, it was stated that an unknown donor gave the rent from a small estate in Devon for teaching poor children of the parish, but the estate was sold and the money raised was used to repair the church. However, the Churchwardens paid out an amount equivalent to the interest on the money used and an annual sum of £1.16s was paid from the Churchwardens' Accounts and was said to have been in operation for at least 100 years. Six poor children were to benefit from this charity and in the accounts we find their names listed and a record of payment of £1-16s to their teacher, Mr. Morgan, 1756, Henry Angel, 1808, Elizabeth Stone, 1811, and Betty Gover, 1826 and 1833.

It was very likely that dames' schools were in existence in the village by the end of the 18th Century. Children would attend these dames' schools paying a few pence each week. It was far more of a minding service than an educational establishment for the dames were not very good teachers, although those more capable, taught some reading and a little Religious Knowledge. In Burton Bradstock one dames' school was recorded to have existed in the corner cottage at the bottom of Cliff Lane and it was said that Magnolia House was once a girls' school, another school at what is now Ingram House. A directory of 1859 lists a Miss Gammas' school for girls. At the turn of the century (1800) there were already Sunday Schools, mostly Church of England, except in Bridport where the Unitarians had first set up a Sunday School. A minute in the Churchwardens' Book of 1813 stated that a Sunday School was to be established in Burton Bradstock and that 4 guineas per annum would be paid out of the poor rate towards the expenses. Richard Roberts, the Flax Mill owner, had mentioned a Sunday School, for the child labourers who worked in his mill, where they would learn to read and say their Catechism for two hours every Sunday.

The first Burton Bradstock School Log Book, which probably dated from the mid-nineteenth century and was written up by the Head Teacher, was presumed to have been destroyed by an incoming head in the 1940s.

There was a large increase in the population in the country from 1801-1871 and in the 12 parishes, within a seven mile radius of Bridport, a survey in 1812 showed that hemp and flax were grown on a large scale and it is known that agriculture was the other main occupation. Many of the children were engaged in these trades and, if they did attend the dames' schools they only did so for a few years for as soon as they were old enough to work (about 7 or 8 years old) they left and began their long labour of life to provide income for the household in which they lived. The average weekly wage for an adult male was no more than 5 or 6 shillings and the few pence a child could earn was not to be lost.

William Gear (1864-1955) left school at 7 years and went to work on a farm. His sisters Lizzie and Polly were ball winders at the mill 3 days a week and attended the Burton School the other 3 days. When education became compulsory William had to give up his work and attend school full time. Fred and Dave Legg, in the 1880s, are known to have left school at 11 years of age.

In some parishes there were evening schools and a report of 1818 stated that there were five schools in Burton Bradstock. Whether they were dames' schools or evening schools, or both, there is no telling. One was most likely the Sunday School. The population of the village was by then 677.

An enquiry set up in 1846/47 reported that there were three schools, a Sunday, a day and an evening school in Burton Bradstock where the population had exploded to 1200, of which 174 were children attending the schools. At Little Bredy there was a thriving night school by 1873 which operated four evenings a week and had 26 pupils on the register.

From 1833 National Assistance was available towards the setting up of schools. The establishment of Church of England schools rested with the clergy, in each parish, who applied for aid and opened schools for those baptised in the Church of England faith, although this rule was not entirely enforced. To qualify for the National Society Aid parishes had to contribute a proportion of the money and local Building Funds were set up. The landed gentry and nobility in the district were usually the main contributors.

In Burton Bradstock a Church of England School was established in 1845. An uncertificated master was appointed and a report gave the leaving age of the pupils as 13-15 years old which was indeed high, as in many other villages children left school at a much earlier age. It seems that a large number of the Burton School children were taken away from school to work on farms when haymaking, harvest and other similar seasonal work was at a peak or put to work as full time agricultural labourers or in Roberts' mill. Because of this, winter evenings classes were held in Burton Bradstock. Some farmers hired a whole family, necessitating moving on from village to village, and the children of these families had no schooling at all. Children who laboured in the fields and factories by day were far too tired when they attended evening classes, so much of the good intention was lost. Many were so poor that they did not have decent clothes to wear to school. Even as late as 1899 some children at Burton School arrived for lessons with no boots on their feet and for this the master, Tommy Milburn, would beat the boys. Children did commence their schooling at an early age. Some were only 3 or 4 years old.

The Burton Bradstock School was opened by the Reverend Templar on land given by Lord Rivers. It would appear that a schoolmaster, Zachariah Chick, was living in a cottage, where the present school stands, in 1841 and it is possible that a school already existed there. Two cottages were demolished for this purpose and the school was built by public subscription and the proceeds of a bazaar held in the Rectory garden. It was 1866 before all the buildings were completed. In Burton, Lord Rivers and Colonel Hussey of Bredy were the main supporters of the Building Fund; Lord Rivers subscribing £40.

The Little Bredy and Kingston Russell School Committee's Accounts state that a government grant of £157 was received and setting up a school, renting a temporary house for the Master and levelling his garden cost a total of £471.

In Burton Bradstock, Nonconformist children were allowed to attend the school but their parents were not altogether co-operative in upholding the good influence of the Church of England school. It is possible that the Dissenters had their own school but it had closed by 1841. The Wesleyans did have a Sunday School and library. Farmers were far from keen to educate the labouring classes. Being, on the whole, uneducated themselves they foresaw only problems, in every direction, if schooling became popular.

Building regulations applied, even then, to the structure of schools being built. The walls were to be of brick or stone and 14 inches thick and floors of wood allowing 6 square feet per child. The roof had to be 10-12 feet high to allow air to circulate and the Burton School building would seem to conform well within these expensive conditions.

*   *   *   *   *   *

When a school was established a Head Master or Mistress would be appointed. Pupil teachers served under the Head and were examined in their work, annually, by the Inspectors. Some of these young people, mostly women found it difficult to control the classes and were not too good themselves at some of the work they were trying to teach. It was the rare means whereby a working class person could climb into the middle section of Society. Reliable and more senior pupils were appointed as monitors and helped the teachers or took over completely. The monitors usually went on to become pupil teachers and the better ones were as well trained as any teachers produced from Teachers' Colleges one hundred years later.

Four early pupil teachers appear in the 1881 Census. They were Elizabeth Notton, Elizabeth Carter, Susan Masters and Isabella Douglas, but the one for whom we have details of her career was Winifred Hawkins. She was born in 1885, a daughter of Richard Hawkins who kept the Three Horse Shoes and combined this with being a village baker and postmaster.

At the beginning of the 1900s she became a pupil teacher at Burton School and in 1903 went to a training college in Southampton where she passed her examinations with honours, taking up her first post in 1904 at Salisbury Green, near Hamble, Southampton Water.

From there she moved to Frampton Cotterell, near Bristol staying 12 years, endearing herself to all her pupils. She lodged with a market gardener and his family who kept a few cows. Being a country girl and quite able to milk she kept her hand in by milking these cows and through this she met her future husband, a local farmer, who arrived one day to deliver a cart load of mangels. She then became a farmer's wife, an easy calling for a Burton woman. By this time her family in Burton Bradstock had come out of the Three Horse Shoes and taken Townsend Farm at the northern end of the village, laying the foundations of a large farming unit. Much of the original farmland at Townsend has been built on in recent years.

*   *   *   *   *   *

At Burton School there were not enough desks for all the children but at least there was adequate floor space where the children could stand and receive instruction from the pupil teachers. A tiered gallery was built at some time and the children stood in rows one above the other. The little ones found this very tiring and often fell asleep. A firm blow from the tyrant Head soon woke them up. Most lessons were learnt by heart and repetition was the method used to instill the lessons "home". Much emphasis was put on reading and learning passages from the Bible, copying texts from the Bible for writing exercises and general Religious Instruction. Slates were used usually for writing and arithmetic and when funds allowed copy books were bought for practising the beautiful copperplate handwriting of that period. It would seem that the children were charged for the copy books. Gradually reading books with a moral bias were introduced, as well.

Arithmetic appeared to be the weakest subject. Some of the teachers were only capable of calculating simple sums. The efficient recording of detail by the Salway Ash Mistress lists the lessons of 1887 as scripture, grammar, arithmetic, including learning the multiplication tables, reading, spelling and composition. Throughout the schools there were plenty of singing lessons and poetry learning. "Home Lessons" were common everywhere. Later still, Geography and History were included in the syllabus and memorising kings, queens, dates and battles was to trouble the mind of the village child. From the mid-century the Head Master's wife taught the girls needlework and this system was still in Burton Bradstock School in the early 1940's. The Object Lesson was introduced — the rabbit, milk, coal, the lion, birds' feet and other similar titles appear in the records.

Pupil teachers could train in Dorchester schools at a cost to themselves of £10 per year and on obtaining their Certificate of Merit they could expect to receive a salary of £40-65 per annum. A certificated Master commanded a salary of £100 per year.

The National Society for Education was not in favour of co-education but this was far from practical in small rural communities. Boys and girls were separated, as much as possible in the school, as far as the syllabus and system would allow. Fees were charged for attending school, based on the number in a family and were usually one penny per week per child. At Netherbury the Head Mistress recorded having difficulty in collecting the "school pence" which was 1½d for a child and 2d a week, for a family. Shipton Gorge charged 2d a week and others as much as 4d. The school's expenses had to be met from the fees and at Burton the fire insurance dredged the funds in 1870.

The school hours were usually from 9 a.m. — 12 noon and 2 p.m. — 4.30 p.m. or 2 p.m. — 4 p.m. in winter, as many children had to walk a mile or two, before dark, to the outlying farms and hamlets. On the whole, the school holidays were governed by Church Festivals and seasonal work. The local schools were similar in that two weeks were taken at Christmas and a week at Whitsun. Good Friday and Easter Monday were holidays, later a longer period was taken at Easter. Two or three weeks were taken for harvesting at the beginning of August. The children stayed away for haymaking, potato planting and picking, gleaning and fruit picking.

Bridport and Beaminster Fairs, village feasts, West Bay Regatta, the circus and other local activities warranted the schools closing as most of the children would have absented themselves anyway. Weddings and funerals of the local gentry justified a day or half day's holiday. The Burton School children enjoyed a half day off on Garland Day.

At Burton Bradstock the new schoolroom was added in 1870 and letters of invitation to the village gentry from the Rector are lodged in the Dorset Archives. To Thomas Fry Legge, Esq. of the (Burton) Farm and Job Legge, Esq. he wrote 'the new schoolroom will be opened on Thursday next (D.V.)

and the school children will be provided with tea and cake on the occasion'.

The pattern of schooling at Burton Bradstock went on in much the same manner for a further 70 years. By 1900 the attendance at the school was often as near 100% as could be achieved. At that time the master was a harsh and inconsiderate man and thrashings were the order of the day. He had no sympathy for poor children or those dogged by ill health. His inspectors only saw and reported on his scholastic achievements at the school and these were good. He was a strict disciplinarian and obviously a good teacher as the Diocesan Inspector for the year ending September 1900 reported that 'the mixed school is splendidly efficient' and of the infants' school 'these classes are in admirable order'. On Religious Instruction he said 'the school is in all respects excellent. Teachers and children are working together most admirably. The intelligence of the answers given is in some cases quite remarkable. The tone of reverence throughout the school is most commendable'.

The school had been open 427 times during the year and the following pupils had never missed an attendance:-

Standard VII — Boys — Stanley Hayward.
Standard V — Boys — Henry Davis, Edward Bartlett.
Standard IV — Boys — John Legg, Robert Legg, Conrad Hawkins, Edward Davis,
Joseph Steele, Robert Cammell.
Girls — Alice Brown, Belle Hayward, Bessie Swaffield.
Standard III — Boys — Stanley Marsh, Reginald Buckler, Alfred Brown, George Payne,
William Dunham, Charles Northover, Ernest Legg.
Girls — Lillie Swaffield.
Standard II — Boys — Fred Norris, James Steele, Douglas Hawkins, William Swaffield.
Girls — Nora Wrixton, Ethel Slade.
Standard I — Boys — William George Dowton, Reginald White, Alfred Northover, George
Dunham.
Girls — May Tucker, Sylvia Marsh, May Williams.
Infants — Boys — Regie Davis.
Girls — Rosie Foot.

Medals were awarded for regular attendance and this produced a keeness in the pupils to go to school for it was a great honour to receive the coveted award. The good health of these children, who never missed a day, was a contributory factor. Ill health certainly kept children away from school a great deal. A contagious disease 'commonly called mumps' swept through West Dorset in 1884 and raged for many weeks. This was followed by measles. Wet, cold and snowy weather kept the children who had a long distance to walk, at home. Poor footwear, and often no outer clothing contributed to this problem. The schools had fires which were lit at the end of October. The meagre allowance of coal did not help the situation. In 1905 James Steele received a medal for seven years' unbroken attendance. Others gained six, five, four and three year medals. These children were hardy and their parents were not dependent on them being taken off school to nurse mother or mind the babies or to do seasonal work, which was still in practice, on a lesser scale, even at the end of the 19th Century.

But this exciting story of Burton Bradstock School has led us too far for we must retrace our steps back to the early part of the century when the village and its inhabitants were facing the difficult days of low wages, long and tedious hours on the farms and in the flax mills and when the depression, following the lengthy war period, was being felt.

XXI

POVERTY AND THE TOLPUDDLE MARTYRS

The one shilling paid out by the Churchwardens of Burton Bradstock for the prayers which were said for the recovery of Our Majesty, from time to time, did not produce the hoped for result and the long reign of King George III ended eventually in 1820. His bouts of madness had forced his eldest son, George, to shoulder most of the responsibilities of Kingship during his father's illness and he was therefore King in all but name, a position he had filled since 1811.

George III's many children were unsuccessful in producing legitimate heirs to the throne of England. His sons set up separate houses with "wives" whose own lines were not such to win the approval of The Royal Consent. Many children resulted from these liasons but none but Princess Charlotte, the legitimate daughter of George IV, could succeed to the throne. Her sudden death in childbirth forced her uncle, the Duke of Kent, to break the long association with his French "wife" and marry Princess Victoria of Saxe-Coburg.

*   *   *   *   *   *

In Burton Bradstock the Royal "marriages" and events of the succession hardly bothered the labourer of the parish for he and his family were more concerned with their own survival and the cost of bread. Bad harvests brought high prices and poverty, the better harvests glossed over the problems of the poor and plans to repeal the corn laws fell behind with those who stood, often at their own connivance and expense, in Parliament.

The blazing hot summer of 1801, and the resultant drought, together with all the other problems of the poor, produced near famine conditions. In Burton Bradstock, as everywhere else in the country, the crops did not develop and mature and the poor had to live on barley and bran or oatmeal. The Government issued a proclamation recommending that bran be mixed with flour when ground and that no person should consume more than 1lb of bread a day and that no bread was to be eaten as well as vegetables with a meal.

The Overseers in Burton allowed 2 pecks of barley a week to poor people and the sum of 4/- per month. They also decided to purchase 80 bushels* of good barley. In October, in preparation for the forthcoming winter, their accounts recorded the buying of the barley at 7/6d a bushel and 200 bushels of coal at 2/- a bushel. Thirty one people received relief from the parish together with several children. Some lame people caused additional expense to the parish and two women were allowed £1 on account of illness.

Inoculation against smallpox, pioneered by a Dorset man and given Royal approval, had lessened the outbreaks of such a vile disease. In Burton Bradstock in 1807 some seventy five children and several adults were inoculated at the cost of 2/6d a head at the expense of the parish. From then this practice became more acceptable.

In 1818 there were 25 parishioners requiring help. During these lean years the Manorial Court continued to meet and little had changed from a century

*4 pecks = 1 bushel (dry measure) approx. 47lbs. barley.

earlier. There was mention of a slaughter house and the dust caused by winnowing of corn. One villager was fined for carrying a lighted candle in the street and a new order was brought in that all horses going through the streets, to water, were to be led and any cattle were to be followed by some person. The rivers, as always, caused problems and there was earth settlement at the New Bridges. There were problems with the sanitary arrangements of the Poor House. The Court was told that the vault belonging to the Poor House was so full that it was a great and offensive nuisance to John Hooper, the Hayward, and his family.

A vault type lavatory would have been a pit over which a wooden box with a cut out seat(s) was erected. The vault was allowed to fill until such times as it was so full that it was necessary to dig out the contents which were usually spread on the garden or an adjacent plot. Those favouring better hygienic methods would shovel lime into the vault from time to time.

The Overseers of the Poor, who were responsible for the Poor House, were given ten days in which to empty the vault. This type of lavatory was common to most cottages well into the present century.

*   *   *   *   *   *

The summer of 1818 brought a bit of light relief in those times of hardship and poverty for the working folk of Burton Bradstock. The celebrations for Victory, after many years of war, were held in Bridport. A long, long procession of floats, followed by workers dressed in the appropriate garb of their trade, paraded through the town. Prominent were the hundreds of flax and hemp workers. A vast quantity of beef and ale was consumed at a feast which followed.

*   *   *   *   *   *

It would seem that people were now living longer. If they survived the rigours of actually arriving into the world, usually into the rude conditions of a humble cottage and the diseases of childhood and adolescence and if they were fortunate enough to escape contracting consumption and hereditary weaknesses then, and only then, might they live a long life.

At the time of the Victory celebrations, the Burton Bradstock Parish Registers record the ages of the following parishioners:-

John Ferry 86, William Tucker 86, Jenny Angel, Betty Camel, Hannah Gale, all 85 years old. Benjamin Atkins, Joseph Chambers, Eleanor Downe, Richard Gale, 84, Joseph Chilcott 83, Henry Angel and Samuel Camel 82, Edith Anning, Joseph Everett and Mary Garland 81 and William Buckler 80 years old. John Hooper (the hayward or smuggler?) born in 1749 "enjoyed" 90 years of life.

These old folk of Burton Bradstock had been born between 1718 and 1749. Their lives had taken them through one of the most difficult periods in the history of the village. They may have been fortunate enough to have enjoyed a better standard of living and/or been engaged in a more healthier occupation than some people. It is interesting to note that there were more old men than old women.

*   *   *   *   *   *

95

Animals and birds, which were classed as vermin then, were trapped and their heads or tails brought as proof to the Churchwardens. Otters, foxes, badgers, polecats, rats and sparrows, the latter being detrimental to thatched roofs, were caught and the reward received for their capture brought in a few pence for the trappers — male and female! Sparrows raised 4d per dozen and a dozen rats 6d. In 1826, 88¼ dozen sparrows netted a total of £2-4-1½d. A badger head was worth the princely sum of one shilling, the hams making a fine meal for some family!

* * * * * *

The church was to be enlarged in 1832 by adding 180 free sittings. Revenue from rented pews had brought in substantial amounts but this was really illegal. Owners of pews painted and decorated, and often locked them, according to their fancy. In 1813 a new gallery, in the north aisle, had been installed in the church and subscriptions collected. The seats and pews were numbered and in the gallery some seats were of the tip up sort. The owners were allowed to paint them if they followed a uniform plan. Amongst the subscribers was Admiral Ingram who required a pew for 4 persons. Catherine Spurdle paid 8/- for a turn-up seat, no. 62, in the middle of the gallery, as did Elizabeth Buckler for no. 63. Painted and lettered fire buckets were placed in the church 'furnished' by the Sun Fire Office.

* * * * * *

Great disappointment was felt by the adults and children alike in Burton Bradstock when their August Feast was postponed in 1832 because of an outbreak of cholera in Bridport. Besides this precaution, notices were posted at either end of the village telling all vagrants to pass through the village without begging and no vagrants were to be lodged at 'publick or beer houses'. All these places were to be cleared from 1 o'clock on the Sunday night for a fortnight and all drains were to be attended to and all nuisances immediately remedied.

After a long period of war, unemployment was another problem. The navy did not need men nor tackle to the extent that both had previously been required and the more general use of machinery in agriculture or manufacturing cost some men their jobs. West Dorset fell victim to the reduction in work.

General unrest prevaded and much is written into our National history with regard to this. Perhaps the farmers of the Bride Vale were not so progressive as their brothers up country for we do not find incidence of machines being smashed in Burton or corn ricks being fired. We do know that the mills were not so productive. This was due to the general fall in the need of sail and tackle for the navy at the same time as the Roberts sons took over the business, on their father's death in 1820.

Very low agricultural wages caused a group of men of Tolpuddle, near Dorchester, to band together. Trade Unions were already in existence in a simple form. Plenty is well written, in great detail, about the Tolpuddle Martyrs and their conviction, transportation and eventual pardon. For certain their arrest and fate was well reported in Burton Bradstock for the

Tolpuddle leader, George Loveless, had a brother, William, working as a flax dresser in or near Bridport. Extensive research by Mr. L. O. Bealing of Bournemouth, over many years, has resulted in an index of some 1100 Loveless names and has revealed an extract from a letter, probably held in George Loveless's wife's family, which stated that his brother, William, was living at Burton, near Bridport in 1834. The Burton Bradstock Parish Registers contain the baptisms of two of William's children. Ann Down in 1824 and George in 1837 (named after his "famous" uncle?)

Yet another brother of the Martyr lived in Burton from 1805, presumably for some years. In a settlement order of 1859 John Loveless declared on oath that he had heard and believed that he was born in the parish of Tolpuddle, about the 14th day of April 1786, in which parish his father Thomas Loveless was a settled inhabitant. He went on to say that in 1805 he was bound apprentice for 3 years to Mr. John Clay of Burton Bradstock, who was a flax dresser, in the employ of Mr. Richard Roberts. Loveless stated that he lived in Mr. Clay's house, was found board and lodging by him and received £4 at the end of the term. By 1859 John Loveless was an old man in his seventies and was being removed back to Burton, by the Bridport Authorities, for parish care, in his old age.

There are other Burton Bradstock connections with the Tolpuddle Martyrs which require further research. At the time of the trial some considered it a disgrace to be connected with the Tolpuddle Martyrs and relationship to them was often concealed. Only in later years when they were granted a pardon and fêted as heroes did more evidence of their families become apparent.

About this time the Poor Law was reformed, much needed, as it had not been amended since 1601. The workhouse system was brought into being and one was set up in Bridport around 1836. Those from Burton, who needed "care" in those early days of the 19th Century, were then sent to Bridport Union Workhouse. Anyone who became an inmate there was said to have gone into the Union. The Burton Bradstock Poor House was no longer needed and became an ordinary cottage. Records of 1861 show that Hannah Knight, born in London, aged 86 years was living there, pensioned off after being matron until its closure and with her lived her servant girl, 19 year old Elvina Davis. Here we can conjure up the story as to how Hannah Knight came from London to Burton. Was she one of Roberts' apprentice girls from care in Westminster?

* * * * * *

In 1837 the church bells of Burton Bradstock rang out once more across the valley, heralding the accession of the young Queen Victoria. She took on a weak and disrespected throne. Her uncles had done little to strengthen the Monarchy but her determination and loyalty to duty, influenced by her husband, Prince Albert, and Subjects, who took easily to following her fine example, eventually inspired a great respect for Queen and Country. During her reign the British Empire doubled and her family married into the Royal households of many other countries, creating a peace with those particular nations.

At the Bridport Workhouse the residents celebrated Victoria's Coronation with beef, plum pudding and a pint of strong beer; a welcome change from the meagre and uninteresting diet they usually endured.

XXII
THE GIRL THAT LOVED A SAILOR

Here now in the early 1800s must be included the story of a real Burton family, the Clarks. Richard Clark, born in 1775, was a fisherman and mariner; earning his living between voyages at sea by seine fishing from Burton Beach. His prospects in life looked good for he took for his bride Elizabeth Killick, a farmer's daughter from Watton, near Bridport; they were married at St. Mary's Church, Burton in 1800. Later he is given as a Pilot, possibly at Bridport Harbour.

Their two daughters, Mary and Caroline, have fortunately left unique mementos which are now in the hands of their descendants.

Mary married into "the business" when she became the wife of Henry Hoskins, a mariner, who haled from Cornwall and who could possibly have put in at Bridport Harbour during the course of his career at sea.

Mary Hoskins was a proper wife and mate in that she went to sea with her husband, living with him in all winds and weather in the cramped and cold conditions of a sailing vessel. Their travels together resulted in the regular arrival of a family — a grand total of ten babies which were often born at sea or in some lodgings in port.

Henry received promotion, rising from Bosun to First Mate, eventually becoming Pilot at Bridport Harbour and then at St. Peter Port, Guernsey where he settled with Mary and their family. Their life was shattered when Henry was lost overboard and drowned. So with her baby, Caroline Ann, in arms, Mary sailed for her last time, alone, for Weymouth Harbour and her parents' home at Burton, 107 Southover.

The elder children were, by then, off her hands, earning their own living but she still had to care for two small boys and a girl and her newly born baby. The Steam Ship Company paid their fare from Guernsey to Weymouth Quay and for Mary and her little girls to travel by horse drawn vehicle to Burton but the boys were not included and these little lads were expected to walk alone from Weymouth to Burton, which took them several days. They were forced to beg for food on the way, eventually arriving at their Grandmother's home, in Southover, very weary and hungry.

The eldest child of Mary Clark and Henry Hoskins' union was Bill Clark Hoskins who at the time of his father's drowning was himself a mariner. Between voyages he made 107 Southover his base but regrettably his life was to be cut short, too, for he was also lost at sea. His descendants possess a portrait of Bill, probably drawn by an artist in some sea port. It is, in fact, the earliest picture that is known of a Burton Bradstock man. That he was also a mariner and from a long established Burton Bradstock family makes the portrait even more unique.

Richard Clark's other daughter, Caroline, born in 1813, grew up in Southover in the village. She spent her time braiding the trawl nets that her father and other fishermen needed.

Her hard work was relieved by thoughts of other things, for she had a sweetheart. No record has survived of his name, although he may have been the man she later married. We certainly know that he was a sailor, for in 1834 when Caroline was 21, on returning from a voyage, he brought her back a token of his love and affection, in the form of a beautiful jug.

In fine condition, the jug is 27½ inches in circumference and is a Sunderland pink lustre jug. On one face is a picture of a sailing vessel and her name CAROLINE CLARK 1834 and on the reverse a piece of verse.

"Here's to the wind that blows
And the ship that goes,
And the boy that fears no danger,
A ship in full sail
And a fine pleasant gale
And a girl that loves a sailor".

Treasured throughout her life, the jug has been passed down in the family through the female line. But Caroline's story does not end there for she married a man named Morris. He was probably a mariner, and most likely the presenter of the lovely jug, although no record of their marriage has, as yet, come to light. Their son Fred followed in the family tradition and took to the sea. He, too, was doomed to die at sea and was reported lost, but his mother would never accept that he would not return and kept her personal trinkets safely locked in a wooden deed-box, together with her carefully written instructions, that they were to be passed on to Fred on his return.

The tragedies in her life were numerous for she was to be widowed as well. Later in her life she remarried and further linked her family with the history of Burton Bradstock by becoming the partner of Zachariah Chick, the village Schoolmaster and later Parish Clerk, himself a widower in 1862, when they married.

A second Burton sailor's jug is preserved in the County Museum, Dorchester. Smaller than the Clark one, this jug is also pink lustre ware and was made at Wear or Moore's pottery in Sunderland. The inscription is to R.A.E. Helyar, 14th. September, 1857. The verses on it are: "The Sailor's Farewell" and "The Ship's Return". The Helyar family's connection with the sea is well known and has carried on well into the present century.

XXIII

A FRIEND FOR BURTON MEN

The following of the Wesley brothers was strong in Burton Bradstock and the establishment of Methodism in the village can be attributed to Dr. Giles Roberts. Giles Lawrence Roberts' Burton Bradstock connections are not as well known as his later business activities in Bridport.

He was born at The Ship Inn, sometimes called !'The Sloop"[1], in Burton Bradstock Parish, at Bridport Harbour in 1766, within the parish of Burton. It would seem that he was the son of Richard Roberts of Netherbury and Mary Lawrence of Burton who were married at Shipton Gorge in 1753. His grandfather was John Lawrence, a gentleman, well established in Burton Bradstock and his great grandfather Solomon Lawrence, a shipwright, who probably built ships at Bridport Harbour. Solomon was a man of some standing as his will of 1727 reveals.

*   *   *   *   *   *

Solomon Lawrence named 'Basins tenament' in Burton and Graston. His pewter was to be divided between his sons Abraham and John and daughter Sarah (Mrs. Hall), equally, by weight.

Abraham received the Basins' tenement and John the one at Graston. The warming pan, pewter platters and plates (his one third weight in pewter, no doubt), long table board and all the chairs in the hall, together with the great 'kittle' went to John Lawrence. He was also to receive the plough tackling and the horse.

Sarah, the daughter, was to inherit the new feather bed and furniture, a pair of stools, a pair of blankets, a rug, bolster and pillow after his wife, Elizabeth's death. The wife had the use of the new feather bed, headboard and curtains (bed curtains) and furniture, in the west chamber, for her life. The bedhead and curtains were to pass to son John on his mother's death.

There was also another estate in Whitchurch Canonicorum which Solomon Lawrence left to his wife, for her life, which was to pass to another son, Giles, together with £200 and the bed and furniture in the east chamber and the round table board. Three grandchildren were not forgotten in the will each receiving £15. Abraham's children received 2 guineas each and Sarah's children £5.

*   *   *   *   *   *

Giles Roberts' father was a mariner but had been wounded in the hand and was forced to take a shore job bringing him to Bridport Harbour as a pilot which he combined with being an innkeeper. Besides their son Giles, the Roberts had two other sons who died in infancy and a daughter who is known to have reached womanhood.

The young boy Roberts showed a clever mind and business attributes as a very small child. Having survived being lowered down a well by an exasperated maid, he enjoyed cooking and making sweetmeats. He set up his own confectionery at a tender age selling gingerbread and other sweets which he shaped into animals and figures.

When he reached working age he was sent to Exeter, apprenticed to a draper, but that was short lived as he was returned home after a month's trial.

The decision to place him with a grocer in Bridport did last a year and from there he went to Shepton Mallet to learn a trade as a tinman and brazier. He also proved good with a lathe, clocks and watches and the art of taxidermy.

He developed a great interest in medicines and his intelligence was satisfied when he qualified at St. Thomas' and Guy's Hospitals, obtaining his M.D. at Aberdeen.

Whether he was related to the Roberts family of the Burton spinning mills still requires further research but there is a great possibility that he was a second cousin to Richard Roberts, the mill owner.

Dr. Giles Roberts took as a wife Phoebe Brown of Shipton Gorge whose family held land and property in Shipton and Burton parishes. Phoebe was a tall, broad shouldered woman of masculine appearance. She towered over her husband who was short and sombre with dark, piercing eyes. On their wedding day the Shipton ringers, who were very well trained, spared no energy in pealing out the glad tidings.

The couple set up home in Burton and Roberts would appear to have turned back somewhat to his skill as a brazier, at the same time displaying medicines in the window of his home in Burton.

He devoted all his energies and money to the Methodist cause and began preaching in the whole Bridport district. At first his object was to 'expound God's truth and show them the way that would conduct them safely to heaven'. He obtained his licence as a local preacher in 1803.

At the cost to himself of £100 Dr. Roberts hired a small building from Mr. William Bishop and fitted it up as a place for worship in Burton. This was used for three years. A Sunday School was started with 60 children but sometime before 1807 the chapel was closed and the school given up. Further preaching took place in a house belonging to Mr. Henry Smith and when Mr. Smith moved, Mr. John Loveless carried on the cause, the Loveless family of Tolpuddle being devout Wesleyans. By 1818 Mr. Thomas Hutchings had hired a cottage to the Doctor for 7 years. It was converted to a chapel and £5 rent was paid annually.

Dr. Roberts' personal life was saddened at the premature and unnecessary death of his 13 month old little girl. A nursemaid had mishandled the child, dislocating her back and injuring the spinal cord. Mrs. Roberts was filled with grief and kept all the little girl's clothing.

Dying in 1810, Phoebe Roberts was buried with all her baby's garments as she had wished, but not before her husband had kept her body for longer than the customary period. She had a great fear of being buried alive.

By this time the Roberts were living in Bridport, in West Street, and from there he moved to East Street where his chemist shop still exists. Thomas Beech, of another strong Methodist family, took over the pharmacy on Roberts' death. Besides his Methodist work, Dr. Roberts taught the poor prevention rather than cure and dispensed medicines at a cost within the means of poor folk at the same time charging the rich for his potions. He became known as the "poor man's friend", dying a poorer man through his

102

ministering and medication.

It would seem that he was particularly interested in gypsies and often visited their camps and talked with them and one would suspect learned much from them in connection with cures and balms, gypsies being well acquainted with natural ingredients for their medicines.

A gypsy king died at Bradpole in 1805 and Dr. Roberts was amongst the large number of mourners (mostly gypsies) who followed the chief to Loders for burial. Hundreds of sightseers came too.

In 1825 a larger building was taken for worship in Burton and a chapel was opened. The house was rented from Mr. James Brown and gutted in order to seat 120 people. It is now used as a branch of the County Library being sold in 1965 for £1000. By 1831 the recorded Methodists in Burton numbered 23 and there were 32 in 1853.

Dr. Roberts did not always find preaching easy. At one time, the Burton Curate, the Reverend Mr. Lambert, attempted to restrict the movement of the Methodists and drive them from the village. In 1811 Admiral Ingram who was a local Magistrate, living in Burton Bradstock, compelled the Methodist preacher to 'desist'. This only inspired Dr. Roberts and others to persist in their work and with their beliefs. The Doctor likened Methodism to a camomile bed, "The more it is trodden the faster it grows", he said.

His success in converting the people was shown in 1803 when Mrs. Green, of London, was overcome by the Glory of God and The Lord Jesus. The Burton chapel was filled with light and she could not see a candle which was burning, nor the pulpit. In the midst of this she beheld the Lamb of God. 'She saw Him and ran to Him and caught Him in her arms.'

Dr. Roberts' death in 1834 brought a great sense of loss to the whole district. Several families in Burton grew away from the faith and left the Society, and the following year the death of Mrs. Robinson, wife of another Doctor and sister of James Brown of Burton, further set back the village Methodist Society. She had provided a library of several hundred books for the benefit of the Sunday School and poor of the village and visited and comforted the sick and bereaved.

Dr. Giles Roberts' inspiration lived on it spite of these set-backs and continued in the village right into the middle of the present century, the Chapel and Sunday School being part of the life of Burton for a long period.

1. Probably the present Bridport Arms Hotel.

XXIV

NAMES, TRADES AND PLACES

Spinning runs in the Northover family, and though Sarah is a spreader and never will be anything else, there have been wondrous good spinners in the clan. This girl is called Milly Morton, and her mother and grandmother spun before her. Her father was Jack Morton, one of the last of the old hand spinners. To see him walking backwards from his wheel, and paying out fibre from his waist with one hand and holding up the yarn with the other, was a very good sight. He'd spin very nearly a hundred pounds of hemp in a ten hours day, and turn out seven or eight miles of yarn, and walk every yard of it, of course. The rope makers swore by him.'

from "The Spinners"
by Eden Phillpotts

Documents for these first years of Victoria's reign record very interesting and valuable information. A Tithe Map drawn up around 1840 depicts all the properties in the parish and an accompanying book lists the owners and tenants. This, together with the first detailed census taken in 1841 enables the researcher to conjure up a vivid picture of the village and inhabitants of that period. The population of Burton Bradstock was then at its peak of 1201.

The principal landowner was Lord Rivers whose tenant was Job Legg at Burton Farm, where the acreage totalled almost 500 acres. Samuel Puddicombe Warren owned Graston Farm and other land there which was in the tenancy of Henry Marsh and amounted to 222 acres. Bredy Farm under the ownership of John Hussey, 359 acres, had Isaac Morey as a tenant. Hussey also owned Hamilton Farm near Shipton Gorge. James Brown had land in the parish totalling some 304 acres. William Roberts farmed Cogden and John Briant (Bryant) was at Berwick, as the tenant of the Duke of Bedford. Mary Marsh farmed at Nether Sturthill, 117 acres and John Burt at St. Lukes, near Shipton. He also rented Magnolia Farm from Lord Rivers. John Pitfield, another tenant of Lord Rivers, had, as bailiff, Thomas Pariss who managed Pitfolds, near Bothenhampton. A further 119 acres were freehold and various small acreages were rented from the Lord of the Manor.

There were two inns in the village where the Anchor and Three Horse Shoes now stand, several beer houses, and at least 2 grocery/drapery shops in the main street. A butcher's shop and slaughter house existed in Bull Lane (now more often called Grove Road), and possibly a second one somewhere in the village. A baker lived right on the outskirts in Common Lane and a carpenter's workshop, (Abraham Mutter, the carpenter), could be found where Shadrach Stores now stands and until its conversion to a fine shop, by Mark Bell in 1962, was always the Estate Carpenters' Workshop.

The tailor, Knight, and his family of 9 children, with the village nurse nearby, had cottages in the main village street, known then as Top Street. (From the Old Blacksmith's shop to Three Horse Shoes' corner). The Shoemaker, also a father of 9, lived and worked with his employees behind the Three Horse Shoes in one of the cottages known, for obvious reasons, as "The Back o' November".

The Schoolmaster, in a cottage where the present school stands, probably held classes in his home — hence the site for the new school. The women who gave their occupations as schoolmistresses may have been responsible for the Sunday School and a separate school in the village.

The Grove Mill, still in the hands of the Roberts family, had reverted to grinding corn whilst the spinning mill continued to produce flax and hemp products.

All the older cottages and houses that make up the present old village of Burton Bradstock were in situ and in fact, many more besides. Over the years a large number of homes burnt down and thus provided the gaps where more modern buildings stand today. Over 200 houses and cottages were in the village in 1841 with others on outlying farms and roads, most with garden and/or orchard.

Fire was a terrible and common hazard. The thatch and old timbers burnt rapidly. Fire fighting was a manual job and often had little effect on a well established blaze which spread rapidly to adjacent buildings. It is recorded that 20 cottages burnt down in 1854 but the church rate list of 1855 records 30 cottages empty and not rated through fire.

In the village of 1841 there were 59 male agricultural labourers aged between 12-60 years. Farm work was the principal occupation and 8 other men termed themselves as general labourers, 16 women likewise. Many of these too, would have been employed in agriculture.

The flax spinning industry took the second place for employment in the village. Eleven middle aged men were flax dressers and 7 were weavers. Samuel Robins, aged 82, was a weaver and 2 boys classed themselves as ropemakers.

Amongst the females of Burton Bradstock 17 were spinners, mostly girls and younger women. Two others were termed as 'breders of netts'.

The sea provided work for at least 16 men as mariners and there were 9 coastguards stationed in the village. Nine other men were fishermen ranging in age from 20-70 years, including a Robert Cammell, aged 35. Some mariners, away from home at the time of the census, do not appear to be listed.

Other occupations were represented as follows:-

Female servants	13	(domestics and dairymaids)
Male servants	2	
Corn Factor	1	
Female Nurse	1	
Housekeeper	1	
Carpenters	8	
Masons	6	including apprentices
Plumber and glazier	1	
Bricklayer	1	
Mechanic	1	(at the mill)
Millwright	1	
Butchers	3	
Male Bakers	2	
Female Bakers	2	

Miller and baker	1
Malster	1
Female grocers & drapers	4 (including employees)
Dressmakers	7
Tailors	4
Mantilla Makers	2
Shoemakers	10 (mainly one family including apprentices)
Blacksmiths	4 (1 at the mill)
Carriers	6
Shipwright	1
Clerk	1
Manufacturer	1
Wheelturner	1 (Joseph Angel aged 11)
Schoolmasters	2
Schoolmistresses	2
Publicans	2

Other child labourers were not recorded on the census.

Mary Gerrard aged 80 and Elizabeth Thorner aged 71 had termed themselves as labourers — other old women in the village of 1841 were Catherine Spurdle 83, Mary Robins 81 and 86 year old Mary Hine who lived in the building at St. Luke's Farm. There were 26 women aged 50-59 years and 25 between 60 and 85 years.

As for the men, the eldest were in their seventies. Joseph Parsons had reached three score years and sixteen, Thomas Rose and John Wraxton were a year younger at 75 and the Patriarch of the village was 82 year old Samuel Robins, the weaver. A total of 22 men were in their fifties and 13 more were aged between 60 and 82 years. People were living longer than one hundred years before.

At Bridport Harbour men were mariners, shipbuilders, sea pilots and one was a Customs Officer and another a tidewaiter. William Swain, aged 55, and his son, 30 year old William, were merchants. A row of cottages in the present West Bay is known as Swain's Row.

The Mill Pioneer's children enjoyed a measure of comfort and prosperity. Between them they controlled the two mills, Grove House, garden, stable and waggon house, the latter now fortunately preserved as stores. Son, Richard Roberts and Eliza, née Pitfield (?) his wife and large brood lived at Girt House. William and Robert Roberts, his brothers, farmed at Cogden. The family rented the withy bed and pond near Lawrence's Mill, and a Miss Roberts, daughter of Richard Roberts who established the mills, had possession of the warehouse and counting house, (now Mill Terrace), and the Mill House opposite.

Another spinster resided at the Rookery, she was Elizabeth Hansford, one of the three daughters of Mary and Royal Navy Commander, William Hansford. A memorial to them can be found in the church. Elizabeth lived until 1847 to the grand old age of 83. Elizabeth Hansford's sister Ann, one of a twin, the other a boy, Robert, dying in infancy, had married Peter Daniells of Yeovil. Charlotte Hansford, born 1770, was the wife of the Rector of Burton

Bradstock, Robert Hunter, as related in a previous chapter.

At Burton Farm House (now Manor Farm House) lived 25 year old Mrs. Mina Legge — presumed to be the daughter-in-law of Job Legg. She had three young children. Listed at Burton Farm was Richard Gale as the Corn Factor, William Haines, Shepherd and Richard Churchill as Dairyman. Three labourers and 4 girl servants lived in at the farmhouse. A total of 30 people were at Burton Farm and a similar number at Shadrach Farm. A Mrs. Mina Legge is recorded on the Tithe Map as the owner of Darby House and its coach house opposite, but Francis Roberts and his family were living at Darby House when the 1841 census was taken.

Southover, the street of mariners, housed a total of 98 people. The coastguards, who now replaced the Sea Fencibles, and their families at the Coastguard Station, near Cogden, numbered 23 and in the three cottages in Cliff Lane could be found other coastguards and a Customs Officer.

Many of the mill workers lived in Mill Street and the Mill Manager at Mill House. Fishermen's cottages were scattered all over the village. Benjamin Williams and Matthew Buckler lived in the Shadrach vicinity and 75 year old William Smith, another fisherman, made his home in Darby Lane. Nearby lived Robert Woodcock, the maltster, where there was a beer house, and from the present Wedge Cottage, George Williams, the village plumber and glazier plied his trade.

The thoroughfare from the Church to Timber Bridge was called Bridge Street and there, next door to Zachariah Chick, the schoolmaster, lived John Angel, a carrier and Mary Coombs who worked on the land. Joseph Grinstead a 40 year old mechanic made his home in High Street and Henry Hutchings, the millwright, in Church Lane. They were very likely employed at the flax mill.

The Tucker family at Shadrach, in a cottage above Girt House, had a variety of occupations. Old Mary and Martha were labourers and Maryann was a dressmaker, as was her younger sister Elizabeth. William, aged 20 was a surveyor. Just up the road at Pound Street another Tucker was a tailor.

The Burwood family could be found in Common Lane in 1841. There was Ann, a twine netter, Ethelinda a flax carder and Abel who was a servant boy and four younger children. Here, too, in other cottages lived Richard Hawkins, a baker and Joseph Woodland, a carpenter and their families, a total of 16 persons. Elizabeth Gale was "mine host" at The Three Horse Shoes Inn and Sarah Conway competed for the sale of ale at the Anchor Inn. At Bridport Harbour two of the inns were in the hands of the Jarvis family.

It will be of interest to mention that some 140 different surnames occur on the 1841 census for Burton Bradstock. Many of the same surnames as were found way back in the previous centuries in the village but others completely alien to the district. The Coastguards introduced new surnames at this time.

*   *   *   *   *   *

This, then, was the busy community of 1841. Completely self-sufficient, many working from their own homes, everyone contributing to the economy and survival of the village. Sadly those industrious people were lowly paid for their skills and craftsmanship. Had they lived today many of them could have enjoyed a high standard of living. It was their masters who benefited from their endeavours and this must not be forgotten when we think of their humble homes and the poverty that some suffered.

Those who had survived the enclosure of the land and remained completely or partially independent were able to own or rent land and/or workshop and home and could enjoy a better mode of living. These people established family farms and businesses, many of which survived into the next century.

* * * * * *

In the autumn of 1847 Queen Victoria decreed from Osborne House that prayers of thanksgiving for the abundant harvest should be read throughout the kingdom in all the churches. At Burton Bradstock Church a bundle of flax was the central feature in the Harvest decorations and it would seem the worshippers from the village continued to display flax as a symbol at the Harvest Service for many more years to come.

* * * * * *

By now the Rectory had been extended. A "New Front", as the villagers called it, was added. It was discovered much later that the drawing room was built over the old courtyard and well. The carriage house had accommodation for a groom and comfortable mahogany boxes, with a hay loft overhead, for the Rector's horses.

Over the old section of the Rectory were three maids' attic rooms reached by a back staircase. At one time a batchelor Rector had built a tunnel from the back kitchens to the servants' lavatory, the tunnel running just inside the wall in Mill Street.

Manor (Burton) Farmhouse had also had an additional wing added but still backed by a courtyard and cottages. Shadrach Farm was improved by its Yeoman occupier and it would seem that Cogden Farmhouse and farm were well established.

The Husseys of Mosterton had taken Bredy Farm by 1804, in whose family it remained for some time. In 1859 the house was rebuilt by the Husseys and an interesting ceremony was held when Mrs. Gowring, a Yeoman's wife, laid the principal corner stone, coins being first placed underneath. The masons and carpenters enjoyed a large quantity of liquor at the celebrations which proved to be a very enjoyable occasion for everyone!

In 1814 Graston had been sold by Sir William Oglander to John Hussey of Lyme Regis. It again changed hands but was repurchased by the Husseys in 1864.

A dairy house could be found where Cheney's Garage now stands, a known haunt for smugglers.

XXV

VICTORIANS

On into the second half of the 19th Century ..... the people of Burton Bradstock saw rapid general changes in social and economic conditions, particularly from 1850-1870. Much was altered that the people had learned to accept as normal. Their horizons were widened by the arrival of the railways and the bicycle but even these modes of transport were not readily available to the working class for some time.

By 1851 the population of Burton Bradstock had dropped slightly to 1181, although the birth rate rose in England from 1850-1870 and the death rate fell a little.

Men received around 10 shillings a week as a wage. Extra labourers, in peak periods, could receive up to 3/6d a day plus beer and on the whole women were paid 10d a day or 1/6d at busy times, together with an allowance of beer. In Burton more men and women termed themselves as net makers or braiders of nets in the 1851 census showing that the flax mill had turned more to this type of manufacturing and some women were obviously working from home again. Flax was still being processed for we find 9 men who classed themselves as flax dressers; men whose enlarged hands worked the golden tresses as finely as any silk worm winds her cocoon. John Tibbs aged 63 and John Chilcott 77, were weavers and John Davis a flax spinner.

The appalling working conditions in England and exploitation of child labour was investigated by Lord Shaftesbury, who headed a five year commission in 1861. This brought many atrocities to light and by 1870 the working day was reduced to 10-10½ hours a day. The weekly hours worked were 60, with Saturday afternoons free. In agriculture this was not easy to adhere to and farm labourers had to work longer hours and feed and milk animals on Saturday afternoons and Sundays. At haymaking and harvest they worked from dawn to dusk. This did not reduce the large congregations attending St. Mary's Church. In 1860 the Rector, the Reverend William Templar, recorded the morning service average attendance as 150 and 300 at Evensong.

*   *   *   *   *   *

Into the homes of our people filtered the Bridport News which was first published on June 23rd 1855. The penny newspaper was intended to bring tidings and news not only to the mansion or country house alone but to the poor man in his cottage.

The advent of the Bridport News heralded reports of the Crimean War, so many thousands of miles away. The numerous black and white sketches and news from the front, for the first time, brought the battlefields into the parlours of the Burton Bradstock cottages. The paper at that time contained much National and International news.

Crime featured widely in the local paper and smuggling tobacco into Bridport Harbour, and sheep stealing, from the fold of Mr. Job Hansford, at Loders, was reported.

Less than half a century earlier sheep stealing was an offence punishable by hanging. This fate befell a labourer who lived in one of the two cottages at St. Catherine's Cross. He had stolen a sheep and buried it in the garden. When the law caught up with him he hid in Cathole Copse where his wife visited him daily with food. No difficulty for the police constables to follow her and arrest the culprit.

For the farmers and butchers, the price of mutton at Bridport Market in 1855 was 7d a lb and pork 10/- a score. Butter was 98/- to 102/- per cwt. and Dorset cheese (Blue Vinney) 68/- to 80/- per cwt. At Whitchurch Canonicorum Corn Market wheat fetched 10/- a bushel.

Mr. John Jarvis of Harbour Road, Bridport, was selling prime French Cider at 7d a gallon in pipes and hogsheads and advertisements appeared for an errand boy 'who can read writing' and a plain cook 'who can make butter and bread'. A cottage in Burton was advertised to let at £6 per annum, the convenient distance from the sea being an important amenity.

5,000 Irish reapers had crossed for the English harvest in the late summer and they were being paid 7/- a day! At Dorchester Crown Court a servant girl was sentenced to three months' hard labour for stealing a yard of silk from her master and another girl received a week's solitary confinement for stealing a handkerchief!

By Christmas of that year the winter and the war were the main topics and at Wootton Fitzpaine Mr. Drew had commissioned his Bailiff to select the best bullock to dispense to the poor fellow parishioners which was most acceptable 'in the present circumstances'.

If the following summer proved sunny and fine 38 year old Mary Helyer could be assured of plenty of work in Burton, for she made straw bonnets and young Mary Brown was kept busy all the year around with her stay and corset making.

By 1861 there was a Police Constable resident in Burton Bradstock. He was Robert Churman and he attempted to keep law and order amongst the 1010 people of the village.

In 1864 Joseph Davis of Burton was apprenticed to David Spooner, a grocer of Bridport, at the cost to the parish of £25 for 4 years. Several other village boys were bound to apprenticeships, one being William Sponsford bound to Henry Whittle to teach him the trade of carpenter and another being Richard Hutchings also to learn carpentry from Mr. G. Hayward at the total cost of £9 per annum, payable from The Broadmayne Charity.

Expenses were paid for young William Welch to go before the Captain of H.M.S. Colussus, a Man of War, in Portland Harbour, in the hope of securing a place in the navy but unfortunately he lost his chance, being just one year over age.

*   *   *   *   *   *

The binding of apprentices was in itself a grave undertaking and the conditions laid down could be likened to the vows taken by people in strict Orders.

Two Indenture of Apprenticeship documents, not connected with the Broadmayne Charity, that have survived, clearly set out what the apprentice would be expected to do, or not do, in return for the instruction given in the particular trade.

In 1840 Alfred Chilcott, son of Alexander Chilcott, of Burton Bradstock, was bound apprentice to Ephraim Matthams and Company, Rope Makers of Bridport Harbour.

The term of instruction, in the art of rope making, was to be seven years, during which time young Alfred was to serve his Masters faithfully, keep their secrets and gladly do their every command. He was to warn his Masters of any damage likely to be done to them by others and not to waste or lend the goods of his Masters.

For his labours, he was to receive three shillings a week during the first year, rising to seven shillings a week during the final year. Also written into the contract was that Alfred should not commit fornication or marry during his apprenticeship, nor play at cards or dice tables, haunt taverns or playhouses or absent himself from his Masters' service unlawfully day or night.

Documents were signed, in this case the apprentice and his father were able to pen their signatures in a good hand, and a fee paid — default on the Masters' part would result in a penalty of £50 and the apprentice would forfeit his right to follow the trade if he broke the contract.

Later in the century, 1897, Frederick White, son of George White of Burton Bradstock was apprenticed to Joseph Rendall, of the Grove Mill, Burton, to learn the trade of miller and baker.

The term was to be for five years, during which time he, too, was expected to serve his Master well and faithfully, his secrets keep and not do or suffer to be done by others, hurt to his said Master. Fred White was not to embezzle, waste or lend his Master's goods or at any time to depart or absent himself without leave.

Joseph Rendall, the Master, agreed to find meal, drink, washing, lodging and apparel for his young charge and to pay the sum of 1/6d per week for the first year which would be increased to 5/6d weekly in the fifth and final years of apprenticeship. In the event of sickness and loss of time the deductions would be made from the wage by the Master.

Frederick White completed the apprenticeship in November 1902, to the complete satisfaction of Mr. Rendall. Then he was a qualified miller and baker and was in a position to ask for the hand of his sweetheart.

*   *   *   *   *   *

A slight increase in the population of Burton Bradstock brought the total to 1036 in 1871 and the line and twine factory, where many villagers still found employment, was run by John and Albion Andrews. The pastoral care of the village still rested with the Reverend William Templar, M.A. and the education at the Church of England National School was in the hands of Miss Bessie Hawker.

By now there were several shops and workshops in the village. The first mention of a shop was in the Manorial Rolls of 1750 but now we find Joseph Baggs, shopkeeper and butcher, Mrs. Anna Holt, a grocer, Henry Prout the baker, James Stevens another grocer who had a draper's department as well, John Knight, a blacksmith (the blacksmith's shop was reputed once to be in the Shadrach area). Other trades were plied by William Knight and George

Brownson, tailors, Francis Foot, mason, and Henry Whittle, builder and undertaker.

The amount of walking and work done by the parishioners provided good business for boot and shoe makers; equivalent today to being in the motor industry! George Buckler, Thomas Thorner and William Trivett satisfied this need in Burton Bradstock.

Richard Hawkins and George Hayward kept the inns and the goods and kind, human and animal, were moved by horse and cart, by carriers Charles Collins and Silas Symes. Miss Ann Jarvis Hayward was a dress maker and had several girl apprentices doing work for the ladies of the village.

Burton Farm was let on a 21 year lease to Mr. Thomas Fry Legg in 1870 whose wife was Mary Bligdon of the Litton Cheney family. On their retirement they moved to The Retreat, which they had named, near the Anchor Inn. The farm tenancy had previously been in the hands of Mr. Job Legg from 1855-65 and in his agreement he was obliged to keep a Field Book, for the last four years of his lease, recording cropping, manuring and cultivation of the fields on this farm of now 534 acres 1 rod 7 perches. He had paid a yearly rent of £700, whilst Mr. Samuel West had paid £399 in 1802 and was not allowed to break up, (cultivate), any of the permanent meadows. By this time the watering of meadows to produce early grass, by digging channels across the fields and flooding them from the river, was well established.

The Rookery came out of the Daniell family of Exeter (descendants of the Hansfords who had owned it earlier) and was sold in 1875 to Mrs. Mina Legge of the Court House, Litton Cheney for £1,050. It was sold again, on her death, by the Trustees, in 1896, to Lt. General Augustus Henry Lane Fox Pitt-Rivers remaining in the Pitt-Rivers' Estate until it went into private hands again, in 1958, to a sitting tenant. Fire insurance coverage at the Rookery was £500 in 1896 at a premium of 7/6d per annum.

*   *   *   *   *   *

Bridport, as a watering place, with the arrival of the railway branch line to the Harbour in 1884 was to attract middle and professional class people to the resort. The name of Bridport Harbour was then changed to West Bay. The working folk came there for the Annual Regatta and the two day Whitsuntide Fair held on the East Beach, travelling in from all the villages around. The traps and carts that brought them were left on the shingle, the ponies being stabled locally or taken out of the shafts and tethered near the vehicles.

Other important fairs were the two in Bridport each year where many sheep and cattle were sold and "cheap jacks" and other stalls lined the streets and one at Lambert's Castle, high above the Marshwood Vale, where pony racing was held, as well. At Toller Down the annual fair was a great event. Hundreds of sheep were sold and farm labourers engaged. With all the "stannins" and other activities on site those who travelled there from all over West Dorset were well rewarded.

*   *   *   *   *   *

From the 1870s the lot of the people was improving, if still hard. They worked in less fear of their masters and in Burton Bradstock they developed a great respect and love for the Lord of the Manor, General Pitt-Rivers. His interest in the welfare of the Estate workers and their families was reflected in the welcome he received on the occasions when he visited the village from his home at Rushmore, North Dorset. It was said that he could travel from there to Burton Bradstock without going off his own land. The landed gentry continued to live in the old pattern but life was far less harassing for the middle and working classes than it had been a century earlier.

The health of the people was improved by the wide use of antiseptics by 1881. This helped combat infection which set in after an injury or surgery and the use of chloroform made the latter and childbirth less of an ordeal but in Burton in the 1890s, a young boy who cut his bare foot on glass in the river whilst tickling trout, was given some 18 stitches without an anaesthetic!

Dentistry, too, was much improved. Pulling teeth by various weird means was still being practised in Burton Bradstock in the early 20th Century.

With less decayed teeth and probably less toothache, the village people could enjoy their slightly improved diet. Most of the cooking was done on an open fire or, in the larger houses, on the Victorian introduction of the black kitchen range. Their diet of potatoes, bread, cheese, fat mutton, swedes, turnips and apples was varied with sea-gull flesh and eggs (for those who were not superstitious), rook pie and occasionally a badger ham supplemented, too, with results of a bit of game, rabbit and salmon poaching. Throughout the 19th Century the food acquired from poaching was a necessity to the working family. Beer and cider were drunk and Indian tea, which was cheaper than China tea. The poorer people could not afford tea when it first became an English beverage. By the end of that century cold tea, in bottles, was often carried by the workers, in the fields, in their envelope shaped, straw, dinner, "nammet" bags, slung across their backs. Furmity was also eaten — a type of gruel made by boiling together wheat, currants and milk. By the end of the century the original knob biscuits were being produced at Litton Cheney in the bakery of Mrs. Bligdon. An Irishman working there brought the "secret" recipe with him and later took it to Morcombelake and the Moores family where these unique biscuits are still manufactured, in vast quantities, and sent all over the world. The knob biscuits were soaked in tea and this pulp usually consumed, as a stomach filler, first thing in the morning before beginning the day's work. Baked apples, Dorset Apple Cake, stewed fruit and milk and suet puddings were standard food and cooked well in the old kitchen range, for those who owned such an amenity, or in the embers, for the cottagers whose sole method of cooking was on the open fire. A typical meal for a working family would be an assortment of vegetables simmered in a pot over the open fire. Topping the vegetables would be a dough which was cooked by the heat of the vegetables and formed a crust. This was known as "skimmer cake" — skimming the top of the vegetables.

Fish was a great bonus, as a food, for the people of Burton Bradstock, for it provided, excellent, cheap, nourishment not available to people who lived away from the coast. Herrings and sprats were salted for the winter months and mackerel, in their season, were often soused, which is done by baking them in vinegar. Fresh caught and fried in butter they were even more delicious!

Eels were eaten by many. The clear, clean river Bride provided an abundance of this delicacy which was within the reach of the village folk, just for the catching. The migratory life of the eel was well known to local adults and children and they knew exactly the right time to wait at the mouth of the river, at Freshwater, to see the elvers come in from the sea and the matured eels go out, for the journey to the Sargasso Sea, so many thousands of miles from the waters of the Chesil, to lay their eggs in deep water.

Trout from the River Bride and plovers' eggs, from the meadows, found their way onto many a cottage table, too.

Some cottagers kept a pig to fatten in a stone built sty at the end of the garden. Much effort was put into providing sufficient food for the animal, which, until its slaughter was a family pet. Viewing it and comparing size was a weekly pastime for neighbours. When the time came for the killing, the sharpening of the knife, to slit its throat, and the boiling of water to scald the skin, for removing the hairs, caused much hurrying and scurrying. The sale of half of the pig usually paid for the barley meal it had consumed and the rest was readily sampled by the family and the remainder salted for the winter. All the parts of the creature were utilised and hardly a bristle or trotter or length of gut was wasted.

XXVI

TRAGEDY AT SEA

Every man in Burton was born with "salt in his veins" and he either became a full time fisherman or combined fishing with his usual occupation or became a mariner. Over the centuries the list of those known to be mariners from Burton Bradstock makes lengthy reading.

The women and families learned to live with the fact that the sea was the Master and that many husbands and sons, who followed this traditional career, often never came back from a voyage.

The winter of 1881 lived up to this fear when the two masted sailing brig., the "Why Not", was lost off the coast of Aberdeenshire.

On board this vessel were five men from the village. They were the Mate of the "Why Not", 58 year old Joseph Gerrard and his 25 year old son Joseph, Simeon Hutchings, a father of five young children,[1] and his nephew William Hutchings who was just 19 years of age. (Reports give the Hutchings men as brothers but the Hutchings' family tree shows them to be uncle and nephew). Another family tie was that the elder Gerrard was brother-in-law to Simeon Hutchings. The fifth Burton man was 52 year old Joesph Gear. Joseph Gear was the son of William Gear, a labourer, born at 47, Darby Lane in 1826. A further member of the crew was W. Tizzard of Maiden Newton.

*   *   *   *   *   *

At the age of 14, Joseph Gear had been soured by the cruelty to a horse, which he witnessed on the farm where he was employed and this decided him to run away to sea — an idea he had cherished for a long time. He confided his intention to a friend and they agreed to set off at the crack of dawn the following day; which they did.

They set out for Poole, where all manner of vessels plied between the Newfoundland Fisheries and the Dorset Harbour. Sleeping under a hedge, the first night, cooled Joseph's friend who decided to pack in the expedition and return home but Joseph Gear carried on, covering the 40 odd miles to Poole by the second evening.

He signed on and worked his passage to Labrador where he spent five years as a whaler living a rough, hard and very often cold life off the Newfoundland caost. Eventually saving enough money for his return passage, he became an Able Seaman in the Merchant Service and returned, after each trip, to Bridport Harbour and his home at Burton Bradstock.

In May of 1859 he married a Burton girl, Jane Coombs, and moved into number 60, Mill Street, where they set up home. In due course he found himself signed on board a coaster, the "Why Not", which sailed between Bridport Harbour and the Channel Islands and along the English Coast.

*   *   *   *   *   *

The "Why Not" was a vessel of 150 tons burden first registered at Shields in 1854 and then re-registered at Bridport in 1861 after she was lengthened. This made her 98.9ft overall with a depth of 11.4ft. She had been built in Malmo, Sweden and was originally named Najaden which translated means "a sprite". At Bridport she was owned by James Templeman, a Bridport draper and was later transferred by a bill of sale in 1880 to Henry Morgan Restarick, a shipbuilder of Bideford. It was not the first voyage that some of these men from Burton had made together on the "Why Not".

Simeon and James Hutchings from Burton Bradstock, had been taken on, with no written agreement, to take her from Bridport Harbour to Bideford, in June 1879, where she was laid up for six months undergoing repairs. When she was ready, Thomas Denty, of Plymouth, joined her as Master and Joseph Gear, who had recently signed off from the "Pride of the Isles", made a fateful decision to sail with him.

By 1880, Able Seaman Simeon Hutchings and Joseph Gerrard, as a cook and seaman, joined the crew. With them, from Burton, went young William Hutchings, who at eighteen, was sailing on his first ship. The vessel's papers, of December 1880, reported the characters of all the crew as 'very good'.

By the New Year, the Captain was a partner in the "Why Not" and did not take a wage but took what he required from the freight. He was, by then, living at East Chinnock, near Yeovil with his wife and 18 month old child.

The crew's signing on was supervised by Thomas Britton at Bridport Harbour and they received sums from £4 down to £1-5/-, according to rank, and duties, on joining the vessel.

The winter of 1881 was one of the worst in living memory. There had been blizzards and bitter freezing weather. The "Why Not" was iced up in St. Peter Port, Guernsey in February of that year and when she eventually got out of port, on Sunday 13th February, her crew was in low spirits. Sailing on a Sunday and the 13th at that was not a good omen, especially as sailors were known to be such superstitious folk.

The gallant ship battled her way up the coast for three weeks, as the seas raged and conditions, generally, stayed appalling. Food, too, had run out. Within sight of land, she was being driven ashore in tremendous seas off the Skerry Rocks, near Petershead, Aberdeenshire, where she had intended to load coal for her return trip.

Seeing her plight, the local coastguards attempted to launch the life saving rocket apparatus but the horses could not struggle enough through the wind and snow to drag the heavy equipment to the shore where it was expected the "Why Not" would go aground. Men and boys took hold of the chains and ropes and dragged the machine through huge snow drifts, in high winds, and blinding sleet and hail — but too late. Before they reached the beach news reached them that wreckage was already being washed ashore. The "Why Not" had struck the Maukies, a ledge of rock, with such a terrible force that she was immediately heeled over and went down stern first.

The two Hutchings men had always vowed that they would clasp each other tightly if they were ever going to drown.

Three men had been seen standing on the deck as the "Why Not" foundered. The bodies of the Captain and William Hutchings were washed up but the others were never found, although two other bodies were spotted floating in the treacherous sea.

The Captain's face was badly bruised and his trousers were in shreds, the right leg being completely missing with no stocking or boot on his right foot.

116

Young Hutchings was unmarked, except for a scar on his forehead. On one of the shirts, probably the Captain's, was tied the Shipwrecked Mariners' Society Medal. Their bodies were taken to the chapel at Burnhaven and later buried. From Burton, people made the arduous journey for the funeral.

Five local families were bereaved that day, although it was some time before the bad news reached Burton. There was then a large number of fatherless children. Simeon's widow and her six children had to move out of the Back o' November Cottage and take a smaller one. The Gerrards and Joseph Gear had left widows and children, too.

Amongst the wreckage washed on shore were the Ship's Articles which included the list of the crew.

One person in Burton was not surprised to learn of the tragedy. She was Joseph Gear's wife. During the bitter cold of that winter she had daily studied the "pictures" in the frost on the window panes and one morning she saw the vessel that her husband was on, sink. Such premonitions are not uncommon happenings for true sea and country folk.

The pang of that tragedy has never been forgotten by the descendants of those brave seamen. The bereaved families were comforted by their great unity and the close knit community in which they lived, where help was always forthcoming.

1. Simeon Hutchings' wife was pregnant with her sixth child when he sailed.

XXVII

THE 1800s ...... FUNERALS AND FLOODS

The detailed Census continued to be taken every decade and in 1881 (the latest census available at the time of writing, the details only being released after 100 years) a similar pattern was evolving to that of 40 years before.

Apart from the Coastguards who had been born as far afield as Ireland and Plymouth, and the Police Constable who was born at Melksham, the butcher, Joseph Baggs, from Liverpool and Zachariah Chick, now stated to be the Parish Clerk and Sexton, a Somerset man, no one recorded had come further than Wimborne or Hazelbury Bryan and, in fact, the majority of people had been born in the village or neighbouring parishes.

There were 243 cottages in the parish of Burton Bradstock, which would have included Bridport Harbour and the population was 454 males and 492 females.

Sixty year old May Symes, Rebecca Dunham, 46, and young Jane Symes termed themselves as field hands and 18 year old Alfred Dunham called himself a plough boy. George Downton reared his nine children on a carter's wage and George Steel was a groom. Forty year old Mary Swaffield gave her occupation as haymaker. We find Richard Thorner, the coal hauler, and William Symes, a village carrier. With him lived his nephew, six year old William Smith, who would eventually continue the business.

Charles Chainey was now the village fish dealer and John Cammel, Henry Moore, William Buckler, Fred Symes, Richard Helyear, Robert Steele and George Gale, men aged from 20-55 years, were full time fishermen.

Young William Morey, a 13 year old lad, was employed as an errand boy and 80 year old William Steel still worked arduously as a stonecracker; the stones used on the local roads for which the parish was responsible. Elizabeth Notton from Southover, was 14 years old, calling herself a Pupil Teacher, as was Elizabeth Carter (18) the daughter of a Coastguard pensioner, Susan Masters, her father a dairyman, and Isabella Douglas (18) who boarded at Darby House with Mrs. Elizabeth Chant. For her six grandchildren, Mrs. Chant engaged Jane Parsons as a Governess.

Mr. William Tucker, the local Relieving Officer and Inspector of Nuisances lived at the Great House. The Post Office, now an important asset to the village, was run by Elizabeth Knight, the tailor's wife and Bridge Cottage Grocery Shop was kept by Isabella Hayward, a mariner's widow and her step-sister.

Another general shop could be found in Darby Lane run by Theadora, the wife of Balshazzar Burwood, a road contractor. Their daughter, Thurza, was a dressmaker, as was Jane Bartlett.

The women bereaved by the sinking of the "Why Not" clearly stated that they were mariners' widows. The lengthy lists of their children followed.

Ann Hitt termed herself as a net braider as did 28 other females. Many of these were married women braiding nets at home. Fifteen young women were mill hands. Two young boys worked as ropemakers, one man was a twine striker, two boys and two older men were twine spinners. Four men termed themselves spinning hands and two, flax dressers. One woman gave her occupation as a mill hand warper. There were three hacklers, a braiding machine worker and two mechanics. The Mill Manager was James Grand (or Grant?).

The village nursing requirements fell to 62 year old Harriet Conway, the wife of a carter and Susan Gale, also in her sixties, a labourer's wife, and at the Rectory the servants listed were a cook, a housemaid, a parlourmaid and a groom.

Caroline Chick, the second wife of the former school master, lived in Anning's Lane and ran her own village laundry, boiling, ironing, starching, goffering the linen for the gentry and washing the vestments for the Rector and Church. Mary Hoskins, her sister, and other members of her family would seem to have assisted her.

Joseph Buckler, still only in middle age, had been blinded in an accident at work from which he would never completely recover, and several other men and women would appear to have been unemployed, probably through sickness or accident. Children at school appeared as "scholars" in the 1881 Census.

Still a thriving village, Burton Bradstock was held together by its handful of gentry, staunch farmers and smallholders and an active business and working community, the farms, factory and fortunes of the sea dominating their lives.

*   *   *   *   *   *

A century ago, in 1882, the children of the well attended Wesleyan Sunday School, in Burton, enjoyed a Christmas treat. A splendid tree was decorated and loaded with over one hundred parcels each containing useful articles of wearing apparel. As the children left the party they each received a bag of sweets. An everyday occurence for the children of today but a rare and welcome gift for many in those bleak days.

The New Year of 1883 was a happy occasion for Captain Hawkins and his wife at Bridge Cottage, Burton, when their baby daughter was born. Ten weeks later, their joy turned to tears at her death, infant mortality still so common.

The Dorset Hunt Ball at the Corn Exchange, Dorchester was the venue for the wealthy of the county. Magnificent decorations filled the hall. Awnings and drapery trailed from the walls and everywhere was festooned with greenery. The refreshments left nothing to be desired and the band of the Royal Artillery played tune after tune for the Valse, Quadrille, Lancers, Polka and Gallop.

Back nearer home there was a move afoot, in Bridport, to install public baths but it was found that women preferred to do their washing at home, in their own houses.

Bad weather in January brought about the death of young Henry Samways at Swyre when he and three other fishermen were washed into the sea by a huge wave, his fate not so horrific as that of the crew of a wrecked schooner off Virginia who were found frozen to the rigging.

The Bridport News, now available for reading in the new Reading Room at Burton, reported the safe return of Hero Private Welsford of the Gordon

Highlanders to Bowood, just north of Bridport. He had been listed as slain at Tel el Kebir, in Egypt, but instead had been badly wounded and maimed. His cottage home still carries the deserving name of Tel el Kebir. Oxford won the boatrace — what oarsmen from Burton could not have held their own against any University crew had they only had the chance?

*　*　*　*　*　*

A 'cloud of deepest gloom was cast over the parish' in October of 1883 when the village was struck down by the sudden death of a well loved friend and benefactor. Whilst presiding over an entertainment in the Reading Room, in aid of funds for the room, Mr. Richard Francis Roberts of Cogden, Solicitor to the London and N.W. Railway Companies and a Director of the Bridport Railway, was suddenly taken ill, just as Mr. Churchill was about to render his second song of the evening. Everyone was cleared from the room and restoratives were brought quickly in the form of brandy, mustard and hot water bottles. Regrettably, these were of no use and by the time a doctor had been summoned and arrived from Bridport, at 11 o'clock in the evening, the huge crowd, which had gathered outside the Reading Room, was informed of Mr. Roberts' death.

The grandson of the mill owner and members of the Roberts' family were by then, very endeared to the people of Burton and the district. His home was in London but he came to Burton for several weeks each year and was described as 'warmhearted to a degree. A man of earnestness, integrity and promptitude'.

An inquest was held at the Anchor Inn before C. G. Nantes, Esq., the Deputy Coroner. *The Foreman of the Jury was Mr. H. Whittle and others sworn at Cogden, where they had previously viewed the body, were Mr. J. Waldron, Mr. Grig Buckler, Mr. W. H. Hayward, Mr. J. Trevett, Mr. A. Bartlett, Mr. G. Carter, Mr. H. Stevens, Mr. E. Stevens, Mr. C. Cousins and Mr. J. Knight* — it would appear all Burton men. Evidence was given by Mr. Roberts' friend, who was a guest at Cogden at the time, and also by an employee of the Railway Company. They both remarked on Mr. Roberts' high colour **and** stoutness and that his apoplectic condition had appeared to worsten of late.

Joseph Buckler, a local man, of about the same age as Mr. Roberts, stated that he had been in the habit of going shooting with the deceased for many years and had done so the day before from 10 in the morning until 2 in the afternoon. He said Mr. Roberts had complained of a pain in his side but was a very good walker and had kept up his usual pace. Other evidence said that Mr. Roberts had attributed the pain to three walnuts he had eaten the day before. On the evening of his death he had walked down from Cogden to the Reading Room — the ladies having gone on ahead by carriage.

The funeral was of an imposing and impressive character. Such a mournful or extensive procession had not been remembered in Burton before. The melancholy cortège left Cogden and was met at the beginning of the village by the main procession. Mr. Knight of the Bull Hotel had provided the horses and carriages and Mr. T. B. Baker the drapery.

A special train was run from London to Bridport bringing the many

120

mourners from the Capital. The funeral procession was headed by the coastguards stationed in the village and the six fishing crews led by their Captains G. Carter, W. Buckler, C. Chainey, R. Steele, S. Gale and R. Hillier (possibly Helyar?) Naval pensioners followed and the tradesmen and inhabitants of the parish led by Mr. R. Hawkins, Senior and Messrs. J. Hawkins, Master, Cousins, Gale, W. Knight, J. Knight, Anning, H. & E. Stevens, Foot, George Buckler and Grig Buckler and many representatives from other villages together with officers from the House of Commons and the Railway Company.

The coffin was of polished oak with brass furniture and was made by Mr. H. Whittle of Burton. It was drawn in an open hearse with no pall or plumes, trappings or drapery but the 'copious wreaths of choice flowers' completely hid the coffin from view.

* * * * * *

No mention is made of the bearers. It can be supposed that at this funeral the bearers were supplied by the undertaker and then certainly would have been local men. For villagers there was never any question about who bore them on their last journey. Sons would carry fathers, brothers carry sisters and friends of the family filled in when there were insufficient men available. The whole village shared in a bereavement, for most families were related to each other in some way. Shouldered from cottage to church to grave, the procession wound its melancholy way through the village streets. For farmers and the like, the coffin was often borne by horse and waggon to the church.

From the Gear Memoirs we learn that when a young girl of 18 died in Burton in the 1870s her coffin was escorted to the grave by six of her girl friends, dressed all in deepest black, acting as pall bearers. Their white gloves made such a stark contrast to that sombre scene. The grave was lined with flowers and more were scattered over the coffin as it was lowered.

* * * * * *

Mr. Roberts was laid to rest beside others of his family overlooking the warehouse and mill that his grandfather had built. The Reverend W.C. Templar conducted the service and gave the address. The blinds of all the houses and cottages were drawn throughout the village and as the cortège passed the Reading Room a group of people, in deepest mourning, could be seen standing there, as a mark of respect. All business in the village was suspended and at Rendall and Coombs' Burton Spinning Mill all work was halted. Shutters were put up at tradesmen's windows in Burton Bradstock and Bridport. The minute bell at Burton tolled.

For a while village life rolled on with every day ups and downs until the close of 1886 when gloom clad in another form struck the village.

* * * * * *

Early on the morning following Christmas Day 1886, which was a Sunday, it began to rain. It rained and rained all day and was also bitterly cold, the wind blowing hurricane force. By late afternoon the rain had turned to heavy snow, the flakes being very large. There were then blizzard

121

conditions in the whole of the Bride Valley, the snow forming huge drifts.

The water which had collected above the valley poured down off the surrounding hills, accumulating in the River Bride. A total of 4.20 inches of rain and snow was measured as having fallen in the Valley between 5.30 am and 9 pm that December day.

It seems that flooding was imminent but no warning could have prevented the disaster that beset Burton Bradstock and other villages in the district in the path of the overflowing rivers.

The thousands of tons of water thundered towards the sea, gathering strength as it approached Burton. Water, too, was pouring into the village off North Hill and by the evening a total of 47 houses and cottages were flooded, in most cases the cold, dirty water reaching to the ceilings. Walls of cottages collapsed and the main bridge was swept away. Mr. Gillett's home, the **Rookery and Magnolia House, where Mr. Edward Rendall, the owner of the** Flax Mill lived, were extensively flooded.

The whole of Mill Street and from the Post Office (now the west end of the Three Horse Shoes) to the Blacksmith's shop and Manor Farmhouse was a turbulent sea of water.

At Greenwich Cottage, presently owned by Mr. and Mrs. W. Cammell, themselves all too familiar with serious flooding, the Symes family escaped death when they were about to leave their home. As they left their cottage **door, a wall of flood water drove them back indoors. The water rushed in** through the doors and windows of their home and sent them upstairs where they remained marooned for over ten hours, in pitch darkness, as the water continued to roar past the weakening walls of their cottage.

Men from the village began rescue operations, carrying people and possessions from the flooded homes, wherever possible. Charles Bugler was **aware that the lives of the Symes family were in grave danger and together** with seven other men he went to the beach, in blinding snow and shouldered a boat back to the village.

It is difficult to calculate which way the men took to reach the beach considering that the fields at Timber Bridge and right back to Arch Bridge and Bredy would have been very deep in water. Knowing that four of the men came from Southover, which would have escaped the flooding, it is probable that they all came from that side of the river.

In their rescue bid the men were unaware that the bridge had gone and Bugler was swept into the water and carried 100 yards downstream and into an eddy where another stream met the main river. Luckily, he was then swept onto ground where he clung to a tree. His cries for help, in the darkness, made his friends realise his plight and without consideration for their own lives, the boat, manned by Jesse Hitchcock and George Hussey was launched into the raging torrent, held back from meeting a fearful fate on a long rope, by the **other men, themselves struggling in deep water. Their swinging lanterns** buffeted by the strong wind. Charles Bugler was rescued suffering extensively **from the terrible cold, his clothes frozen to him. Taken to a nearby cottage,** **which had escaped the floods, his frozen clothes and those of his rescuers were** **peeled off them.**

The Symes family remained in the upper rooms of their cottage until the next morning when daylight made it possible to attempt another launching to rescue them. By then the storm was abating and the waters receding so that a boat was not necessary. Snow lay deep and drifted, after continuously falling throughout the night.

Grocery stocks at the village shop were destroyed or badly damaged and animals drowned. Fortunately, no human life was lost, as could so very easily have been the case. The Symes family were overwhelmed when they heard what had happened that night and expressed their gratitude, which Mr. Symes said, was all they had left to give. It is known that Jesse Hitchcock received a Life Saving Award for this daring rescue. Whether all, or any of the other men were acknowledged for this is uncertain.

Scores of trees had been blown down in the apple orchards. Bradpole, Loders, West Milton and Netherbury suffered similar flooding that day, as Burton and those other villages did in subsequent floods. There was also considerable damage to parts of Bridport that lay near the rivers. The older village folk, recalling the flood caused by a tidal wave sweeping in from the sea, were certain that the water on this occasion, 1886, was at least a foot higher than that of 1824. This devastating flood has been known ever since as "The Great Flood".

Charles Bugler later wrote a letter of appreciation to the Bridport News publicly expressing his heartfelt gratitude to the seven brave fellows who rescued him, saving him from being swept to his death that night. The letter names the men as Jesse Hitchcock, George Hussey, John Cammell, William Thorner, Edwin Buckler, Joseph Buckler the younger and William Sponsford.

Mr. Lovibond, a London Gentleman who often visited Burton, had received news of the 'fearful flood' and some weeks later arranged for his friends, Captain and Mrs. Parr, who lived in the village, to organise a dinner and entertainment for the villagers.

There was great excitement and the children could not wait for the appointed time and were already at Mr. Symes' carriage house, now dry and clean after the floods, long before the doors opened. This Mr. Symes was known locally as "The Duke" because of his autocratic ways. Mrs. Symes had cooked a sumptuous meal and the decorations were very attractive. A banner displaying the words "Welcome to All" and a large Red Ensign greeted the arrivals. The interior was lighted with large pendant lamps and Chinese lanterns. Over the Chairman's seat was another banner proclaiming "Health and Happiness". Mrs. and Miss Parsons entertained with songs such as "Eight Hundred Years Ago" and "Beautiful May" and "The Rosy Morn". The children left before the adults and were given an orange each to be 'a pill before bedtime' and the entertainment continued to 10.30 p.m. when more refreshments were served and the old folk given plenty of tobacco.

*   *   *   *   *   *

The year wore on and the village Cricket Club took to the field, firm and green again. By the 1880s cricket and football were more organised and far less vicious. The previous wet weather had resulted however, in thousands of tons of rocks falling from the Burton cliff onto the beach below.

The Bath and West Show which was held at Dorchester was blessed with fairly good weather, required for the visit of the Prince of Wales. Special trains were laid on for the double event. Attending such a fine exhibition of cattle, sheep, horses and dairy products, with the added bonus of a visit by the Monarch's eldest son, was too good to miss. The Bridport train was so full that hundreds of people had to be left behind at Toller, Powerstock and Maiden Newton. Sections of the Guard of Honour for the Prince were formed by the Lyme and Charmouth Artillery Volunteers and the Bridport Rifles, under the command of Major Whetham.

*   *   *   *   *   *

The time had now come in June 1887 for the Golden Anniversary of the Queen's accession to the throne of England and the dressmakers of the district were busily sewing gowns for the local ladies. Fine silks were in high fashion and there was certainly going to be far more gaiety than usual. The village girls were buying pretty coloured ribbons to trim their dresses and hats, as ribbons were superseding flowers for adornment. Little girls, whose parents could afford it, were being dressed in book muslin.

The Jubilee Day dawned and a large flag fluttered from Burton Church tower. The village was decorated everywhere with bunting, flags and garlands. A service was held at the church at 2 o'clock with Miss Parsons at the harmonium. From there some 600 people gathered at the base of Bind Barrow hill to enjoy a free tea. The school harmonium had been transported by waggon to the site and the children sang suitable pieces. Sports for all followed, well into the evening and at 10 pm the beacon on top of Bind Barrow was lit and rockets sent up. Other beacons were fired on Allington and Bothenhampton hills and at the Bridport Workhouse the inmates had **eaten such a large dinner that they could hardly move out into the garden where they enjoyed the pipes of tobacco supplied to them!**

Shortly after, the parish received a copy of the Queen's letter of thanks in which she said ".... the sense of duty towards my dear Country and Subjects who are so inseparably bound up with my life will encourage me in my task, often a very difficult and arduous one, during the remainder of my life".

Fig. 32

*SOUTHOVER SHOWING THE DOVE INN, ORIGINALLY A BEER HOUSE, WITH ITS
SIGN OVER THE DOOR.*

Fig. 33

*MR. E. T. STURDY, EARLY TRAVELLER AND PHILOSOPHER AT NORBURTON
WHICH HE REBUILT IN THE EARLY 1900S*

Fig. 34
THE FLAX SWINGLING MILL (L) AT THE END OF GROVE LANE, BUILT BY ROBERTS IN 1803 AND THE ARTIFICIAL WATER-WAY CUT TO PROVIDE POWER FOR THE SPINNING MILL.

Fig. 35
WOMEN BRAIDING AT THEIR DOORS IN MILL STREET.
THE WAREHOUSE CAN BE SEEN CENTRE (L) AND FACTORY CHIMNEY, AT ITS LOWER LEVEL.
MILL HOUSE (R CENTRE) – SHADRACH(K) DAIRY HOUSE FRONT (R).
IN DECEMBER 1916 THE WALL WAS BREACHED TO ALLOW CATTLE TO ESCAPE FROM RISING FLOODWATER.

Fig. 36

MACKEREL ABOUT ON THE FRESHWATER SIDE OF BURTON,   C 1912

Fig. 37

MRS. REBECCA DUNHAM WEARING THE WORKING DRESS OF THE DAY AND THE
BURTON BRADSTOCK BONNET – C 1914.

Fig. 38

C 1900 THERE WERE OVER ONE HUNDRED PUPILS AT THE VILLAGE SCHOOL. A TIERED PLATFORM WAS USED WHERE THE CHILDREN STOOD FOR LESSONS. ANY WRITING WAS USUALLY DONE ON SLATES WHICH WERE TAKEN HOME AT THE END OF EACH TERM IN ORDER THAT THE WOODEN EDGES COULD BE SCRUBBED "WHITE".

BACK ROW: L to R. SID BOUCHER (FROM WEST BAY), EMILY AND ANNIE WRIXTON, DOLLY SYMES, SIS VINE, MAY CHURCHOUSE, FLO TREVETT, BIRDIE PAUL, CARRIE CAMMELL, MILLIE CASE.

SECOND ROW: MR. MILBURNE (HEAD MASTER), CHARLIE NORTHOVER, REGINALD BUCKLER, ———, SILVIE MARSH, NORAH WRIXTON, ———, ———, GLADYS MILBURNE, ———, DAISY STEVENS (TEACHER)

THIRD ROW: STUART JACOBS, ALF BROWN, STAN WHITE, FRANK WRIXTON (AGED 87 IN 1982 WHEN HE IDENTIFIED MANY PUPILS IN THIS MIXED AGE GROUP), ———, ———, UNA WRIXTON, ———, RALPH NORTHOVER, ———, ———, TINY BANKS (TEACHER)

FRONT ROW: HERBERT MARSH, ———, HAROLD NORTHOVER, TOM PERRIN, ALF NORTHOVER, ———.

Fig. 39

THE CHILDREN MAYPOLE DANCING C 1918.

FRONT: L to R. (anti-clockwise)
DORIS LANE, RON GUYATT, KATHLEEN BUCKLER, ARTHUR THORNER (Centre Front), LILY HUNT, LOUIS WHITE, FREDA ELTON, SID RUSSELL, VIOLET NORTHOVER, ARCHIE MITCHELL, MRS. HOWARTH (TEACHER), IVY HYDE, BOB HOWARTH JNR., ENA FOOT, STEVE NORTHOVER, ENA NORTHOVER, TOMMY BRINE, OLIVE LAWRENCE, FRED ELTON, DORIS HITT, RON BUCKLER, DAPHNE LEGG, WILL BURWOOD, OLIVE HITT, BERT WILLIAMS, ADELE BATHOL, BERT SAMWAYS.

Fig. 40

HAYMAKING WHEN ALL HANDS WERE NEEDED. THIS SCENE IN THE 1920S HAD BEEN ENACTED FOR GENERATIONS.
FRONT (L) STUART JACOBS, (R) EDGAR HAWKINS.

Fig. 41

DAVE LEGG, WITH A THREE HORSE TEAM, HARVESTING BARLEY, ON MANOR FARM. C 1930

Fig. 42

THE WEDDING GROUP OF FREDERICK WHITE AND ALICE BUGLER. TAKEN AT THE TOP OF
DONKEY LANE. EARLY 1900S. BRIDESMAID (L) MINNIE WHITE, BESIDE HER IN FRILLED DRESS
IS HER SISTER BLANCHE (NIECES OF THE GROOM). TO THE LEFT, FRANK WHITE AND ABOVE,
WILLIAM WHITE, IN BOWLER HAT, (BRIDEGROOM'S BROTHERS). (R) OF BRIDE HENRIETTA
BARTLETT, BRIDESMAID. JOE WARD SAILOR (EXTREME R). BILL BUGLER, WITH PIPE
STANDING BEHIND FRED BUGLER (BRIDE'S BROTHERS). BILL BARTLETT, BAKER'S BOY AT
THE GROVE MILL, SEATED FRONT (L). REG WHITE, SEATED (R).

Fig. 43

THE WEDDING GROUP OF JANE GIBBS BARTLETT AND
JOHN CAMERON MACLEAN. EARLY 1900S.
EXTREME BACK: WILLIAM LEGG IN FISHERMAN'S CAP.
BACK ROW: L to R. MRS. JULIA LEGG, MRS. MINA THORNER, ———, ———. BRIDEGROOM'S
BROTHERS EITHER SIDE OF WILLIAM BARTLETT, ANNIE BARTLETT, FRED, NED AND HETTY
BARTLETT, ———.
SEATED: MRS. ERMANTRUDE BRETT (née SWAFFIELD), MINNIE BARTLETT, ELFRIDA BUCKLER,
BRIDEGROOM, BRIDE, MABEL HUSSEY, CHARLOTTE PAYNE, EMILY BARTLETT (née PITFIELD), RALPH
BARTLETT.
CHILDREN FRONT: WILLY BARTLETT, LESLIE LEGG, DOROTHY BARTLETT, ALPHONSO BARTLETT.

Fig. 44

*THE PURCHASE OF A BICYCLE FOR AROUND £18 WIDENED THEIR HORIZONS.
MRS. ELIZABETH BUCKLER IS PICTURED OUTSIDE MAGNOLIA HOUSE IN 1905*

Fig. 45

*THE OLD POST OFFICE AND SHOP ADJOINING THE THREE HORSE SHOES INN.
HERE IN THE STREET THEY DANCED ON FÊTE AND FEAST DAYS.*

*"THE CANARIES" BURTON BRADSTOCK FOOTBALL TEAM RE-FORMED
AFTER THE FIRST WORLD WAR.
BACK ROW: L to R. BERT WILLIAMS, FRED MULLINS, TED HITT, REG
BUCKLER, RALPH BARTLETT, WILL WARD, BOB HOWARTH.
MIDDLE ROW: THE REV. STEVENS, STAN WHITE, JESSE JACOBS, AND
BOB SAUNDERS (FROM SHIPTON)
FRONT ROW: RALPH NORTHOVER, JIM STEEL, GEORGE LEE, JACK
CAMMELL, PHONSO BARTLETT, AND THE TEAM'S MASCOT, JESTER,
THE GOALKEEPER'S DOG, BROUGHT HOME FROM INDIA AFTER THE
WAR.*

Fig. 47
*MRS. HETTY BARTLETT STANDS OUTSIDE HER COTTAGE, DECORATED TO
CELEBRATE THE VICTORY OF THE FIRST WORLD WAR*

XXVIII

MACKEREL AND HOLIDAY MAKERS STRAYING

The weather of 1887 continued to improve and good catches of mackerel were made. On July 15th several boat loads were sold at West Bay and sent off on the 8.20 a.m. train.

The villagers always received a signal to alert them that fish were being landed. A long cow horn was blown to summon them to the beach, either to assist in hauling in the nets, or to purchase their next meal. The horn carved with the name of Thomas Hutchings, a mackerel, sailing ship and other engravings is still in the possession of his descendant Philip Hutchings, of Burton. Mackerel straying and the resultant catch caused as much commotion in the village as if the place was on fire.

The route to the beach was via a track up from the village to the top of the cliff and down over to the beach. The present Cliff Lane was only blasted out from the rocks at the turn of the last century (called then "The Cutting").

Horses and carts were used to transport heavy loads of fish back to the village or men carried baskets on their shoulders. Once donkeys were the means of transport, kept by a man at the top cottage, at what is now known as Donkey Lane. These donkeys bore bushel-baskets full of fish. The donkeys were used by their owner to turn the wheel of a well at the cottage, also their loud braying was acceptable as part of village life then!

For some time, fishing had been a full time occupation for a number of crews in Burton and all along the Chesil Beach. Great rivalry existed between them, not so much for the success of getting the largest catch but for the fact that their livelihood depended on the number of fish caught. The crews often waited long hours for fish to stray. The captain of the boat was the owner and took six shares of the proceeds, one share for the boat, four for the net and one for himself and the remaining shares were divided between the crew which could be as many as 20 men for mackerel fishing. The share-out at the village hostelry, an important occasion at the end of each week.

Much earlier records state that the boat owner took two shares, two more for the net and the crew one share each and a string of fish for the other helpers.

An idea of the amount of fish being caught can be obtained from a record of 1905 when 2321 bushels of wet fish were caught at Burton from April to September, valued at £296 and £6 worth of shell fish (crabs and lobsters).

The specially built boats designed for the Chesil waters were made by the Forseys of Eype and were known as lerrits, 20 feet long and double ended (At Swyre the skipper of the boat and seine had entertained his crew of 18 men to dinner on Jubilee night).

The fishermen's wives not only helped to braid and mend the nets and pull them in, but trudged miles and miles with huge baskets on their arms selling, or hawking, the fish. It was nothing for them to journey the 15 miles inland to Maiden Newton and back in a day. The 1881 Census records 39 year old Annie Hussey and Hannah Cammel, 53, as fishmongers.

Men had earned a full living from fishing since 1841, for certain, as the records reveal and the census of 1871 lists William Chillcott as a fish dealer, indicating the more organised method of catching and marketing the fish. Fish caught at Swyre, Cogden and Burton often would be rowed to West Bay and sold to dealers. A Powerstock lad was apprenticed to a fisherman in 1749 who agreed to provide the boy with meat, drink, wearing apparel and lodgings. It seems there were full time fishermen always! Other men were part-timers and could earn as much in a good fishing season, by that means, as from their normal occupation.[1]

A man would be posted on the top of Burton cliff at the point always known as "look out" and on sighting the fish straying — that is moving along in the water in a shoal, often preceded by bait or pursued by gulls he would give a special signal and wave his cap in the direction in which the fish were moving.

The speed and accuracy with which a waiting crew could put to sea and get their net cast was a work of art, each man doing his particular job to make a successful and rapid launch down over the steep, shifting curb of shingle. Few of them could swim!

When times were hard and fish did not appear to be straying and the men needed a bit of cash they would try a "venture shot". This was a chance launch in the hope of getting a few fish. If they were lucky and caught a couple of dozen then they would stow the seine net into the boat and try again.

Crews signalled to each other along the beach by means of an oar set up vertically in the boat on which a jersey or jacket would be hung. This meant that the crew who had hoisted the signal were about to try a shot.

Their characteristic mode of dress and their weathered skins gave them a tough and leathery look. Likewise their women folk, in long skirts and aprons splattered with fish scales, their shoulders draped with shawls and their pretty cotton frilled and tucked bonnets symbolised an era and way of life which is now so sadly gone for ever from the Chesil Beach.

The harvest of the sea was an important part of village economy and early in the season a service was held on the beach to bless the boats and to pray for good catches. On May 12th flower garlands were made and taken around the village by the children, who sang at the doors of the gentry and hoped to be given a few pennies. This custom possibly coincided with the old calendar date of the beginning of May, a time for renewal of life. Once the garlands were strewn on the sea, as is the custom still at Abbotsbury, but this later died out.

*   *   *   *   *   *

Another type of income was being obtained from summer visitors. Towards the close of the 1880s several of the larger cottages and houses were being used to accommodate business and professional families for the summer holidays. A whole family stayed for one to two months. So important was the arrival in the locality of these families that lists were published. Some houses were holiday homes, as they are today, and kept solely for that purpose. We find Alpha and Beta Villas, Sunnyside, Montrose House, Darby House, Grove House, The Retreat, Cliff Cottage and Post Office, the Anchor Hotel and Providence Cottage all accommodating anything up to a total of 100 people during August. By 1894 Mrs. Elizabeth (Bess) Buckler at Magnolia House and a few years later, Mrs. Kate Hutchings, at Vine House, were taking professional families — giving them full board with six course dinners and employing servants to cope with all the cooking, serving, laundry, cleaning, and filling the oil lamps.

Other visitors came to Burton and the beach for the day or afternoon and could take tea at Mr. Collins'. One such party met with an unfortunate accident on returning to Bradpole when the waggonette they had hired overturned on rounding the Anchor corner at 6.45 pm, one fine August evening. The dozen or so occupants, including a child of 4 and an 85 year old woman, were thrown out and two women seriously hurt. They were bleeding profusely and quite insensible. The driver of the waggonette sat on the horse as it struggled to get up until it was released from the shafts and harness. Luckily the horse was unharmed and once he had obtained a fresh set of harness the driver galloped to town for medical aid.

The account in the Bridport News went on to say that the two seriously injured women had not regained consciousness for several days and were cared for in the village. The outcome was probably fatal.

Death from accidents caused by horses, both ridden and driven was very common. A bolting horse, a cart turning over or being crushed by waggon wheels gave little chance of escaping death or very serious injury. The roads were rough, full of holes and strewn with sharp stones and boulders. In the 1890s it was easier to cycle to Marsh Barn across the fields near Freshwater than along the rough road.

Drunken and careless driving of horse drawn vehicles was punishable by fine or imprisonment. Once a man from the Bride Valley was fined 4/- for driving without reins.

---

1. Blanche (née White) Everett's father could earn 12 shillings a week as a part-time fisherman in the 1890s which was as much as he earned as an agricultural labourer on Burton Manor Farm.

XXIX

AT THE CLOSE OF AN ERA

The last two decades were not without their moments of phenomenal weather, for besides the threat of flooding, usually a yearly occurrence, both 1881 and 1891 came in with appalling cold and frost. In 1891 there had been the longest period of frost since 1813 which eventually gave way to very sunny May-like weather in February, although having lower temperatures than the spring month and no rain. March came in like a lion and snow fell heavily and without cessation. The storm grew to a hurricane. By the morning of March 2nd there were drifts 10-12 feet deep at Burton and throughout the district. The hedgerows were completely covered and hundreds of sheep were buried. All outdoor work was suspended and the men set-to, digging out sheep and clearing roads. The schools were inaccessible and trains were stuck in drifts at Grimstone and Powerstock. It snowed continuously for two days, and on the third and fourth days further high winds caused even more drifting. No one could reach Burton from Swyre and Abbotsbury and the only route to West Bay was via the beach. The wedding of Miss Alice Lenthall of Belshay, near Bridport, had to be postponed as the carriage driver could in no way reach her home, to convey her to Loders Church and a young man who had set out from Swyre, on the first day, to deliver goods to Abbotsbury, was almost frozen to death when his trap turned over in a drift and he was forced to try to make his way to the beach in high, freezing wind and blinding snow. A search party set out to look for him without success. Eventually he arrived safely back at Swyre, with one arm completely frozen, and his coat buttons ripped off in the storm. He had taken eleven hours to make the four mile journey.

When the storm abated a snow plough was brought into use in Bridport. Drawn by four horses, it had been previously used after a similar blizzard in 1881. In addition to problems on land there were terrible disasters at sea owing to the hurricane force winds.

*   *   *   *   *   *

An outbreak of influenza swept through the country a few weeks later. Mr. Slade, the butcher, of Burton Bradstock, was the first to fall victim to the illness in West Dorset and his absence was noted for several weeks at the Bridport Market. His condition was aggravated by erysipelas and opthalmia and his recovery was slow.

The ladies who escaped the epidemic turned their thoughts to the fashion of the day. Cloth gowns were "in" for dressy afternoons and pale shades of pinkish lilac, heliotrope, aubergine and dove grey were the latest colours. Skirts were two inches from the ground and jackets tight fitting, with turned back velvet lapels. The choice of the Princess of Wales dictated much that became fashionable.

*   *   *   *   *   *.

By now the mills were in the hands of new owners, the Roberts grandsons having taken to the sea. The Grove Mill was owned by Mr. Joseph Rendall, miller and baker and the spinning mill was producing flax and hemp nets and twine in the hands of Messrs. Rendall and Coombs.

The major landowner was by far the Pitt-Rivers family, after some three hundred years as Landlords of Burton Bradstock. Practically the whole parish was under their umbrella and this included all the land both sides of the road from Cogden to West Bay, together with many properties.

In 1880 under the will of the second Lord Rivers, his heir, who was the youngest son of a younger son, was required to take the name Pitt-Rivers. Hence, General Augustus Lane Fox, who was then 53 years old, took the title by which he was known to his tenants.

*　　*　　*　　*　　*　　*

The Queen's Diamond Jubilee in 1897 even superseded the celebrations of the Golden Jubilee. Throughout the Kingdom services of thanksgiving, parties and illuminations took place. The length and breadth of the country was ablaze with bonfires, as darkness fell at 10 o'clock. In London such a procession and pageantry had never been witnessed before and the strains of the band playing "Rule Britannia" and "God Save The Queen", lustily sung by the vast crowds, quite moved the Old Lady to tears.

From all the ports the fleet mustered for a Review by the Prince of Wales, in the Solent, on June 26th. Men from Burton were on board several of Her Majesty's vessels, including Dick Conway serving on the Royal Yacht. This great spectacle conveyed an idea of the power, magnitude and grandeur of the Navy.

*　　*　　*　　*　　*　　*

The Victorian compulsion to rebuild and restore churches did not escape Burton and the church was completely restored and rebuilt in 1897. The total cost of this work amounted to £1.721-6-3d. The architect's fee was £195 and Mr. Fred Kerley, the village blacksmith, charged £20-15-7d. Messrs. Bartlett and Hayward, local builders, carried out the main work. Donations were received from the Duke of Bedford and the Roberts family and Col. R. Williams M.P. A concert raised £7-0-4d. Village people donated sums of 2/6d to 2 guineas and 3/- was received, 'a widow's mite'.

*　　*　　*　　*　　*　　*

Throughout the ages the younger generation has been told of the disasters that have beset the people and village and it is at our grandmother's knee that so much history has been heard. So it is for Burton Bradstock, for the floods and fires mark the years of life far more readily than any calendar.

The 1890s brought further consternation to Burton in the form of a destructive fire on Tuesday 13th. September, 1898. That unlucky night six cottages in Southover were completely destroyed when a fire broke out in the centre of the block, which was the cottage of Mr. John Thorner.

The summer had been exceptionally dry — good weather for fishing — but not so good for thatched buildings which were, by then, tinder dry.

Some of the villagers smelt the burning reed and set up the alarm which brought virtually the whole village to the scene. Men and women soon organised a human chain and over one hundred buckets were passed back and

129

forth, by hand, to the appalling blaze.

The event was serious enough in itself but it was all the more heart rending because some of the cottages were occupied by old and feeble people. Old Mrs. Kerley, the blacksmith's wife, lay seriously ill and had to be carried out, as did old man Cheney and his wife. Mr. Cheney was completely helpless and his nephew had great difficulty in reaching him. In another cottage lived old Joseph Buckler, now completely blind and his ailing wife, Ann. They escaped from the burning inferno and when questioned did not know what, if anything, had been saved from their home. Their daughters, Alice and Sophie, who were braiding at the time, fled to safety with them.

William Thorner and his wife had to leave hastily, in an almost naked condition, being in bed at the time, and old Mrs. Hussey, in an adjacent cottage, had just said her prayers when she smelt fire. All she had on that belonged to her were her stockings, she said. When asked what she had lost, she replied, "I have lost everything. We have lost all our drifting nets and I suppose they were worth £20". A ring which her old mother had given her and three watches were gone and thirty shillings saved up for the rent. "I would not have lost my poor mother's ring for £20", she lamented.

The blazing fire was fanned by a very strong wind and lit up the sky for miles around. The glow could be seen clearly from Bridport and many people rushed over to view the spectacle.

The fear that adjacent rows of cottages would ignite was primarily in the minds of their occupiers and the village constable, P.C. Hansford. He was later congratulated on organising another human chain of buckets, of water, to throw on to the roofs, to act as a protection.

In one nearby home lived a woman, named Harrison, who lay close to death and could not be taken out. The eventual arrival of the Bridport Fire Brigade saved the situation as they doused the building with water from the river.

The rescuers were hampered in their efforts to save furniture and other belongings by the dense smoke. The scene of six cottages fully ablaze and the sad human suffering caused by such a catastrophe is difficult to imagine.

It seems that the fire started when some burning embers were thrown on to the ash pit which almost touched the back of John Thorne's cottage. The homeless villagers spent the night with relatives. None of their belongings was insured and the desolation the next morning was pathetic. It was not until half past midnight that the blaze was brought under control. Three and a half hours of terror. In later years the village could sport its own hand-worked fire appliance, manned by local men.

*   *   *   *   *   *

As the century closed in, a concert in the Reading Room, proved a great attraction as a gramophone was used, manipulated by Mr. Mercer. At Christmas the school children sang songs and received bags of sweets and good things and countless interesting puzzles and pictures paid for from the subscriptions collected.

The Parish Council Elections resulted in Messrs Thomas Brown, Alphonso Bartlett, Vile, Hallett, W.T. Milburn, Levi Gale, John Churchouse,

A. Marsh, Thomas Richards and Fred Symes being elected. The Parish Council now an energetic body since the inauguration of Local Government in 1894. No women eligible to vote, as yet.

The Churchwardens saw to all Church affairs with a Board of Guardians administering In and Out-Door Relief. A Coal Fund Committee was now providing winter fuel for the needy and another "Body" collected weekly small sums of money which acted as an insurance in the event of sickness. There was also a village Clothing Fund run on similar lines. From the money subscribed, warm clothing was purchased for the 'cold winter' and in Burton there were 58 people in that scheme at this time. In cases of prolonged illness concerts were held to raise funds for the patient and his family. Surviving records show that during the Winter of 1874/75, 306 cwts. of coal were purchased at a total cost of £22-16-5d and in 1886/87, 425 cwts. were bought at 1/2d a cwt! What pittance did those miners receive for their labour? The Directors of the Spinning Mill contributed 10/- to the Burton Coal Fund.

In Birmingham, in 1899, a member of Parliament was asking, "What is to become of the poor Dorsetshire labourers?" That the working man's lot was still hard goes without saying and as there had been an agricultural depression many had sought work in other fields. The decline in the net and twine industry had resulted in movement from West Dorset and the naval dockyards at Southampton and Portsmouth held more attraction for the men to continue in their trades as net and rope makers. The railways too, lured many to other towns.

For the boys and men of Burton the navy was, as always, a ready means of earning a living. Like their fathers and forefathers before them they were never slow to go to sea.

The Portland Quarries provided work for a number of men from the village too. That, indeed, was arduous work -- long hours with much physical exertion and the long trek to Portland from Burton on a Monday morning before dawn and the return walk after work on Saturday. Earlier in the 19th Century, building the Portland breakwater also gave employment and effected a certain amount of movement away from villages.

The ship building at West Bay petered out after the launching of the last ship to be built there named the "Lilian" in 1879 and some shipwrights moved to the larger shipyards.

For those who chose to stay behind the hoeing and mowing, sowing and ploughing, reaping and threshing at the farms filled their every working hour.

The Dorset Horn Sheep were still thickly spread on the hillsides and the predominating breeds of cattle were the Shorthorns and Devons, the mottled and various colours of the Shorthorns and their curling horns being a major feature, the Devons, rich red, with thicker and longer horns. Fat pigs were popular on the farms and hens, ducks and geese wandered aimlessly around the homesteads.

The farmers' wives and servants churned out pounds of Dorset butter and Blue Vinney cheese and carried this produce, together with eggs and live and dressed poultry to Bridport Market every Wednesday and Saturday and the twice yearly fairs. Many vats of butter and cheese were sent to

London, by ship, from Bridport Harbour and later by rail.

At Manor (Burton) Farm, Henry Lenthall, known locally as "Spotty" Lenthall, had taken over the tenancy from Joey Rawles, employing anything from 15 to 18 men who earned a weekly wage of 13/-. The breed of cattle kept were Devonshires, of the Dorset type, which were good milkers. Some 800-1000 sheep grazed the pastures of Manor Farm and three carters worked and cared for 12 heavy horses. Three or four old horses were also kept for general carting around the farm, although it was nothing for a farmworker to carry a large sack of corn or a truss of hay on his back across fields. A shepherd would more often move the hurdles himself, shouldering anything up to half a dozen, spiked on a hurdle stake, across his shoulder.

"Spotty" Lenthall was born at Kingsland Farm, Salway Ash and took on that farm at 11 years old, with his mother, on the death of his father, Eli.

Wet days could present him with a problem at Manor Farm, Burton with so many employees and so the "Flax Shop" was kept full, at Freshwater, where the men would work the flax when it was too wet for some of them to get out on to the land.

Already full-time workers at Manor Farm were the two Legg brothers, Fred and Dave, who had left Burton school at the age of 11. Fred worked on another farm for a year before going on to Manor Farm in 1893. One of his brothers, Dave, followed him in 1897. They served the three generations of the Lenthall family remaining on the farm until their retirement. Between them they contributed some 140 years' service. Fred who had gone out to the meadows very early on warm summer mornings with a scythe, one of a team of mowers, built and repaired the dry stone walls that skirt the village, made hedges, dug ditches, hoed acres of root crops, reaped and stitched corn and pulled flax, walked miles to and from the part of the farm where his work took him, regular and punctual, loyal and reliable, ended the last days of his lifetime's work on Manor Farm tending the vegetable garden, reluctant to be pensioned off, as did his brother Dave. Dave lived on to be 90 after retiring from Manor Farm where he had been carter for many years. His straight eye and steady hand had guided his beloved heavy horses over acres of the farm, ploughing, harrowing, dragging and rolling the many fields from Burton to West Bay, Shipton to Bothenhampton, the steep slopes and heavy clay a challenge to his strength and that of his horses.

The brothers' years of loyal service to agriculture were rewarded by Long Service Medals which were awarded to them by the Melplash Agricultural Society. It was men like this that were bred in Burton and they fashioned the landscape over those years, leaving a picture for us, which if left unspoilt, will be a permanent memorial to them and their kind.

Two more generations of the Lenthall family were to farm at Manor Farm until Mr. J. M. (Bunny) Lenthall, grandson of Henry Lenthall, emigrated to Australia to farm at Bradstock Downs, Albany, in 1967.

*　　*　　*　　*　　*　　*

Some seventy or so men and women were employed at the Spinning Mill. Their working conditions vastly improved after the rebuilding of the mill, burnt down in the 1870s, from what it had been for their great grandparents.

The building had been raised, with sky-lights inserted in the roof, but the dust and din created inside was far above any level that would be tolerated today, the whirring belts and machines unguarded. The factory chimney dominated the village and belched forth smoke; too much one day in 1902 when sparks drifted in the wind to the thatched cottages below the school. The quick action of Joseph Buckler saved his home, Magnolia House, from being engulfed by flames. Seizing a special tool kept for the purpose he cleared a vertical strip of thatch between the burning cottages and his home and prevented the flames from spreading across. From her cottage upstairs window Mrs. Hetty Bartlett, well advanced in pregnancy, watched horrified as the cottages were consumed by the fire.

The fishermen and women could still be found at the beach. Their patience and toil usually rewarded in what seemed to be long, hot summers which were good for fishing. Several crews worked from Burton. The fish dealers (or jutes) also waited long hours. They travelled to the village from the Somerset borders in high pony traps and spent their waiting time either at the inns or on the cliff playing cards and "shove half-penny", consuming ale and cider to the advantage of the publicans and brewers.[1] In 1899 Palmer's beers were selling at 1/6d a gallon and Irish and Scotch Whisky from 3/2d to 4/- a bottle.

*   *   *   *   *   *

Somehow there was time for other things and the people of Burton made much of entertainment and recreation.

The village cricket team, under the Captaincy of the Rector, with several of his family making up the numbers, in a match against Bridport, fielded the following team:- *The Reverend F. T. Harrison, I. G. Harrison, W. Harrison, G. W. Dibben, A. Churchouse, A. M. Harrison, E. Banks, The Reverend M. Forbes, M. Bullock, A. H. Dibben and A. F. Dibben.*

A football team was not formed until a few years later when the new Schoolmaster, Mr. R. B. Howarth put Burton's name on the football map.

The village "Veäst", which had been held for centuries, was an exciting event. Stalls lined the verge outside Manor Farmhouse and Mill Street and in later years there were roundabouts on the Pound. Sports and competitions provided much amusement for spectators and participants, winning the long jump or pole vault being the most sought after prizes. There was skittling for a pig, which had replaced bowling competitions. The prize was usually the runt of a litter, called locally, "the nestle tripe". Holding a greased piglet, whilst trying to render a song, caused much hillarity.

In the evening everyone flocked to the Post Office corner, lured by the sound of a concertina. Then they took their partners and danced in the street, whirling and twirling, up the sides and down the middle.

The local branch of the National Deposit Friendly Society held an Annual Dinner, at the Anchor Hotel and a village fête. Sometimes the dinner was held in a marquee off Anning's Lane.

The streets and cottages were again garlanded and decorated floats, drawn by ponies, paraded through the village. The Townsend Showmen brought the roundabouts to Burton and 87 year old Mr. Frank Wrixton remembered them being sited in the Anning's Lane fields.

One cottage in Burton Bradstock holds a souvenir of the days of the Burton Feast. A china sailor boy, with nodding head, proudly sits out the years on a shelf with other treasured knick-knacks. He was brought to the home, he has been in for a century, from a stall in the street on "Veäst Day".

Concerts in the Reading Room and Schoolroom and dances, where the "Four handed Reel" and "Lancers" set everybody's feet tapping, were regularly held. The Church Choir was another activity for anyone with the required talent. Bell ringing was a prized pastime and still the bells were a means of conveying the news of life and death, joy and calamity to all within earshot.

The boys of the village amused themselves by forming gangs — one being the "Black Hand Gang" who left their mark wherever their simple misdeeds happened to be carried out. Their main occupation was to steal apples from the walled gardens and orchards. The boys enjoyed helping with hauling in the nets or hunting rabbits. They cut ash poles and spent hours vaulting across the many streams and looked forward to the excitement and danger of Bonfire Night, the smell of bromide wafting in the cold night air, from their home-made fire works.

Once a gang of lads found a basket of laundry — a common sight in any village doorway. Seizing the basket they lugged it off to the top of Bind Barrow where it remained undiscovered until the following morning when curiosity brought some folk to the top of the hill to see what huge bird was perched up there. Some thought it must be an eagle!

The village lamplighter received little peace from the Black Hand Gang as they pursued him on his nightly mission lighting the paraffin oil street lamps.

The girls led more sheltered lives and were early put upon to help in the home and mind the younger children. They were particularly used to assisting with the braiding that their mothers did, readily filling the needles with the twine for net making. The women sat at their cottage doors in fine weather, their work fixed to a hook in the door post. In the winter and dark evenings they braided in their kitchens, the hook screwed to the kitchen table. Girls learned to sew and some later were apprenticed to dress makers and milliners in the village.

On Sundays and Christmas Day the older girls would take the family dinner to the bakehouse which was next to the Carpenter's Workshop. The bakehouse and ovens were in front of the cottage that has recently been renamed rightly "The Old Bakery". Here many dinners of meat and a multitude of home-grown vegetables were roasted for those who did not have ovens in their cottages. When the meals were collected and carried through the street, the aroma signalled the regular Sunday ritual when all the family collected together for the week's best and biggest meal.

Another Religious Event brought about the custom of Panshard Throwing by the young people. This was on Panshard Day (Pancake Day) when the family was supposed to feed itself well, prior to fasting during Lent.

Once the feeding was over, the crocks (shards) were symbolically **smashed, as meat dishes were not required through the fasting period.**

134

In the story of the Gear family, Dorothy Mansfield writes of her father, William Gear, 1864-1955, recalling Panshard Throwing. The children would call at houses hoping for a few pennies or a piece of cake. If the rewards were not forthcoming then the shards were thrown and smashed at the door of the householder. It would seem that this custom had died out in Burton by the end of the 1890s.

Lucky children had an iron hoop which they bowled along, even to school, where the hoops would be parked along the school wall. Some were fortunate enough to have wooden toys and a few little girls had wax dolls.

Gardening, for necessity, was an every day occupation and the men tilled long strips of garden and often an allotment as well. The Pitt-Rivers' Estate rented land to the parish which was sub-let. The first allotments were below Common Knapp.

There was a little more time and energy for growing flowers. The cottage windows were choked with geraniums and outside, narrow borders, "flower knots", of forget-me-knots, hollyhocks and phloxs prettied up the village. Creepers clung to most of the cottage walls and old fashioned rambler roses wound their way round walls and hedges. The pungent scent lingered in the air as workers made their way to work at the crack of dawn or women sat braiding at their doors on summers' evenings.

At the larger houses, walled gardens held choice fruit and vegetables — medlars, quince and peaches trained on south facing walls and asparagus and artichokes grew well in the loamy soil. The dessert and cooking apples such as "Tom Putts and Buttery d'Ors" grew in abundance, their flavour never completely replaced by modern, heavy cropping varieties. Exotic shrubs and plants were now well established, in the larger gardens, since being introduced by travellers returning from the warmer climates and Eastern World.

Other travellers passed through the village, vagrants, like a hundred years before, tramping from place to place. Showmen and entertainers passed through and sometimes stopped to perform with their puppets or the live dancing bear on a chain. The Volunteers held their summer camp on the cliffs, spurring on little boys to play at being soldiers, especially during the years of the Boer War, when the Bridport News again brought battle news right home.

The greatest excitement came when the new fangled motor car travelled through the village. Driving through the main street was easy enough but the hills surrounding the village presented the early motorist with problems. The bigger boys would run beside the vehicles and then lend willing strength to push them when they conked out going up over Common Knapp or Mixen Gate Hill.

*   *   *   *   *   *

About this time the Shipton building firm of Bartletts was engaged to build Norburton on behalf of Mr. Edward Sturdy — a philosopher and traveller, particularly interested in the Buddists of Tibet and also a designer of the early aeroplane.

This fine house was built, on the, then, very secluded site, of the former North Hill Farm, the new house featuring in Eden Phillpotts' book "The Spinners". It is believed that the architect was Mr. Sturdy's brother-in-law.

The trees planted at Norburton at the turn of the Century now form a forest around this lovely house.

Mr. Sturdy's interest in Tibet is written for posterity on the mantelpiece in the hall. In Sanscrit are the words *SATYAT NASTI PARA DORMA* which translated means, *"Truth is nearest to God".*

He was a motoring pioneer and enjoyed driving at maximum speed, heedless of crossroads and turnings, maintaining that anything coming in the opposite direction would have to get out of the way! Mr. Sturdy also claimed to have died. In the 1914-18 war the serious outbreak of influenza killed many people. He caught the virus and was very ill. His nurses laid him out and left him for dead but he later believed that their throwing open the windows brought him back from the "other side". Living well into his nineties, he revealed he had no fear of really dying for he had travelled to a beautiful world.

1. Roger Guttridge mentions fish dealers coming to Burton from Sussex. (Buying for London markets?)

XXX

BUSY TIMES FOR BELLRINGERS

Time had travelled on too and now the bells were tolling out the old century and ringing in the new. A new century has something hopeful, inspiring and enquiring about it which only those alive at the time can understand.

A change was inevitable, everyone knew that the Queen was in the evening of her life. The war with the Boers was uppermost in the minds of the people. It was not over by Christmas 1899, as expected, but the people were sure, wrongly as it happened, that victory and peace were not far off.

In Burton Bradstock the battles and victories were recorded for ever in he Parish Registers. The baby daughter of Mr. and Mrs. Albert Marsh was christened Colenso May. This child, with rich red hair, was to grow into an elegant and clever young woman. She, like others before her, was to be educated at the village school and become a pupil teacher. She taught the three Rs thoroughly to at least two generations of Burton Bradstock children. Another child was named Dorothy Pretoria Mary Bartlett and there was also baby Colenso Wills, christened in 1900.

The war was still raging by 1901 and the Bridport News continued to recount the events, some horrific. More troops were embarked for Africa in January 1901. By the end, of what proved to be an eventful year, in other respects, the numbers of captured Boers were given in the local newspaper. The appalling conditions in the English concentration camps were excused by blaming much of the death and disease on the disgusting habits and methods of the women there, so many of them and their children dying from disease.

* * * * * *

But the Victorian age was over. 'So great a sovereign had never reigned since the days of Alfred the Great'. Queen Victoria was dead. In London the Lord Mayor read the Prince of Wales' telegram to an awe stricken crowd.

On the day of her funeral, Burton Bradstock, like every other hamlet and village throughout the Kingdom, was in deepest mourning. Blinds were drawn and the shutters put up. A service was held in the church at 2 o'clock and the pulpit, reading desk, lectern and communion table were draped in black. The Reverend F. T. Harrison conducted the service and the chosen hymns were sung with intense feeling. Miss Mercer, at the harmonium, played the Funeral March.

This long and impressive reign had now to be commemorated and in Burton Bradstock a committee was formed to discuss what form a memorial should take in the village. To raise funds, Mr. Gillett of Darby House, was given a mammoth task as its secretary.

Various suggestions were put forward which included a pulpit, an organ, fencing and laying out the ground surrounding the sycamore tree on the Parish Green, fixed seats and a shelter near the sea and a drinking fountain at the beach, perhaps all of these.

A letter of appeal was sent to everyone in the village and the surviving list is also a register of those living in Burton Bradstock at the time. The recipients were asked to state how much they were prepared to subscribe and for which item(s). People associated with the village, living elsewhere, were also invited to donate. These included H. K. L. Pitt-Rivers, Esq., Miss Roberts, and the Earl of Ilchester.

About the same time Christ's Hospital School, usually known as the Blue Coat School, was moving from its long established premises and a clock that had been in position there was sold to Blount and Sandford, Housebreakers of Camberwell. The Reverend Harrison, Rector of Burton Bradstock, had a son who had passed an examination to the Blue Coat School and had heard of the sale of the clock.

The Harrison family decided to purchase it in the hope that the Memorial Fund Committee would consider placing it in the church tower as a memorial to the late Queen.

The clock face measured 5'6" across and struck the quarters. It worked in conjunction with a bell 25" in diameter and was made by A. Thwaites, Clockmaker, London, in 1780. (Its value £30 in 1901). Estimates were received from Bartlett and Sons (late Henry Bartlett) a firm established over 100 years, builders and contractors and sanitary engineers of Burton and Shipton.

It was finally decided, by the Committee, to purchase the clock but to sell the bell. This Mr. Sturdy of Norburton was much against as he wished the bell to be retained. He promised to pay a further £5 if the bell was kept. 'It would have been a great historic suggestion to have heard the bell daily to which tens of thousands of hurrying souls have listened for so long', he wrote, to Mr. Gillett. He went on to say, "I really forget how I stand. Whether this is the second or third subscription I have promised and what I have paid".

An amount in the region of £70 was required to buy and install the clock and this was to be raised by donations and sales. A jumble sale netted £5-2-3d and the sum received from the sale of the bell was £14.

Thwaite and Reed of London packed and despatched the clock but they would not undertake to keep it in order as it was an OLD clock. They later sent a can of clock oil, by parcel post, to Burton, at a cost of 2/6d for the oil and 4d for the postage.

Bartlett and Sons' account for the work was as follows: drawing holes, fixing bearings, labour, fixing clock, fixing platform on floor for weights and carriage £7-14-0d. The carriage of the clock from West Bay railway station was itemised at 2/6d.

Further letters were sent out in order to obtain nine subscribers to complete the amount required for the Memorial Fund. Rendall and Coombs, of the Spinning Mill, refused to contribute, preferring to give 1-2 guineas to the Coal Fund to make winter more bearable to a portion of the villagers. Mr. Hussey, of Merriott House, Crewkerne stated, "I really cannot give anything more towards the Clock Fund. It has been nothing but a continual appeal for subscriptions for one thing and another". W. Colfox, Esq. of Westmead did not see how the clock justified as a memorial but sent 2 guineas. R. Williams, Esq. of Bridehead wrote, 'The ways suggested to me of showing our appreciation of the late Queen are getting rather numerous'.

The clock and its fixing was finally paid for and its prominence on the north side of the church tower has for eighty years metered out the days and nights for three generations. How many of the hundreds of Burtoners have observed a peculiarity that the clock possesses would be interesting to know, for at 12.45 p.m. the clock sometimes strikes two notes instead of the usual six, at three quarters to the hour.

It would seem that it always possessed this deficiency but recently the present Rector has attempted to set the clock right, only partially succeeding. Having called the boys, including Coleridge and Lamb, of the Blue Coat School to luncheon at 12.45 p.m. long ago and for so long and maybe misled many a Burtoner about the hour of his "nammet", the old clock does not intend to be changed for change's sake.

*   *   *   *   *   *

The census for 1901 gave the population of Burton Bradstock as being 574 (this did not include West Bay). A directory published at the time records the private and commercial inhabitants of the village, the trades and business activities of the community.

Some working families were still finding life difficult and illness and accident, through no fault of their own, often left a family fatherless or motherless or even absolute orphans. Large families still lived in what today would be called tiny cottages. The women folk were thrifty and made the most of small wages and fruit and vegetables grown in the garden and allotment. All of them knew the methods of cleaning and cooking the local fish. They could all braid and were good needlewomen, and so they reared large families under difficult conditions without a lot of grumbling and with great dignity. They usually accepted their lot and station in life. They took particular care of their old folk and aged parents lived on with the family, or nearby, during the last years of their lives.

One exception to this was the case of two young men — one living in Burton, who failed to support their ageing parents. They were brought before the Magistrates and ordered to pay 6d a week, each, for the upkeep of the old people.

*   *   *   *   *   *

The August of 1901 was a joyous occasion. A relief from the sombre atmosphere which still gripped the people who had followed the Victorian custom of prolonged mourning.

Miss Harriett Emily Catherine, the eldest daughter of Mr. J.J. Mercer of The Mount, Shipton Lane, which he had built around 1880s, was married at St. Mary's to Mr. David Fraser, M.D., of North Wales. The Mercer girls worked hard for the church and Miss Harriett was the Sunday School Teacher, a district visitor and member of the choir.

This grand wedding took place on a beautiful summer's afternoon — a Tuesday. The church was packed and a crowd lined the church path. The service was fully choral. The Victorian influence for light coloured wedding dresses was reflected in Miss Mercer's beautiful gown of chiffon. Her train was trimmed with lace, caught with large chiffon roses and the hem of the gown was finished with chiffon ruching. The bodice was slightly pouched and inserted with lace with a tucked chiffon yoke and sleeves and a folded belt of

139

silk trimmed her waist. The neck of the gown fell rather low, finished with chiffon ruching. The tulle veil, embroidered with true lovers' knots was fastened with a wreath of orange blossom. Miss Mercer wore a spray of orange blossom on the bodice of her gown and a diamond and ruby heart and opal and ruby butterfly brooch, the bridegroom's gift. She carried a 'handsome shower of exotics'.

Attended by a page and six bridesmaids, the charming scene must have been the most breath-taking the village had ever witnessed. The bridesmaids were all dressed in gowns of pretty lily leaf green glacé silk, with trains. The skirts were deeply flounced with silk, edged with écru lace and trimmed with several rows of black bébé velvet. A hanging pocket of silk was also trimmed with the black velvet. The yokes were transparent and the undersleeves of fine écru lace. The waists finished with narrow black velvet ribbon and steel buckles. They carried pink and white choice flowers. Their hats were of black fancy straw trimmed with black chiffon, pink roses, ostrich plumes and steel buckles.

The black hats and trimming were a mark of respect as the Country was still in mourning for Queen Victoria but, even so, the materials, style and colouring of the gowns of the bride and her attendants must have been spectacular.

The village children showered the happy couple with rice and the bells peeled as they entered their carriage and drove to The Mount, where the reception was held. A splendid cake, made by a firm in Oxford Sreet, was cut.

For her going away dress the bride chose turquoise and blue taffetta trimmed with narrow frills and black velvet ribbon. The bolero was finished with cream appliqué revers over ivory satin. Her hat of black fancy straw was trimmed with chiffon, cream ostrich plumes and a paste buckle. Mr. and Mrs. Fraser left by horse drawn carriage for Dorchester to take the train to London, en route for Scotland.

The occasion had been a most memorable one for all the people in Burton. It started with the day being ushered in with a peal of bells and the whole village was in celebratory mood. The bells were pealed at intervals throughout the 'glad day'.

The numerous wedding gifts had been displayed at the bride's home, for all to see and included amongst many cheques and other valuable presents, paintings by Miss Mercer's talented sisters, a silver crumb scoop from Mrs. Gillett, together with a bread fork and tongs, silver salts in a case from Mrs. Bradford. Mrs. and the Misses Dease chose silver cayenne pepper castors, a silver and cut glass scent bottle and a silver stamp moistener as their gifts and the Burton Bradstock Church Choir gave a butter dish in a silver stand.

Weddings of village folk could also be grand occasions and none the less were those of Frederick White and Alice Bugler and John Cameron MacLean and Jane Gibbs Bartlett at the beginning of the new century.

Two old Burton families were united when Fred White and Alice Bugler wed. They had grown up together and knew from their early youth that they would marry, as soon as they had saved enough to set up home and rent a cottage from the Pitt-Rivers' Estate.

Alice chose Boxing Day for her wedding and by a quirk of fate she was to be buried on a Boxing Day, many years later.

Frederick White had completed his apprenticeship as a miller and baker, under Mr. Joseph Rendall, at the Burton (Grove) Mill and was now a Journeyman. The Pitt-Rivers' Estate offered him the tenancy of number 57. Burton, at £2 per annum. Like other industrious men of the village he considered that life would not be complete without an allotment. Fred was able to secure the tenancy of one at an additional 1/3d a year. Later on, in their married life, Fred and Alice moved to number 13, Burton, the Old Bakery. The rent of that cottage being £8 per annum, with the Landlord paying the rates. (One month's notice on either side.)

Alice kept house for her brothers and so was fully occupied with all the household chores. With so much to do at home she did not go out to work elsewhere. She would have been a good needlewoman, like most of the other village girls, and could easily have made and embroidered her beautiful wedding gown. However, she followed local custom and had this very special dress made professionally.

For several weeks before the appointed day the village dressmaker was busy making Alice's gown and those of her bridesmaids and the other women close to the bride and groom.

When the great day came Alice walked from her home in Southover to St. Mary's Church to be given in marriage by her brother. Her gown of grey silk had a high neck and yoke of white lace and the sleeves were ruched, falling to embroidered cuffs trimmed with lace. The flounced skirt, decorated with an embroidered band, had true lovers' knots worked in raised stitchery along the hem. Alice's large hat was trimmed with ostrich feathers and net and her bouquet was of chrysanthemums.

The somewhat serious appearance of the wedding group, in a photograph, belies the fun and gaiety that followed to celebrate the event.

Jane Bartlett's wedding caused great excitement for she had fallen in love with a young man from Liverpool (a world away to many Burton folk). John MacLean had first come to Burton in the early 1900s as an engineer for the telephone company when this fairly new instrument was being installed in the district. The telephone first came to the Bridport area in 1899.

He lodged at the Post Office not far away from the cottage, in Mill Street, where Jane and her family lived close by the mill where her father was employed. John's family were in business as undertakers in the north. They also had a fleet of carriages which could be hired for weddings.

Wednesday September 4th dawned bright and sunny and there was much activity at the Bartlett cottage and at Magnolia House where the bridegroom's family were staying and where the reception was to be held.

The bride rode to the church in a horse drawn carriage supplied by Mr. Knight of the Bull Hotel, Bridport. As the journey from Mill Street to the Church was so short the bride was driven around the village first. All the people turned out to see her go by and gasps of admiration echoed from door to door, of the cottages, as she passed.

Jane's gown was of ivory silk trimmed with silk broderie anglaise, lace and ribbons and the customary "true lovers' knots". She chose to wear a veil of Brussels net instead of a hat and a wreath of orange blossom and white heather adorned her hair. Her beautiful bouquet was the gift of the bride-groom.

The bridesmaids were Minnie Bartlett, Elfrida Buckler, Mabel Hussey and Charlotte Payne who we learn were 'daintily attired'.

The bride gave the groom a signet ring on which was engraved the wedding date. The wedding presents were 'numerous and handsome' and the bridecake was made by Miss Spiller of the Bakers and Confectioners, West Street, Bridport.

The families were photographed under the magnificent fig tree, on the lawn at Magnolia House. Nothing had been spared to make this a splendid wedding. The dresses and hats of the lady guests were elegant and beautiful, their jewellery prized family heirlooms. The suits of the gentlemen and their headgear of top hats and bowlers befitted such an occasion.[1] Little Alphonso Bartlett was also exceedingly well turned out. He wore a navy velvet suit trimmed with mother of pearl buttons. His white stockings and cavalier hat completed the picture.

The young couple later left Burton, by carriage, for the train which eventually connected to take them to Liverpool.

They made their home in Brighton but Jane's anchorage at Burton was never fully severed for she continued to visit her home and family, later bringing her little daughter Vera to stay. She had inherited the tenacious spirit of true Burton women for when she realised that her only child possessed talent as a dancer and entertainer she let nothing come in the way to stop the little girl getting every chance.

Vera MacLean was awarded a medal for work during the 1914-18 war as a child entertainer. Afterwards she was auditioned and selected from hundreds of juveniles to play one of the "Babes in the Wood" on the London Stage, at the age of twelve, going on to enjoy a remarkable career.

1. William Legg refused to wear any other headgear than his fisherman's cap.

XXXI

THE MAN ON THE LOOK-OUT

'Midst all the events of the earlier part of 1901 and the celebration of the weddings in Burton Bradstock the care and conditions of those sick and destitute had to be considered. To the poorer village people went funds similar to the old Poor Rate to assist them in their old age or trouble and Mr. Richard Moses Gillingham, who lived at The Magnolias, was responsible for handing out the money. This was done from a cottage in Darby Lane which backed onto his garden.

For those for whom "out of door relief" was insufficient aid there was the Workhouse or "Union" in Barrack Street, Bridport, as austere a building as its purpose dictated.

In Bridport, Andrew Spiller, later Mayor of Bridport in 1928, had been on the Board of Guardians for six years. He had been returned unopposed in 1898 but when the election became due again in 1901 he was opposed by Mr. F. W. Knight. A Public Meeting was held in the Town Hall, presided over by Mr. T. A. Colfox. In his address to the packed audience he spoke of Mr. Spiller having devoted much time to the office and his able administration of the very complicated Poor Law which required a lot of time and considerable study. He went on to say that Mr. Spiller had undertaken his duties fearlessly and had done much sifting.

This last statement was the probable reason as to why Andrew Spiller was having to fight for his re-election. He had worked very hard to improve the conditions at the Workhouse and for the poor generally. Supported by two lady guardians and others on the committee he had left no stone unturned to weed out the Dickensian conditions and attitudes. Because of this some were afraid that he would spend too much of the ratepayers' money or bring fiddling and swindling of the funds to light. Supporting his election, Henry Legge, Esq. of Litton Cheney said, "We thought you would scatter outdoor relief broadly and indiscriminately but we soon altered our opinions in a very short time. You have sorted out imposters and malingerers and saved public money".

It transpired, that during his six years in office, Spiller had replaced the very inexperienced workhouse nurse with a qualified one, sold for scrap the old 2′ 6″ iron bedsteads (which had the edges of the iron upwards instead of down) and replaced them with more comfortable beds, wide enough to turn a person. Partitions had been taken down and let in light to the building allowing a view to West Bay. He was anxious to provide out of door relief as often as possible and not to put people into the workhouse against their will or unnecessarily and he was keen to board out orphan children rather than subject them to a life of institution, as in the case of the Monkton Wylde children sold to the gypsies by their father. He had also uncovered a 'meat shindy'.

Andrew Spiller had the old Tramps' House removed. It had been only big enough for two but as many as nine a night were locked up in there from 9 pm - 8 am, with no sanitary arrangements. Even by 11 am he had been unable to persuade any of the Committee to inspect it in the mornings. These tramps moved freely with the inmates of the "Union" and one tramp was found to be suffering from smallpox on his arrival, the next evening, at Chard.

At a cost of around £500, new quarters had been provided for tramps and they were obliged to work one day in order to receive two nights' lodgings. They had a plank bed each, were given a bath, bread and cheese and a little soup and tea. These arrangements revolutionised workhouse amenities for tramps and as a result of the new move in Bridport their conditions and the "tramp question" was considered nationally.

In summing up the case for Spiller's reappointment, the Reverend C.O. Watson praised his courage to speak out. "He turned himself inside out as he was confident in the strength of his own backbone. Let the Master, of course, keep his hand on the tiller, but the man on the look-out had better be Spiller", he said!

Andrew Spiller was re-elected unanimously and continued to serve his native town and the poor of the district for many more years.

XXXII

THE NEW GENERATION

Those early years of the 20th Century were to be, perhaps, the most tranquil and idyllic that the many generations of the people of Burton Bradstock would know.

The end of the Boer War in June 1902 was soon put behind most of them. For others, who lost husbands and sons, war is never forgotten and so it was for the Mercer family. So shortly after the happy occasion of their daughter's wedding, news came through that their only surviving son had died in South Africa. For the children of Burton the Boer War had been a game to play. "shooting" each other with pop guns and the English always being the victors.

The news of peace did not reach the village until the next day. Peals of church bells rang out, yet once more, across the valley and a service of Thanksgiving for Peace was held in St. Mary's Church.

Now it was to be a time of joy again. The Coronation of Edward VII was imminent but his sudden, serious illness and the postponement of the ceremony was an anxious time for all his family and subjects.

The people of Burton Bradstock had always been very Royal and anxiety prevailed in the village, as it did everywhere else. The Rector reminded his congregation that, 'Man proposes, God disposes'.

*   *   *   *   *   *

Dorset history managed to find a niche, even in this unusual event, for one Frederick Treves, a Dorset man, had been appointed Surgeon Extraordinary to Queen Victoria in 1900 and it was he who was called upon to perform the delicate operation on the Sovereign.

Treves was known to have lived over a furniture shop in Dorchester. Born in 1853 he attended Barnes' School for boys there and at twenty three became a medical officer at the Royal Navy Hospital. By the age of thirty one he was a full surgeon. Later he lectured and had a consulting room at No. 6, Wimpole Street. It was here that this distinguished man came to Royal notice.

After the successful operation on the King, Treves was made a baronet and lent Thatched House Lodge, Richmond. He died in Switzerland in 1923.

*   *   *   *   *   *

The villagers were not to be denied another exciting day. The Coronation took place, unusually on a Saturday, August 9th, 1902 and after a Special Service in the morning the rest of the day was spent, just like it had been on so many similar occasions, over the years, in jollifications. This time the sports and tea took place in the field behind the Villas and Mrs. Harrison distributed the prizes and memorial medals to the children.

The boys who ran and jumped and sang and rejoiced that day had just a dozen years left before some of them and so many of their generation were to be cut down in their prime in yet another war.

Now war was far, far away from their minds. The pop guns were put to other imaginary uses and the children had different activities to fill their time.

At the village school Mr. Milburn, the Head Master, had succeeded in producing a very high standard of work and attendance from his pupils and the reports from the Inspectors were excellent. His retirement in 1907 was marked by a presentation of a silver tea service. He had been Head Master for 17 years, ably assisted by Mrs. Milburn. It was to be the boys of a Weymouth School who were now to feel the sting of his cane and come under his rigid discipline.

For the Burton Bradstock school children a younger man, with more modern ideas, was to succeed to the Headship. Mr. R. B. Howarth had been appointed and through his hands were to pass three more generations of the youngsters of Burton. With the firm support of his wife, Alice, he was not only to keep up the educational standards of his predecessor but to introduce a wider school curriculum. He involved himself in so many village and local activities and organisations over the next sixty five years making a vast contribution to the quality of life in the village and district. He was an extremely keen footballer and the village team he formed continued to exist in the village throughout his lifetime.

The wars interrupted sport and took away the young men who played but after each time the team was re-formed. How often do the youngsters who play for Burton Bradstock today consider that they are the grandsons and great grandsons of R.B.H.'s early teams?

Mr. and Mrs. Howarth were both certificated teachers and at the time of his appointment to Burton School Mr. Howarth was Head Master at Swindford School, near Rugby. The North of England being his home, somehow over the years he managed to bridge the wide gap between the North and South of the country with the many tales he told of life and lore in his "cold", hard part of the world. His physique was as strong as his character and it was certainly the good hand of Fate that brought him to Burton Bradstock.

During this first decade of the new century the Parish Registers recorded the births of babies who, at this time of writing, are the Senior Citizens of Burton Bradstock. Their first cries were made under the thatched roofs of the mellowed stone cottages, in sight of the spinning mill and the green meadows and the sound of the pebbles drawing back and forth on the Chesil Beach. Their mothers were aided in their hours of labour by the village midwife, Mrs. Jessie Hitt, known locally as "The Angel". These mothers and mothers before them, knew no other type of midwifery than a local woman could give, her knowledge gained by experience and common sense alone.

As the first children of the century came into the world so we read of the passing of those whose names were first recorded in the 1841 Census.

Mary Ann Tucker born in 1818, a young dressmaker in 1841, had stitched many yards of thread by the time she died at 86 years of age. Of the men, Ben Williams, the old fisherman, whose life had spanned the period from 1819-1901 was laid to rest where the cry of seagulls was never far from his grave and Abel Burwood, who once was a servant boy. would never be bidden again. John Knight, another old Burtoner, was 81 when he died. His devotion to the church and his 'firm hold on the truths of religion' were those that so many of the Victorians held. He had performed the duties of Beadle of the Church for many years and it was he who had summoned the members of the Court Leet to attend. With him closed a chapter of the history of Burton Bradstock for he had known The Office of Beadleship when it was at its most authoritive and not just a symbolic duty.

Mary Bartlett who lived 92 years and Mary Foot who died at 90 were both born in 1816. Two years later Jane Travers, Harriett Conway, Fanny White and Samuel Gale were born when the Court Leet still met and used its powers, when men built their own cottages in the village, with no concern for planners, and yet made a good job of it.

All these old people had been given first hand stories of the threatened French Invasion and the successful victories at Trafalgar and Waterloo. They knew all about the village Poor House and how, men and women alike, worked for as long as they could, well into their seventies and eighties, and children toiled in the fields and at the looms.

At the beginning of the 20th Century they could say they had been born in the reign of George III and lived through the reigns of George IV, William IV and Queen Victoria.

In the late 1820s, as young children, they were the first generation to have a village "bobby". They lived through the abolition of slavery, the Great Trek of the Boers, the Crimean War, the Indian Mutiny, the seizing of Khartoum and the Boer War. During their lives they had witnessed the replacement of wind and water power by coal and iron for machines and steam. They had seen the arrival of the railways and steam ships, the telegraph system, the car and the bicycle. During Victoria's reign they saw the increase in the kitchen range, the mangle and sewing machine, in the larger houses, making the life of servants a little easier.

Big changes in the Parliamentary System and the Poor Law had taken place during the lives of these Burtoners. They saw their grandchildren attend school and all of them knew of the vast improvement in medicine by the end of their days. What a wealth of information and local history, for that period, was buried with these old people.

Another era closed with the death of Alfred Walter Finnis, a Coastguard from the Burton Bradstock Station, in 1908. He was buried with full honours in the new burial ground in Shipton Lane, the first person to be interred there. Contingents of Coastguards from Abbotsbury and West Bay marched through the village, with muskets reversed and three volleys were fired over the graveside. This marked the end of over one hundred years of service by the Coastguards in Burton as the Station was then closed, their cottages let for holidays.

This was a decade for the children though, and they so enjoyed their School Concerts and Christmas parties and outings.

In July 1906 the Sunday School children were taken by waggon to West Bay for their treat. The waggons were lent by Messrs. Cleall, Cousins, Lenthall and Smith and many people gathered to see the procession set off. All were clad in their Sunday best. With their teachers, the party numbered around 80.

On their arrival at West Bay they attended a service at St. Andrew's Mission Church, Miss Gluning presiding at the organ. An excellent tea was provided by Mrs. Bartlett of Clarence House, after which they made their way to a field for cricket, games and races.

Perhaps a young boy peeped at the games of cricket and races on one such outing. He was to become a man with great capabilities of leadership and sportsmanship. Young Louis Mountbatten, later Earl Mountbatten of Burma, spent a holiday at West Bay shortly before the First World War, recuperating from whooping cough and bronchitis.

It was 7.30 p.m. before the tired Sunday School group reached Burton. "God Save The King" was sung under the tree and three hearty cheers were given for all who subscribed to the treat and organised it.

Their older brothers and sisters, in the Church Choir, enjoyed outings to Swanage, Exmouth and Bournemouth in the new fangled motor brake. Once, at Weymouth, some viewed the gruesome convict hulk!

Christmas, even then, was a great occasion for children, and the families made their way to the church for the celebration of the Nativity. There were all the outward signs of joy and the bells pealed forth once again. Flags floated from the church tower and holly and evergreens adorned the interior of the church.

In May 1909 Empire Day was observed at the school. There were speeches and patriotic songs, sung with great fervour and the flag was saluted. What a sharp click to attention the hob-nailed boots of the boys would make; especially as the rest of the day was a holiday.

A few days later a concert was given by the school children to raise money for prizes for the Day and Night Schools and the School Boot Club. A packed room heard Edgar Hawkins sing "De Ring — tailed Coon", Winifred Buckler trill in her sweet voice "The Poppies", William Smith recited and William Williams let rip with "The Merry Miller". There were other duets and recitations, Square dancing by the infants and drill with sand and lusty choruses. The children were dressed as pierrots and encore succeeded encore.

For the following summer treat the Sunday School children enjoyed their tea in the Rectory garden and moved off to Vine's field for sports and games and two displays of Maypole dancing, given by the children, who had been carefully trained by Mrs. Howarth. They marched back to the Village Green to render the National Anthem and the annual cheers. This rounded off a successful period for the schools and the children and their teachers.

In 1908 the school received the coveted County and West Dorset Shields for the best attendance in the county with the superb average attendance of 99.3%. It seemed that the habit of regular attendance at school had now become the rule.

There were 84 children on the register and 46 of these received prizes and medals for unbroken attendance. Sixteen pupils were awarded certificates for 400 or more attendances out of a possible 426. In addition to the Day School there was also a busy Night School for the young men and women of the village, organised by Mr. and Mrs. Howarth.

As this story concludes, the names of those children of Burton Bradstock who were honoured that day must be recorded, for it is such names, and that of their families, on which the village was founded and on whose shoulders the future rested.

Norris White, Edgar Hitt, Eva Williams, William Buckler, Edward White, Gladys White, William Brown, William Woodsford, Mabel White, Blanche Davis, Alice Gillingham, Colenso Wills, Dorothy Bartlett, Frank Wrixton,

Ralph Northover, James Norris, William Smith, Stewart Jacobs, Thomas Knapman, Ralph Bartlett, Robert Gale, Reginald Woodsford, Martha Steel, Elizabeth Brown, Ethel Legge, Charlotte Payne, Gladys Hitt, Cecil Legge, William Bartlett, Harold Northover, Reginald Gale, John Dowton, Edgar Hawkins, James Williams, Reginald Davis, Winnifred Buckler, Sylvia Marsh, Ellen Gilbert, Alice Hitt, Minnie Bartlett and Gertrude Tompkins.

*   *   *   *   *   *

In 1914 the fathers, uncles and sons, which included most of the older males who attended those school celebrations of 1908/9, went off to war. They enlisted and volunteered without question. It was to be the "War to end all wars". Some never returned, like the Robert Buckler whose name first inspired this village history to be written. He lies thousands of miles from his home of Burton Bradstock, having gone down with his ship, "H.M.S. Monmouth", in the Falkland Islands' engagement, on November 1st 1914. Twenty five other men from Burton gave their lives in the Great War in order that their homeland and their patch of England could be free.

Their sacrifice and that of the next generation, in the Second World War, was worthwhile, for the happy laughter and chatter of the Burton Bradstock schoolchildren and the glad peal of the church bells can still be heard echoing across the Bride Valley, a permanent reminder of the continuity of life.

———————

Burton's sons were always brave,
On the land or ocean

Song of The Loyal Volunteers of
Burton Bradstock.

XXXIII

AND THEN

Much water has gone under Bride's Bridge since the Great World War. Many other events, sad and sunny, have occurred in Burton Bradstock.

The first great change came to the village in the 1930s when the spinning mill closed and the spinners had to find employment in Bridport and elsewhere. The married women continued to braid at home, their work brought out to them from the factories in Bridport. Now, only a handful remain in the village who can ply that ancient craft. No more do little girls have to fill the twine needles.

Following a miserable depression, farming prospered in the Second World War and even then there were still several smallholders left — a carry over of many hundreds of years from the days of the Manorial System. Very few cottages in the 1980s have a plot of land that went with the tenancy. Most have been swallowed up with the new building schemes. Men do still till allotments, striding through the village with their spades across their shoulders and large baskets on their arms. There are others who prefer to motor to their "ground".

No cattle or carthorses plod through the streets. Burton Manor Farm is no longer the principal holding and caravans "graze" many acres throughout the parish. Fortunately, a few fishermen still fish from Burton, for a hobby. The excitement felt, when there is a good catch of mackerel, remains unaltered.

In the years that have passed there have been many good times. There has been dancing in the street, processions and presentations. Happy children still trip the complicated twists around the maypole. Bells ring, flags fly and beacons blaze.

No one is poor anymore. Old Age Pensions and National Assistance do not carry the stigma that the paupers of long ago felt when they received the equivalent from the Poor Rate. Few, who read this, cannot trace an ancestor, of three or four generations ago, back to the labouring poor of some village.

The Second World War cut short the lives of more young men from Burton. Because of this village life goes on unfettered. Through those awful years there was some laughter, too. Solemn and serious the men who were left behind joined the Home Guard, the A.R.P. and the Special Constabulary. They contributed much to the security of our vulnerable shores but they also managed to make light of some of the incidents that occurred.

Twentieth Century "invaders" came to Chesil's Bank. British soldiers were stationed all along the beach and around the perimeter of the village. They were followed by the Americans and finally the prisoners of war. Evacuees, from London, lived alongside the local children. After the war we welcomed again the annual invasion of holiday makers. Gladly we share the beauty of our coast and countryside, ever conscious that our economy depends on their coming.

The second change that really altered life and lore in Burton Bradstock was the sale of the Burton Bradstock section of the Pitt-Rivers' Estate in 1958. Practically the whole of the village, and much of West Bay, came under the hammer and since then nothing has been quite the same. The Lord of the Manor was more then generous and aided his tenants to purchase the freehold of their properties and land which in many cases had been in the same families for generations. Of the present population they form only the minority.

Modern technology has not prevented the once or twice in a lifetime experience of terrible flooding in the village and cottages can still catch on fire. Twice in recent years the village has been cut off by blizzards, but there are still men and boys who will launch a boat, strip off smouldering thatch or dig through deep drifts; but these are all stories for another time.

THE OCCUPATIONS OF THE BURTON BRADSTOCK PEOPLE
excluding Bridport Harbour

	1841	1881
Agricultural Labourers	59	56 (In 1881 this included: 7 carters, 3 shepherds, 6 grooms, 4 dairymen, 1 ploughboy)
General Labourers	24 (of which 16 were women)	21 (4 women)
Corn Factor	1	1 Farm Bailiff
Flax Mill Hands	35 (17 women spinners)	26 (17 women)
Ropemakers	2	1
Braiders of nets	2 (more women probably braided at home in 1841 than recorded their work)	29 (nearly all older married women)
Mechanics	1	2
Mill Manager	1	1
Manufacturer	1	1
Full time fishermen	9	8 and 2 women fishmongers
Fish dealers	—	2
Mariners	16	6 (4 others had recently drowned)
Female Servants	13 domestics and dairymaids	13
Cooks	—	3
Male servants	2	2
Gardener	—	1
Female nurses	1	2
Housekeepers	1	2
Carpenters	8 including apprentices	6
Masons	6 includes labourers	1
Builders	—	3
Plumber and glazier	1	1 painter and glazier
Bricklayer	1	—
Blacksmiths	4 includes apprentices	3
Whitesmith	—	2 includes apprentice

Butchers	3	3 one also grocer
Male Bakers	2	1 also a grocer
Female Bakers	2	—
Miller and baker	1	1
Draper and Grocers	2	2
Storekeepers	—	2
Milkmen	—	2
Dressmakers	7	11
Tailors	4	3
Tailoress	—	1
Milliner	—	1
Mantilla makers	2	—
Boot and Shoemakers	2	2
Carriers	6	1
Innkeepers	2	3
Schoolteachers	4 (includes evening & Sunday school)	4 pupil teachers
Governesses	—	2
Police Constable	—	1
Coal Hauler	—	1
Road Contractor	—	1
Stonecracker	—	1
Postmistress	—	1
Clerk	1	1
Laundresses	— (excluding washerwomen)	5
Coastguards	9	7

BURTON BRADSTOCK POPULATION

Taken from Census returns:

1801	654
1811	677
1821	854
1831	1068
1841	1201
1851	1181
1861	1010
1871	1036
1881	946
1891	724
1901	574
1901	522
1921	624
1931	634
1941	no census taken
1951	687
1961	602
1971	804
1981	759

Prior to 1891 the figures appear to include the part of Bridport Harbour within Burton Bradstock Parish.

KNOWN MARINERS FROM BURTON BRADSTOCK

The following list has been collated during research. It is therefore not the total number of mariners from Burton Bradstock. Those known to have been lost at sea have been listed.

B.H. — living at Bridport Harbour   b.b. — believed born

**Date stated
as mariner**

1682	John Beere
1690	Samuel Polden
1730	Robert Angel
	Hezekiah Thurman
	John Tibbs
1734	John Angel
1739	William Hansford
1741	Henry Angel
	Joseph Waldron
1742	Joseph Maniard
1755	Joseph Miller
1757	Andrew Topp
1760	Robert Akerman
1762	Henry Angel
1763	John Horseford
	Thomas Russel
1765	Edward Thurman
1768	Samuel Cammel
	Bernard Gover
1769	James Hardy
	John Summers
1776	Aaron Hooper
1780	Francis Roberts
1784	John Anning
1789	Thomas Akerman
1790	Nicholas Ingram
1794	Robert Symes
1799	John Buckler
1800	Richard Clark
1805	Francis Roberts
	Richard Roberts
	— Hawkins
1810	Richard Buckler
1815	John Lawrence
1820	George Chilcott
1821	John Edes
1827	Henry Cork
	Samson Shepherd
1828	Thomas Hutchings
1830	Matthew Buckler
	Alexander Chilcott
	James Williams
1832	Robert Knight

1833	Henry Hoskins
	John Manele
1837	James Knight Hutchings
1839	Joseph Warre
1841	onwards may include some coastguards
	John Baggs
	John Bartlett
	Robert Chant
	Thomas Chant
	Edward Cole
	William Coombs
	Richard Down
	— Ferry
	Elias Ferry
	Thomas Helyar
	Edward Hitt
	John Hitt
	Elevi Keech
	John Keech
	Thomas Kimber
	William Parsons
	William Ridge
	Richard Rixon
	Robert Rixon
	Thomas Rixon
	Francis Roberts
	William Smith
	Charles Soper
	George Squib
	— Stevens
	John Still
	Joseph Symes
	Stephen Tapper
	Charles Travers
	John Waldron (senior and junior)
	Thomas Williams
	John Woodcock
	Joseph Woodcock
	James Whittaker (Customs Riding Officer)
1844	Samuel Smith
	Samuel Stevens
	George Thorner

1845 George Hounsell
1846 David Pidding
1847 George Chilcott
     Thomas Pollard
1850 Robert Knight Chillcott
     John Gerrard
     William Good (B.H.)
     Daniel Jacobs
     William Ponsford
1851 Edward Boucher
     Thomas Cole (B.H.)
     Joseph Gerrard (lost on the
       "Why Not" 1881)
     John Hellyar (B.H.)
     William Holmes
     Ben Simpson
       (Coastguard Master)
1854 John Churchill
     Bill Clark Hoskins
       (drowned at sea)
1855 Edward Cole
     William Ferry
     Fred Morris (drowned at sea)
     James Mundy (B.H.)
     John Steele
1857 Thomas Jarvis (B.H.)
1858 Joseph Thorner
     James Williams
1859 William Hounsell (B.H.)
1861 Edward Boucher (B.H.)
     George Clark (B.H.)
     Joseph Gear (lost on the
       "Why Not" 1881)
     William Hayward
1863 George Pitcher (B.H.)
1864 Lewis Knight
1866 Henry Hitchcock
     William Paull
1869 Joseph Gerrard (junior?)
       (lost on the "Why Not")
     Thomas Rashleigh
1870 William Clarke
1871 — Bartlett
     — Hoskins
     Simeon Hutchings (lost on the
       "Why Not")
     James Tait (b.b. Aberdeen)
1872 William Symes
1874 John Hurrell (b.b. London)·
     James Hutchings
     Richard Wheeler
1875 Richard Hoskins Hitchcock
       (Adventurer. Ran away to sea)

1876 William Hayward (died Liverpool
       aged 15 from effects of
       shipwreck)
     — Hayward
     William Ward (b.b. Portsmouth)
1878 John Bowden
1879 Charles Northover
     William Smith
1880 Eli Churchill
     Frederick Hansford
1881 Azekiel Brown
     James Foot
     George Hussey
     Thomas Hutchings
     William Hutchings (lost on the
       "Why Not" 1881)
     — Welsh
1882 William Hawkins
1885 Simeon Brown
     Alfred Chard
1887 Fred Symes
     John Collins (born Essex, came to
       Burton in 1920s, wounded
       1916)
1888 John Waldron
1889 John Motyer (b.b. Portsmouth)
1890 John Northover
1891 Samuel Dean (B.H.)
1892 Walter Cliff
     John Wilson (b.b. Exmouth)
1893 Alfred Turner
     Samuel Williams
1896 Thomas Knapman
     Frederick Williams
1897 Richard Conway
1899 Ernest Steel
1900 Robert Buckler (lost at sea 1914)
     Frederick Hitchcock
     John Hitchcock
1902 Arthur Bell
     William Morey
1903 Henry Burwood
     Henry Ferry
     Joseph Forsey
     William Wilkie
1905 Thomas Brine
     John Buckler
1906 Edward Stewart
     Simon Brown
1907 Herbert Elton
     James Williams
     — Thorner
     — Symes

C1910 — 1920

The following were either full time mariners or served in the 1914-1918 War.

Thomas Brett (lost at sea 1914-18 War)
James Brine (marine serving on HM ships)
Thomas Brine
Edward Buckler
Charles Bugler
Jack Bugler
Charles Bullock
Robert Cammell
William Churchill
Charles Cliff
Walter Cliff (jnr.)
Wilfrid Cliff
Walter Cox
Jack Downton
William Elton
Douglas Hawkins
Frederick Hoskins (believed navy died 1914-18 War)
Robert Howarth (Headmaster — served 1914-18 War)
Ephraim Hussey
Simeon Hutchings
Jesse Jacobs
"Ned" Jacobs
Walter Legg (Submariner)
Cecil Legge
Herbert Marsh
William Marsh (lost at sea 1914-18 War)
William Morris
William Nethercott (born Devon — Submariner 1921)
Harold Northover
Joseph Northover
Alfred Oliver (believed navy — died 1914-18 War)
William Partridge
Thomas Perrin
William Perrin
William Smith
Louis Sponsford
Thomas Swaffield
John Thorner
Louis Thorner
Walter Tucker
Joseph Ward
Thomas Ward
Jack Williams
James Williams
Stanley Williams
William Williams
Alfred Wrixton
Charles Wrixton
Frank Wrixton
Frederick Wrixton
Harry Wrixton

Five brothers: a fitting
finale to this imposing list
(lost at sea 1914-18 War)

MAIN SOURCES OF INFORMATION

The Burton Bradstock Parish Registers 1614-1907
The Churchwardens' Accounts, 1699-1926 and Overseers' Accounts, 1755-1858 for Burton Bradstock.
The Pitt-Rivers' Family Papers which include the Burton Bradstock Manorial Court Rolls.
The Burton Bradstock Tithe Map with details of owners and occupiers for C1840.
The Burton Bradstock Parish Magazines 1900-1909 — presented by Mrs. M. Ouseley.
Roberts' Letter Books Vols. I and II — presented by Miss D. S. Roberts.
Notes on Burton Bradstock by Maurice Ouseley, M.A. — presented by Mrs. M. Ouseley.
Transcripts of Dorset Lay Subsidy Rolls 1322 and 1327, Dorset Hearth Tax Assessment 1662-1664, Dorset Tudor Muster Rolls.
Askerswell, Chilcombe and Symondsbury Parish Registers of the 18th Century.
Kelly's Directories 1859-1907.
Salway Ash, Little Bredy and Kingston Russell, Bothenhampton and Netherbury School Log Books.
Courtesy County Archivist, Dorset County Record Office, Dorchester.

Census Returns 1841-1881.
Three Dorset Captains at Trafalgar, Broadley and Bartelot (1906).
Nelson's Hardy — His Life, Letters and Friends — Broadley and Bartelot (1909).
Dictionary of 2285 English Emmigrants to New England 1620-1650, by Charles Edward Banks.
Hutchins' History of Dorset Vol. II, 3rd Edition.
Victoria History of the County of Dorset Vol. II, edited by Wm. Page, F.S.A.
Survey and Inventory by Royal Commission of Historical Monuments (Vol. I West)
Survey of Coast of Dorsetshire for the purpose of planning scheme of defence 1798.
The Dorset County Library Reference Dept., Dorchester, Dorset.

The Bridport News Archive, East Street, Bridport, Dorset.

The Chilcott Family Tree
The Clark Family Papers and Tree
The Hutchings Family Tree } Privately held
The Symes Family Tree
William Gear 1864-1955, by his daughter, Dorothy Mansfield
The Sinking of "The Why Not" Notes by Dorothy Mansfield (Bridport Museum).
The History of Wesleyan Methodism in Bridport and its Vicinity — John Stevens (1857), held in the Methodist Archive, County Hall, Exeter, Devon.

For the Second Edition of this book information has been provided by Mr. Campbell Edwards, Mrs. D. Lee, neé Hitt, Mr. W. R. Nethercott and Mr. J. H. Wyatt.

BIBLIOGRAPHY

BAYLEY, A.R., The Civil War in Dorset 1642-1660 (1910).
BOSWELL, EDWARD, The Civil Division of the County of Dorset, 1795 (1833).
BOSWELL-STONE, W.G. Prehistoric and Roman Remains in West Dorset (1893).
BRONSTED, JOHANNES, The Vikings (1960).
CHAPLIN, E.L., Shipton Gorge (1981).
COKER. Dorset's First Book, Survey of Dorsetshire, 2nd EDITION with afterword by Rodney Legg (1980).
COOKSEY, ALFRED J.A., The Telephone in Dorset (1974).
CULLINGFORD CECIL N., A History of Dorset (1980).
DAMON ROBERT, Geology of Weymouth, Portland and the Coast of Dorset (1884).
DAVIES HUNTER, William Wordsworth (1980).
DORSET COUNTY TREASURES, Dorset Workhouses (1980).
EDWARDS, ELIZABETH, The History of Bournemouth (1981).
GIBBS, W.F.E., Elementary Education in Dorset, Vol. I (1960).
GOOD, RONALD, The Lost Villages of Dorset (1979).
HAMPDEN, JOHN, Francis Drake, Privateer (1972).
HAWKINS, DESMOND, Cranborne Chase (1980).
HORSFALL, MARY, Life in Bridport 1898-1918 (1969).
HUISH AND ALLINGHAM, Happy England (1903).
JACKSON, B.L. AND M.J. TATTERSHALL, The Bridport Branch (1976).
KERR, BARBARA, Bound to the Soil (1968).
LENTHALL, J.M., The Bradstock Flock History (1965).
LONG, E.T., Our Heritage, the history of St. Mary's Church, Burton Bradstock (undated).
MARLOW, JOYCE, The Tolpuddle Martyrs (1971).
MASKELL, JOSEPH, The History and Topography of Bridport, Dorset (1855).
MATTHEWS, A.W., West Bay (1901).
MILLER, A.J., Baccy, Rum and Tea from Poole (1979).
PHILLPOTTS, EDEN, The Spinners (1918).
POOLE, H.S., Powerstock (1979).
ROWSON, J.W., Bridport and the Great War (1923).
STRANGWAYS ESTATE, Trustees of, An Appreciation of Abbotsbury (1973).
TEMPLE, The Mighty Oak (1974).
TROTMAN, CANON F.E., The Rectors of Longbredy, 1300-1815 (1968).
WEINSTOCK, M.B., Old Dorset (1967).
WOODWARD, Sir LLEWELLYN, The Age of Reform 1815-1870, 2nd Edition (1962).

OTHER SUGGESTED READING

BAILEY, C.J., The Bride Valley (1982).
COPPLESTONE, BENNET, The Treasure of Golden Cap (1922, reprinted 1982).
CUNNINGTON, PAMELA, A.R.I.B.A., How old is your house (1980).
EASTWOOD, JOHN, The Burton Bradstock Book (1972).
EASTWOOD, JOHN, The Mole Race, Life as a Dorset Fisherman (1981).
HAWKINS, DESMOND, Concerning Agnes, (daughter of General Pitt-Rivers) (1982).
SHORT, BASIL, A respectable society — Bridport 1593-1835 (1976).
SHORT, BASIL and SALES, JOHN The Bridport Book (1980).

BURTON BRADSTOCK ROLL OF HONOUR 1914-1918

William Bartlett
Thomas Brett
Robert Buckler
Wilfrid Cliff
Reginald Davis
Harold Foot
John Gale
William Gape
Conrad Hawkins
Richard Hoare
Frederick Hoskins
William Jacobs
Robert Legge

William Marsh
Henry Mitchell
Alfred Oliver
William Sanders
William Sponsford
George Stevens
Charles Thorner
Albert White
Ernest White
Reginald White
Harry Williams
Kenneth Winterflood
Frederick Wrixton

1939 — 1945

Peter Bishop
Theodore Bulmer
Alfred Cammell
Lloyd Fletcher
Cyril Fletcher
Cyril Northover
Geoffrey de Pury

John Speak
Gordon Ward
Lewis White
Frederick Williams
James Williams
Nellie Piper (Civilian)

A donation from the sale of each copy of this book will be given to the Bride Valley Branch of the Royal British Legion.